LIBERATING CYBERSPACE

LIBERATING CYBERSPACE

Civil Liberties, Human Rights and the Internet

EDITED BY LIBERTY

LONDON • STERLING, VIRGINIA

in association with

Liberty
(The National Council for Civil Liberties)

First published 1999 by Pluto Press
345 Archway Road, London N6 5AA
and 22883 Quicksilver Drive, Sterling,
VA 20166–2012, USA

British Library Cataloguing in Publication Data
A catalogue record for this book is available from the British Library

ISBN 0 7453 1299 3 hbk

Library of Congress Cataloging in Publication Data
Liberating cyberspace : civil liberties, human rights, and the Internet / edited by Liberty.
p. cm.
ISBN 0–7453–1299–3 (hardcover)
1. Computers—Law and legislation. 2. Privacy, Right of.
3. Freedom of information. 4. Internet (Computer network)
I. Liberty (Great Britain)
K564.C6L53 1999
342'.0858—DC21 97–44923
CIP

05 04 03 02 01 00 Impression: 5 4 3 2

Designed, typeset and produced for Pluto Press by
Chase Production Services, Chadlington, OX7 3LN
Printed in the European Union by Athenaeum Press, Gateshead

Contents

PART II

Notes on Contributors

Yaman Akdeniz (lawya@leeds.ac.uk) is currently a full-time PhD student at the CyberLaw Research Unit, Centre for Criminal Justice Studies, University of Leeds, and his thesis title is 'The Governance of the Internet'. He has written several articles related to the Internet and is also the founder of Cyber-Rights & Cyber-Liberties (UK) (http://www.leeds.ac.uk/law/pgs/yaman/yaman.htm), a non-profit civil liberties organisation, which opposes the DTI encryption initiatives. Its main purpose is to promote free speech and privacy on the Internet, and it is a member of the Global Internet Liberty Campaign.

Caspar Bowden (cb@fipr.org) is Director of the Foundation for Information Policy Research (http://www.fipr.org), an independent non-profit organisation which studies the interaction between information technology and society, identifies technical developments with significant social impact, and commissions research into public policy alternatives. He was formerly a consultant specialising in Internet security and e-commerce, senior researcher of an option-arbitrage trading firm, a financial strategist with Goldman Sachs, and chief algorithm designer for a virtual reality software house.

Cathy Bryan is a new media consultant with Informed Sources. Previous publications include *Cyberdemocracy: Technology, Cities and Civic Networks* (Routledge, 1997), of which she was co-editor.

Nick Braithwaite is a partner with Bindman and Partners and heads the firm's digital media group. Recent work includes a defamation claim brought against an Internet service provider. He has written and lectured widely on new media legal issues and is editor of *The International Libel Handbook* (Butterworth-Heinemann, 1995).

Kate Burke has a history of activism with organisations such as Amnesty International, Anti Apartheid and various women's groups. She has also worked for *City Limits* magazine and Liberty. As editor of AVIVA (http://www.aviva.org) Kate's mission is the promotion of equality for women everywhere, through the dissemination of information, contact and co-operation. She can be contacted at kateb@aviva.org

Penny Campbell is Deputy Head of Research at the European Institute for the Media in Dusseldorf. She specialises in European Policy on developing the information society. She is currently working on a project addressing problems of access to the information society for older people in Europe. Previously she worked for nine years in the telecommunications sector. She is a graduate of Manchester University and has an MSc in Science Policy. She can be contacted at penny.campbell@skynet.be

David Capitanchik is Special Projects Adviser at Aberdeen College and Honorary Senior Lecturer in Politics at Aberdeen University. He is a member of the Research Board of the Institute of Jewish Policy Research, the Royal United Services Institute for Defence Studies and a member of the Institute of Petroleum. He has published numerous articles, research papers and book reviews on such diverse matters as Middle East politics, Israeli elections, military sociology, international affairs, social policy in the UK, the Internet etc. He can be contacted at d.b.capitanchik@abdm.ac.uk

Simon Davies is a specialist in privacy and surveillance. He is a visiting fellow in the Computer Security Research Centre of the London School of Economics and is Director of the watchdog group Privacy International (http://www.privacy.org/pi/)

Andrew Ecclestone is a researcher and Website editor for the Campaign for Freedom of Information (http://www.cfoi.org.uk). He was co-author of the Campaign's 1993 report *The Environmental Information Regulations and THORP*. He can be contacted at admin@cfoi.demon.co.uk

Conor Foley is a writer and human rights campaigner. His previous publications include *Legion of the Rearguard: the IRA and the Modern Irish State* (Pluto Press, 1992) and *Human Rights, Human Wrongs* (Liberty/Rivers Oram Press, 1995).

Phil George currently lives and works in East London where he is the Secretary of Gaia: The Society for Research and Education in Earth System Science. He can be contacted at p.george@uel.ac.uk

Angus Hamilton is a solicitor practising in London. His firm specialises in matters relating to computers and the law, and within the sphere of criminal litigation in sexual offences, indecency and obscenity. The firm's Website is at www.btinternet.com/-hamiltons.

He writes regularly for *PCPro* and *Gay Times* on legal issues, is currently Chair of the Board of Trustees of the National Aids Manual and is a long-standing volunteer with the Terence Higgins Trust. He was appointed as an Assistant Stipendiary Magistrate in 1998.

Clem Herman is Director of the Women's Electronic Village Hall, a training and resource centre in Manchester specialising in promoting the use of ICTs and the Internet for women. With a background in community education, she worked in database development for Poptel before co-founding the Women's EVH in 1992. She is passionately committed to empowering women through the use of technology, and can be contacted at clem.herman@mcrl.poptel.org.uk

Ian Hosein is a researcher in the Computer Security Research Centre of the London School of Economics and is a coordinator with Privacy International. He can be contacted at gus@privacy.org

Emmanuelle Machet is a researcher at the European Institute for the Media (EIM) based in Dusseldorf, Germany. She has a degree in media law from the University of Poitiers (France) and has carried out post-graduate work in European studies at the

University of Aachen. She is the secretary of the European Platform of Regulatory Authorities (EPRA) and has recently published together with Serge Robillard *Television and Culture: Policies and Regulations in Europe* (European Institute for the Media, 1998).

Adam Newey is a writer and journalist who specialises in freedom of expression and cultural affairs. He worked at Index on Censorship for five years, where among other things he edited the magazine's Internet news service.

Charles Oppenheim is Professor of Information Science at Loughborough University. He writes frequently on copyright, data protection, liability for information provision, the electronic information industry and related topics. He has previously worked in academia, the information industry and the pharmaceutical industry.

Sherry Turkle is Professor of the Sociology of Science at the Massachussetts Institute of Technology and a licensed clinical psychologist, holding a joint PhD in Personality Psychology and Sociology from Harvard University. Her other publications include *Life on the Screen, Identity in the Age of the Internet* (Orion Phoenix, 1997), and *The Second Self: Computers and the Human Spirit* (Simon and Schuster, 1984). She lives in Boston, Massachussetts.

Michael Whine is the Director of the Defence and Group Relations Division of the Board of Deputies of British Jews. He is also the Administrator of the Community Security Trust. He is a member of the Royal Institute of International Affairs and the Royal United Services Institute for Defence Studies, and writes regularly on extremist politics, terrorism and anti-Semitism. His latest publications are *Racism on the Internet* with David Capitanchik for the Institute of Jewish Policy Research and 'The Far Right on the Internet', a chapter in *The Governance of Cyberspace*, edited by Brian Loader (Routledge, 1997).

Acknowledgements

Liberty would like to thank the Joseph Rowntree Charitable Trust for the grant which made this book possible. We would also like to thank Zoe Gillard, Alex Hamilton, Katie Scott and Caspar Bowden.

Introduction

Since the beginning of its exponential growth in the early 1990s, ambitious claims have been made for the Internet. It will be the great democratiser, levelling the playing field of knowledge and access to ideas. Like Gutenberg's printing press, it will give to the many the knowledge which was previously confined to the few. It is impossible to censor, its global reach presenting a seemingly insurmountable challenge to would-be regulators. It is a tool of liberation, the medium through which marginalised views can reach a wider audience – not only free of state censorship but unmediated by the decisions of publishers or broadcasters. Strong encryption can provide absolute privacy and security for information sent via the Internet – as vital for political dissidents as for commercial transactions. And, of course, it can be used to enhance government transparency and accountability, and to improve the quality of political participation.

Yet there is another side to each of these claims. The opportunity to play on the level field is open only to those with access. At the time of writing, some 130 million people are 'online': around 2.4 per cent of the world's population.[1] It could be argued that it merely deepens the gulf between the information rich and the information poor. For the information rich, the quantity of material on the Net is vast: some is invaluable, but without editorial control or discipline, some of it is useless. The knowledge and ideas which are so suddenly and overwhelmingly accessible are of variable reliability, authority or veracity. Rumours, hoaxes and simple inaccuracies are fairly commonplace: by what criteria do we assess the truth? The tensions between rights and liberties are thrown into sharp relief by concerns about the use of the Net to further anti-social or even potentially harmful aims: children gain access to inappropriate material; far-right organisations circulate racist hatespeech. The benefits of a free market of ideas clearly outweigh the disadvantages, but this does not mean the latter can be easily dismissed. As well as enhancing privacy and security for encrypted information, the Net provides another arena for state surveillance. And of course improving the individual's access to government information and services can go hand in hand with improving the government's access to the individual.

Is it possible to reconcile the imperatives of free speech with the minimum controls necessary to protect vulnerable minorities? Can the requirements of law enforcement be reconciled with the individual's right to privacy? Will technological developments alter the relationship between the citizen and the state? Will the future development of the Net enhance or reduce inequalities? These are just some of the questions facing us in 1998, which are explored in some depth by the contributors to this book. Many of the questions are far from new, and derive directly from parallel debates in 'real life'. But the development of this unique medium requires new and creative answers.

The book is divided into two main areas: policy and practice. First, the specific impact of the development of the Internet on privacy, freedom of expression, and freedom of information is explored in considerable detail, and a further chapter outlines recent developments in European policy. Additionally, the implications for the law of copyright are analysed. Second, these discussions are complemented by a number of case studies which illustrate the workings of the Internet in practice. These studies do not provide a comprehensive exploration of all the issues raised – many others could have been included – but they do offer a snapshot of the Internet in 1998, covering moral panics, hatespeech, gender, protest and political participation.

The essays contained here are necessarily eclectic. They range from detailed and technical accounts – like the chapter by Caspar Bowden and Yaman Akdeniz, which examines encryption – to the highly personal and anecdotal, such as Kate Burke's chapter, which describes her experiences of setting up her own Website. The purpose of creating this balance between thematic issues and specific examples is to enable the reader with a general interest to gain an insight into some of the current Internet debates. At the same time, the book is organised to allow readers with a specific interest to focus on their areas of concern.

Adam Newey's essay on free speech provides a thoughtful and inspirational argument for opposing attempts to regulate or censor the Internet. As he points out, the international nature of the Net by definition means that it is difficult if not impossible to impose national controls. Where such attempts have been made, they have so far proved largely unsuccessful, the most striking example being the decision of the US Supreme Court to strike down two statutory provisions enacted within the Communications Decency Act (CDA) 1996 to protect minors from 'indecent' and 'patently offensive' communications on the Internet.[2]

That Supreme Court decision is worth a closer inspection. The Court upheld the decision of the District Court which found that the word 'indecent' and the terms 'patently offensive' and 'in context' were so vague as to be unconstitutional, and the legislation was worded sufficiently broadly to 'chill the expression of adults'. To this extent, the decision is a landmark judgment in relation to free speech. However, perhaps more significantly, and of particular pertinence to this collection of essays, there was a recognition that as the Internet is 'the most participatory form of mass speech yet developed' it is entitled to the 'highest protection from governmental intrusion'.

The Court recognised that different considerations apply to the Internet and cyberspace from those applicable to terrestrial forms of media. The District Court, when deliberating the case, specifically found that 'communications over the Internet do not "invade" an individual's home or appear on one's computer screen unbidden'. The Court also recognised that the risk of accidentally encountering indecent material on the Net is remote because almost all sexually explicit images are preceded by warnings as to their content, and specific affirmative steps are required to access information.

In striking down the relevant provisions of the CDA, the Court affirmed that governments have a genuine and legitimate interest in protecting children from harmful materials, but they pointed out that 'regardless of the strength of the Government's interest' in protecting children, 'the level of discourse reaching a mail box simply cannot be limited to that which would be suitable to a sand box'. The Supreme Court therefore upheld the District Court's conclusion that 'the CDA places an unacceptably heavy burden on protected speech' and that the speech restriction at issue amounted to 'burning the house to roast the pig'.

In reaching its decision the Supreme Court recognised the unique qualities of the Internet, and that whilst its use by a small minority for distributing offensive material may be deplorable, this cannot, of itself, be used as justification for censoring human expression on the Net. The Court reaffirmed that freedom of expression is essential for a pluralistic and democratic society. Adam Newey's chapter continues these arguments and develops them in full. As he contends, while there may be a legitimate need to ensure that people, including teenagers, are not exposed to offensive or potentially damaging material, this is more appropriately and effectively achieved through self-regulation and the development of more sophisticated technology.

Andrew Ecclestone's essay provides a thorough examination of the potential of the Net for improving access to information held by government: unlike the UK, most 'wired' democracies have a Freedom of Information Act. Arguing that we must first establish our rights in the concrete world and then make them work for us electronically, he suggests that the government has the opportunity to make transparency the foundation of the future electronic delivery of public services, as well as the means by which it is held accountable for the performance of its functions. With examples of good practice both from the UK and from other countries, he looks at the disparity between government departments' adaptation to rising expectations of greater public access to information via the Internet. He also examines the possibilities for enhancing public ability to influence government; statutory restrictions on access to information; charges for information, commercial confidentiality, and privacy and data protection issues. At the time of writing, recent reports have suggested that the government may be planning to water down some key elements of its long-awaited and widely welcomed proposals for a Freedom of Information Act: it remains to be seen how far the workings of government will be revealed to us in the future.

At the same time as seeking to censor aspects of the content of the Internet, or retain control over information, governments are becoming increasingly concerned about the use of the Internet for carrying out criminal activity beyond the offensive. As Simon Davies and Ian Hosein argue, a hastily drafted encryption policy designed to assist the detection of major crime might easily be hijacked to control basic freedoms: widespread abuses of phone tapping technology throughout the world provide a sombre reminder of this reality. Furthermore, they argue, governments of developing nations rely on first world countries to supply them with technologies of surveillance – the uses of which are of course far more damaging in countries which effectively have no 'contract' between the individual and the state, than they are in liberal democracies. Illegal, uncontrolled use of wiretaps by police, defence and intelligence agencies is widespread in over 90 countries. Consequently, human rights groups around the world, such as those in Ethiopia, Central America and China, rely on encryption to protect their communications and files. They conclude that the responsibilities of developed countries – which inevitably set a precedent for the rest of the world – would be better exercised in promoting and selling privacy-enhancing technologies rather than technologies of surveillance and control.

Caspar Bowden and Yaman Akdeniz examine the policy dilemmas arising from the brute fact that computers cannot prise open the 'strong' encryption now possible. The growth of the information economy will be built on the regulated issue of 'digital passports', as market forces enforce a convergence towards inter-operability of signatures, encryption, electronic cash, and electronic copyright management systems. Meanwhile, the uniform technical standards of the new networks will be intrinsically capable of supporting computer-automated mass-surveillance and traffic analysis of all digital communications. Should the cryptographic infrastructure be designed so that future implementation of mass or even selective surveillance is either possible or impossible? Can abstract data protection principles provide an effective check on abuse?

They emphasise the seriousness – and in particular the sheer *finality* – of decisions to be made: 'the inter-penetration of this new medium with every aspect of society will mean that basic technical choices affecting the degree of anonymity and confidentiality possible in mass market systems may actually determine (albeit in ways hard to predict) the evolution of democratic political culture'.

Contrary to the popular perception that computers abolished privacy long ago, cryptography offers the possibility of strong bulwarks to privacy. They argue that proposals currently under discussion to license and regulate Trusted Third Parties (TTPs) for the provision of encryption services are a cause for concern. The need to safeguard the integrity and confidentiality of electronic information competes with the requirement of intelligence and law enforcement agencies to fight serious crime and terrorism. Clearly the authorities should not be able to swoop down on any encrypted message at will and unscramble it. But even legislation allowing keys to be subpoenaed under warrant will raise difficult questions: what will constitute *prima facie* grounds for issue of a warrant, to recover evidence that is by definition unknown? Will a judge be able to draw adverse inferences from a suspect's refusal or inability to produce a key to unlock information which the prosecution believes to be incriminating? What if a suspect has genuinely lost their key?

It is worth noting that in opposition the Labour Party argued that attempts to control the use of encryption were 'wrong in principle, unworkable in practice, and damaging to the long term economic value of the information networks ... it is not necessary to criminalise a large section of the network using public to control the activities of a very small minority of lawbreakers'.[3] Again, as with the Freedom of Information proposals, how the Labour government responds to competing pressures now that it is in power remains to be seen. The dilemma is succinctly dealt with in the conclusion to their chapter: 'The fork in the road is clear. One path leads to an infrastructure capable of an unprecedented degree of state surveillance limited only by perpetual government self-restraint; the other leads to a dilution of power and strengthening of privacy but with compensatory reforms to assist law enforcement.'

Because this volume is intended for the lay reader rather than the expert, a primer on cryptography is also provided at the beginning of the chapter.

The civil liberties implications for the Internet are not confined to the tensions between privacy, free speech, freedom of information and the need to control crime. The development of the Internet also poses new and potent challenges to the law of copyright. Nick Braithwaite and Charles Oppenheim have both produced chapters looking at the implications for copyright in a post-cyberspace world. The problems are self-evident. How do authors and publishers enforce copyright and, more importantly, royalties, with the advent of this new medium to which the concept of intellectual property is alien?

The chapter by Penny Campbell and Emmanuelle Machet examines the response to date of the European Union (EU) to the issues arising from the development of the Internet. A central focus of this essay is the influential Bangemann report. As the chapter shows, the European institutions have recognised that overly restrictive regulation is likely to hinder the progress of the Internet as a medium for international transactions. And of course there are concerns that any national attempts to regulate the Net may breach Community law which guarantees the freedom to provide or receive services.

The case studies begin with an evaluation by Cathy Bryan and James Tatam of the Internet's possibilities and limitations in improving political participation. Focusing on the individual's role in the political process, rather than the political implications for institutions, they divide this into: voting, communicating with an MP, political party or government body; applying pressure or influence; accessing, retrieving and disseminating political information; and local political activity. Rejecting technological determinism as naive, and liable to distract attention from deeper analyses of impediments to political participation, they argue that what politicians really need to address are the deep-seated feelings of distrust and ineffectiveness that are at the heart of political apathy. The Internet is only a partial technological solution to what is in essence a societal problem.

Angus Hamilton demolishes some of the Internet myths

generated by 'moral panics': the Net is not strewn with offensive material, nor is the law helpless to act. As his case studies illustrate, we should be far more concerned about the impact which over-zealous policing can have on the free speech and expression of sexual minorities.

David Capitanchik and Michael Whine, of the Institute for Jewish Policy Research, consider possible approaches to dealing with hatespeech. While recognising that the benefits of a free and uncensored Net outweigh the disadvantages, they draw attention to the problems arising from both the publication of racist material and the organisation of far right activities – for which the Net provides an attractive and convenient environment. Counterspeech and 'flaming' are not, they argue, sustainable long-term solutions to the transmission of hate material; voluntary codes of practice need to be developed as a medium-term solution. In the longer term, they propose an independent watchdog along the lines of the Press Complaints Commission or Broadcasting Standards Authority.

Clem Herman and Sherry Turkle's chapters both consider the gender politics of Internet use, though from widely differing perspectives. Clem Herman argues that although the proportion of women using the Internet is steadily rising, greater attention should be paid to the cultural and economic factors which underpin gender inequalities, both in terms of initial access and the quality of active participation. Sherry Turkle's chapter focuses primarily on the fantasy world of Multiple User Domains (MUDs). She examines the potential which this provides for individuals wishing to experiment with a different gender identity from that of their 'real life': a liberating and sometimes challenging experience for both men and women. Kate Burke, meanwhile, provides a practical and personal account of setting up her own Website which is now used as a resource by individual women and women's organisations all over the world.

A chapter has also been provided by the McSpotlight Campaign, whose Website played a crucial role in the 'McLibel' case, brought by McDonald's against two individuals who had distributed leaflets criticising the company. Legal Aid is not available in libel cases, so Dave Morris and Helen Steel conducted their own defence throughout the longest court case in English legal history. The Website was used during the case as a means of acquiring and distributing information, and of ensuring greater public participation in the campaign.

The final chapter prepared by Conor Foley draws together some of the differing threads of the book. He looks at the democratic potential of the Net, in particular its use in relation to protest and dissent, and argues that we need some form of international agreement such as a new UN Covenant to protect electronic freedom of expression.

It is difficult to think of any recently developed technology which has attracted comparable hype, enthusiasm and anxiety, and for which so many competing claims have been made. But it is more than just another technological development, and more than just an unregulated virtual world where the usual rules are suspended. The inter-penetration of the medium with every aspect of society means that some of the policy decisions made over the next few years will be irreversible.[4] It is essential that such decisions are underpinned by the highest respect for human rights and civil liberties, and fully informed by intelligent public debate about the implications – or we may all regret it for a long time to come.

Liz Parratt and John Wadham, November 1998.

NOTES

1. Percentages on a country by country basis range from 45% (Iceland) or 30% (USA) to 0.05% (China) and 0.02% (India). (Sources: Gallup, Intelliquest, Yahoo/Reuters, Wired.)
2. *Janet Reno, Attorney General of the United States* v. *American Civil Liberties Union et al.*, Appeal from the United States District Court for the Eastern District of Pennsylvania No. 65 – 511, Argued 19 March 1997, decided 26 June 1997.
3. *Communicating Britain's Future*, The Labour Party, 1995.
4. See Chapter 4, by Caspar Bowden and Yaman Akdeniz.

PART I

1 Freedom of Expression: Censorship in Private Hands

Adam Newey

A great deal has been claimed for the Internet: that it can extend and enhance democracy, giving previously marginalised viewpoints unprecedented access to a broad audience; that it is a tool of liberation, particularly for those people living in societies where information is tightly controlled; that it provides a genuinely free market in ideas. At the same time the Internet has also become a stock cliché for the media, who have demonised it as a haven for pornographers, terrorists and political extremists who can ply their poisonous trades with impunity, corrupt our children, and all for the cost of a local phone call. On this view, the Internet encapsulates all that is wrong with Western post-industrial society.

The diversity of those claims is remarkable, not just for its own sake, but because each of them bears directly on different notions of freedom of speech.[1] One of the distinctive characteristics of the Internet, as compared with other media, is that it has become a strong focal point for debate on the nature and scope of freedom of expression itself. At the time of writing, the question of Internet regulation is a matter of urgent policy debate in the United Kingdom and Europe, where attention has been focused on some of the least acceptable forms of expression (most notably child pornography and other forms of sexual exploitation) and the putative links between the currency of such material and the incidence of physical abuse of women and children. At the same time, highly publicised child murder cases in Belgium have helped to raise the political heat and provide greater urgency to calls for Internet regulation.[2] The media debate on regulation has not simply revolved around questions about the permissible limits in the new media. It has also helped to recast questions about permitted speech in society as a whole and, by extension, about the strength of the values which govern the communities in which we live.

In this respect there is something importantly new about the Internet. It provides, at least potentially, a far more direct and undistorted reflection of social norms, thoughts, prejudices and attitudes than any previous medium has been able to. If the purpose of media in general is to hold, as it were, a mirror up to society, then the Internet has the capacity to do that more directly, and in a less distorted way, than any other medium. Some say that this model of the Internet as a kind of perfect *agora* overstates its democratising potential. But much of the backlash against Net-hype[3] risks not only ignoring the potentials of the new media, but also misconstruing the problems to which they give rise. With regard to questions of content, that can lead to misguided attempts at regulation. Those attempts are misguided not because they are ill-intentioned, but because they are unworkable.

Much of the public debate about regulating the Internet has centred on the well-worn issues of obscenity and racial hatred; and as we see below, some of the statutory provisions governing those kinds of expression may indeed be applied fairly straightforwardly to the Internet. At one level, then, the Internet debate – what should governments, regulators or societies in general 'do' about the Internet? – is just another part of a more general debate about the limits of tolerability (of behaviour, of expression, of attitude, of values, and so forth) that goes on in society all the time. To the critic, the Internet is one more piece of evidence of a long-term breakdown in societal cohesion (along with video nasties, football hooliganism, pornography and drug addiction), and another deplorable result of deregulation in the communications market. One writer has put it thus:

> Because, for instance, the Internet is an area of freedom entirely unconstrained by 'society', it holds up a mirror to those nasty human impulses that are normally constrained by the sanction of collective morality. It is a playground for sociopathic fantasies in which, for example, a huge volume of paedophile pornography can be circulated. The men who facilitate this exchange, the service

> providers and the anonymous remailers who disguise the source of the material, defend themselves with the language of the liberty of the market and freedom of expression. It's an argument that, back in a social environment in which children are real and cherished parts of a whole, is seen as specious and immoral.[4]

On the contrary: Internet freedom, I argue, is worth defending precisely because it does facilitate that mirroring, even at the cost of giving expression to 'sociopathic fantasies'. And nor does the Internet provide an area 'entirely unconstrained by society'. Electronic communication, like any communication, is a *social* phenomenon: like any other human activity it is subject to the mores, values and moral pressures that regulate transactions in the social arena. What is new and special about the Internet is its global, mass-participatory nature, and this throws new light on traditional assumptions about liberty, censorship and the toleration of differences within and between communities. The fact that it involves communication mediated by computer networks does not efface the social dimension, and I will argue below that some notion of community is essential if we are to understand how to impose any effective regulation on the Internet. It might seem obvious, but it is often forgotten that Internet users do indeed operate in a real social environment, not some imagined, utopian or dystopian cyber-reality.

In this chapter I will outline the difficulties involved in attempting to regulate the Internet for content. I will also sketch a positive line of argument, which is that, by virtue of its nature, the Internet deserves a wider margin of licence than we would be happy to allow in newspapers or on television. And finally I want to suggest that the Internet challenges us to revise our notion of censorship itself, by giving the user and reader the power and responsibility to decide what he or she wants to access and what to block. Broadly speaking, this is in line with a general policy trend in the industrialised democracies: as the welfare and regulatory provisions of the state are rolled back, so the responsibility for censorship devolves to the level of the local user, the family or service provider, and away from any constituted state authority.[5] This is what I mean by censorship in private hands.

First, however, a note about definition of terms is necessary. Anyone with even a passing familiarity with the vast and growing volume of literature about the Internet will be struck – or just plain confused – by the imprecision and inconsistency with which terminology is employed. This inconsistency is due in part to the broad gulf that exists between technical usage and the language as employed in the mainstream culture of news reports and magazine articles. 'Information superhighway' is often used when 'Internet' is meant; 'cyberspace' and 'virtual reality' have become practically synonymous, as have 'the Web' and 'the Net', and so forth. All this is made more difficult by the knowledge that media convergence is only going to increase, and the correct meaning of terms is not fixed for all time.

I make no claims to technological expertise but, nevertheless, I will try to employ my terms accurately and consistently: most of what I say will be directed at the global network of computer hosts, telecommunication paths and gateways linking those hosts, which are known as the Internet. Properly speaking the Internet is not a medium at all, but a network through which a plurality of media can be accessed: e-mail, Usenet newsgroups, the World Wide Web, Internet Relay Chat (IRC) and so on. These are linked by the term 'computer-mediated communication' (CMC) which, though it has the virtue of exactness, is intolerably clumsy, and I shall use it only when needing to distinguish between the Internet and other forms of CMC. When I refer to the Internet I mean my comments to generalise across different Internet media. Much other material will deal specifically with the World Wide Web or with Usenet, but I will distinguish where necessary.

CENSORING IS HARD TO DO

Information, so the saying goes, wants to be free. Put up a dam in one place and it simply finds a way to flow around it. Likewise, Internet users are united by a fierce desire to keep the network as free as possible from official interference. Why is the Internet so resistant to content regulation?

The answer lies in the nature of the thing itself, and the ways in which the Internet differs from traditional media. For a start, the Internet blurs geographies: like the telephone, it allows interactive communication between groups of users, regardless of locality, in real time. But unlike the telephone, the Internet allows single individuals to communicate instantly (and cheaply) with large groups of people, effectively turning any user of the network into a potential publisher by greatly extending the reach of his message. Whereas in traditional media there is a very small elite of proprietors, editors and producers who determine output, the Internet shifts the locus of editorial control away from the broadcasters and publishers towards the viewers and users. It is this aspect of the Internet which has generated claims about its capabilities for empowerment and democratisation.

The Internet also has an unparalleled ability to draw people together on the basis of their similar interests, concerns, or points of view. Hence the immense popularity of Usenet, which, while far from the most technologically sophisticated part of the Internet, remains one of its most popular applications. The benefits of Usenet are straightforward and well known: people far and wide with a common interest in, say, fly fishing, soap operas, or vintage cars, can 'get together' on a Usenet newsgroup and exchange ideas and observations. Individuals are not limited to the geographical community in which they find themselves. Usenet enables and encourages the creation of common-interest communities, more or less regardless of location.

Problems arise, of course, when common-interest communities start being built around forms of behaviour or expression which are illegal in one country but not another – some kinds of sexually explicit material, for example. Legal systems, by and large, are tied to a particular geographical area in just the way that the Internet is not. Jurisdiction tends to hold within the borders of the nation-state (or sometimes within a supranational entity like the European Union (EU)), whereas the Internet is by its very nature international. This has led some to claim that the Internet could put an end to national legal systems as we have known them.[6] Such claims might be far-fetched, but they do at least point up the severity of the legal questions that the Internet is raising.

Again, this is in part due to the very nature of the thing: on a digital network which breaks information down into small quanta or 'packets' for speed and ease of distribution, not only is it possible to reproduce, say, an obscene or defamatory message almost endlessly, it can be copied between different parts of the network almost without being traced. Compare the relative ease of disseminating libel or obscenity over the Internet with doing so through a newspaper or a television network, and the problems become obvious.

This is not to deny, however, that some of the already existing laws governing permissible expression can be applied fairly straightforwardly to the Internet. In the United Kingdom, for example, there are provisions in Section 1 of the Protection of Children Act 1978 which outlaw the distribution of 'indecent pseudo-photos' (which includes digitised images) of children under the age of 16. Section 160 of the Criminal Justice Act 1988 similarly outlaws their possession. Indeed, the Criminal Justice and Public Order Act 1994 expressly extended the concept of publication contained in the Obscene Publications Act 1959 to include computer transmission.[7] However, even if these provisions – and others against defamation or incitement to racial hatred – do apply to computer-mediated communications, there are far more serious difficulties associated with enforcement, establishing liability, and determining jurisdiction. These problems are closely interrelated.

The enforcement problem comes down to the question: how can you tell whether anyone is doing anything illegal or not on the network? Given the vast amount of data that is currently circulating on the Internet – 30 terabytes, according to one recent estimate[8] – setting up an effective surveillance operation for the whole thing is not possible. And the size of the network is only expected to increase, in which case targeted surveillance is the only sensible way for states to maximise the enforcement potential of applicable laws. This, in effect, is what happened in 1995 with Operation Starburst, in which suspected paedophiles were placed under surveillance and an international child pornography ring was cracked.[9] Clearly, a mass surveillance operation for the sake of locating other forms of obscenity, or defamation, or copyright violation, is just not going to be feasible; and even if technological advances should make it feasible, it is not going to be worthwhile for the state to devote such resources to tracking down and prosecuting individual Internet users.

But there are far more serious problems than this if we are trying to work out how the restrictions we already live with might apply to the Internet. Given, again, that the Internet is an international network, we are faced with the question: whose restrictions are we going to apply? Jurisdiction can properly only be exercised by a national court system governing the territory where an offence is alleged to have taken place (or by a cooperating jurisdiction which might choose, under certain special circumstances, to apply the laws of another nation-state). With a speech-related offence committed on the Internet, by no means is it always clear within which jurisdiction the offence has been committed. In the words of an American guide to potential legal pitfalls online:

> Generally the laws governing ownership and control [of a host computer linked to the Internet] are the laws of the place or jurisdiction where the host is physically located – typically a state or country. However, the governing laws also can be those of the legal home of the host's owner – for example a corporation in Delaware can operate a computer in New York, and the laws of either state (or both) may apply.[10]

This is less than helpful to the user who wants to know what risk they run of getting a knock on the door from the local constabulary. A good real-world illustration of the difficulties is provided by the Website operated by the well-known Holocaust denier, Ernst Zündel. The Zündelsite, as it is known, is housed in California, but it is evident that some of the material it contains is illegal under German laws which ban any denial of the historical truth of the Holocaust and the dissemination of Nazi propaganda. It has proved impossible to bring charges under German law against Zündel and his colleagues, since they are working within a separate jurisdiction where the material they are providing is legal. Unless Zündel wanders into German jurisdiction or a friendly territory, that will remain the case.[11] It may indeed be possible to bring a case for possession against a user in Germany who accesses the site, but this is still going to be subject to the kind of enforcement problems outlined above. The group set up by the British government to look into Internet regulation foresaw this difficulty in its report of February 1995:

> Practical objections to censorship include ... the global nature of the network. The UK government could only introduce legislation that affects UK users and service providers, and not overseas providers where 'obscene' material may be quite legal. In any case, definitions of 'bad', 'harmful' and 'obscene' tend to be subjective and non-consensual.[12]

To say the least! All the old questions about where to draw lines of permissibility, difficult as they are within one nation-state, become far harder when projected onto the international level. It is hard, for instance, to see how the Miller test (the established obscenity test under US law[13]), which takes its yardstick as the 'local community' standard of acceptability, could have any meaning at all on the Internet.

Rather than retreat in the face of these difficulties, the regulators may be tempted to try to extend international controls over expression. That temptation is present in the European Commission Green Paper on the Protection of Minors and Human Dignity in Audiovisual and Information Services. In Chapter II the Commission correctly points out that the right to freedom of expression as guaranteed in Article 10 of the European Convention is subject to certain generalised restrictions, and that different Member States have established different standards with regard to how they interpret the scope of those restrictions. Nevertheless, says the Commission, one can extrapolate from those different cultural and legal traditions, certain categories of material that are unacceptable throughout the European Union:

> Prohibitions on general categories of material detrimental to human dignity, such as material that is obscene, contrary to sound morals or indecent, exist in most Member States ... And the same concept

> may be used to underpin both a blanket prohibition and a more flexible situation in which material is restricted depending on the potential audience or on the medium used. Given all these factors, it would appear possible to identify certain types of material which are generally prohibited in the Union.[14]

The example given is that of child pornography, which is subject to 'the most unanimous ban' among Member States. This is uncontroversial enough, but what follows is a perfect example of slippery slope thinking. 'A further category of material subject to outright prohibition in a significant number of countries', says the Commission, 'is incitement to racial hatred or violence (or both). The terms used and the degree of precision of national legislation vary widely, but there is evidence of a common objective, which is to combat all kinds of material that directly or indirectly incite to hatred, discrimination or violence against persons or groups of persons on grounds of their race, nationality, skin colour, sex or religion.'[15] If there is any such common policy objective, it is such a broad and ill-defined one as to be almost meaningless for legislative purposes. British measures against incitement to racial violence, for example, and German laws criminalising denial of the historical truth of the Holocaust, vary hugely in scope, application and intent, but could both come within the Commission's vague definition of 'a common objective'. But more alarming is that the differences between existing national laws are cited by the Commission as evidence of the need for the development of a pan-European standard of what material should be treated as unlawful. This goes directly against the jurisprudence of the European Court of Human Rights, which has always firmly resisted trying to impose any strict European standard on matters of taste, decency and public morals. Furthermore, in using the notion of the protection of human dignity as justification for restricting the right to freedom of expression, the Commission is opening the way for the kind of laws that have been enacted in Canada to protect women from the 'dehumanising' effects of pornography (see below).

In terms of jurisdiction, of course, the problems are closely analogous to those relating to the transmission of illegal material through the postal system. But, as we saw earlier, the Internet has an almost infinite capacity for reproduction which makes the problem for law enforcement agencies far more acute.[16] This was clearly illustrated in Canada by the Homolka case.

In 1993 Karla Homolka was convicted of the manslaughter of two young women in Ontario. The judge imposed fairly broad reporting restrictions on her trial, including a blanket ban on the presence of foreign media in the courtroom. The purpose of the restrictions was to prevent any possible prejudice in the forthcoming trial of Homolka's husband for his part in the same killings. Inevitably, Usenet became both a venue for discussions about the rights and wrongs of reporting restrictions generally, and also a means to undermine the particular restrictions on the Homolka trial. The information embargo was already a leaky one anyway – a fair amount of information about the trial seeped back into Canada from US newspapers. But the main source of information for those who wanted it was the newsgroup alt.fan.karla-homolka which, in standard Usenet style, contained a Frequently Asked Questions list as well as a whole range of information gleaned from printed and broadcast sources across the world.

This shows how hard it can be to proscribe information that exists on an interactive digital network like the Internet. Several Canadian universities cut their students' access to the alt.fan.karla-homolka newsgroup, for fear that they might be exposing themselves to liability for contempt of court if they took no action to block the material. However, even if the university was the students' only means of accessing the Internet, it was still easy enough for them to find the information because much of it had already been cross-posted to other Usenet newsgroups.[17] Perhaps information really does want to be free.

Whatever the rights and wrongs of it, the Homolka case is also a casebook demonstration of how futile it can be to attempt censorship in the teeth of popular opposition. The absurd over-broadness of a measure like the US Communications Decency Act (CDA)[18] is a salutary reminder to governments that standards of behaviour cannot simply be imposed from above, without reference to pre-existing standards within the community. The fight over, and subsequent defeat of, the CDA is one more in a long list of bannings that degenerated into farce, from *Ulysses* in the 1920s, to *Spycatcher* in the 1980s, where state-imposed proscriptions were so widely flouted that the authorities were forced into a humiliating climbdown. What it also points up is the fact that banning can actually stimulate a demand for the proscribed material which did not exist before. This has been observed in connection with pornography, as we shall see in the next section. The 'forbidden fruits' effect, as it has been called, appears to be even more marked with the Internet than with other distribution channels, partly because, as we have seen, the technology makes it so easy to circumvent any ban, and partly because the culture among users is a strongly libertarian one.

There are other problems aside from jurisdiction, in terms of extending the kind of regulatory systems we have known up until now to the Internet. The question of how far the chain of liability for online material extends – to the Internet service provider? the viewer? the author of the material? to the phone company over whose wires it is transmitted? – has been very widely aired, and I do not propose to address it here, except to point out that the liability question is further complicated by the jurisdictional question, because different countries have already established quite different chains of liability. Whatever the answer, governments will be unable to impose direct control over the content of the Internet unless, as in Singapore, they simply monitor all incoming and outgoing phone lines – impracticable in any state larger than a city.[19] In this case, I believe, the debate must shift to a different level, to the level of policy, where there are complicated questions about the desirability of restricting certain categories of speech.

THE GREAT PORN DEBATE

Western governments have not as yet found a way to solve the regulatory problems. The EU might yet decide on regulation at the regional level, although the CDA experience showed the inadequacies of the legislative approach. But just because the

Internet is hard to regulate, that does not mean we should just give up and say 'anything goes', does it? Outside the US, governments have tended to be a little more realistic about the problems they face in formulating policy with regard to the Internet. The UK's Ethics Collaborative Open Group, as we saw above, gave a frank assessment of the prospects for regulating the network. And in Canada, an Information Highway Advisory Council (IHAC) report in May 1996 called for greater clarity on questions of liability and outlined 'the need to strike a balance between freedom of expression and protection against offensive content'.[20] At the time of writing, the policy debate is still being thrashed out and it is clear that until that happens, no coherent regulatory approach can be established. So what are the issues surrounding speech on the Internet? What are the interests that governments are trying to balance? And what lies behind calls in the press and elsewhere for greater restrictions?

IHAC's notion of a balance between freedom of expression and protection against offensive content would, I suspect, strike many as a model of reasonableness. They may be wildly overplayed in the traditional media, but nevertheless there are serious concerns about some of the material which finds its way onto the Internet: not just the wilder fringes, such as child pornography, so-called 'bride-trafficking' or bomb-making manuals, but more mainstream forms of obscenity or indecency, material about illegal drugs, or messages inciting religious, racial or ethnic hatred. There is no doubt that some or all of this material is circulating on the Internet, and that it can cause genuine offence. It may even cause real harm to real people, though this is harder to substantiate.

Questions of offence and harm are important questions. Is causing offence sufficient to justify restrictions on freedom of expression, on the Internet or anywhere else? On one hand, the idea that expression causes actual harm would appear to provide a stronger justification for restricting that expression than mere offence. On the other, it is always going to be harder to prove the existence of actual harm than it is to prove the existence of offence. This debate is most familiar in terms of access to pornography, which many people – women and men – find offensive in the extreme. Regardless of what the obscenity laws allow or restrict, some argue, pornography should be banned on the Internet because it causes actual harm to women as a group by defining them as submissive sexual objects, thereby reflecting and reinforcing their subordinate status in society at large. This is one way, it is argued, in which pre-existing structural inequalities are perpetuated, and the disbenefits that accrue to all women from the consumption of such material outweigh the disbenefits from restricting the free speech rights of the purveyors and consumers. According to Susan Easton, it is not so much a choice between allowing free speech and averting harm, so much as realising that a permissive approach can sometimes harm the cause of free speech itself:

> The pornographer's free speech means in reality the loss of speech for others. The First Amendment [to the US Constitution] and pornography have quite distinct aims. The aim of the former is to promote freedom of expression, while the latter silences women.[21]

On this basis, argues Easton, absolutely unfettered freedom of expression might be possible in a society which lacks the economic, cultural and political inequalities of contemporary liberal democracies, but until we arrive at such a situation some temporary, targeted restraints on speech are necessary to actively encourage the expression of non-dominant viewpoints. Pornography harms women by forcing them to shut up; therefore it should be banned.

Harm, as noted above, is hard to prove. At the most straightforward level it has not been possible to establish any causal connection between consumption of pornography and a disposition to commit sexual crime.[22] At the broader societal level, however, the issue becomes more complex. In Canada the courts have upheld the view that some types of pornography should be restricted on the basis of causing social harm to women.[23] The trouble is that the notion of harm which this embodies ('dehumanising and degrading') is so amorphous as to be practically useless for the purpose of determining precisely what should be banned and what permitted. The class of material which this kind of restriction could rule out is incredibly broad. More importantly, however, there is no reason to believe that restricting on this basis does actually have the consequences claimed for it – namely that it effectively stamps out pornography, that it greatly reduces exposure to violent sexual imagery and that it has a discernible impact on deeper societal inequalities.

The harms argument, of course, can also be applied to other forms of social discrimination – against blacks, or Jews, or gays – and in each case the difficulties with it are analogous.[24] But the most fundamental difficulty in each case is that attempting to restrict expression only makes expression a scapegoat for deeper social problems. Speech does not *cause* sexism, or racism, or homophobia, and nor, in any real sense, does it perpetuate them. The causes of racism, for example, lie in a multitude of historical, sociological and psychological factors including exclusion, class, poverty, identification and so on. Criminalising racist speech does exactly nothing to address those factors.

Worse than that, though, criminalising unwelcome forms of expression is actually counterproductive. Anti-censorship feminists argue that the pornography problem can be turned around by saying that concentrating on the manifestation ignores the causes of inequality and helps to define women as victims. We saw in relation to the Homolka case how futile it can be to try to outlaw speech, particularly on the Internet, but there are ways in which censorship can actually harm the cause that restriction is supposedly trying to advance. According to Nadine Strossen, president of the American Civil Liberties Union and one of the main lobbyists against the Communications Decency Act:

> [T]he evidence suggests that censorship of any material increases an audience's desire to obtain the material and disposes the audience to be more receptive to it. Critical viewing skills, and the ability to regard media images skeptically and analytically, atrophy under a censorial regime. A public that learns to question everything it sees or hears is better equipped to reject culturally propagated values than is one that assumes the media have been purged of all 'incorrect' perspectives.[25]

Exactly so. We help no one by restricting speech and claiming that we do so on behalf of other interests. That can have two consequences: either it strips the viewer or reader of any responsibility for what he sees or reads and, more importantly, for his response to what he sees and reads, because that response has been pre-sanctioned ('this material must be okay because if it wasn't, I wouldn't have access to it'); or, alternatively, it simply serves to sharpen the appetite for what is forbidden.

But Susan Easton's concern about pornography silencing women does raise a central issue, and one which is of particular importance here, namely the degree to which a set of media like the Internet permits the reflection of a full range of viewpoints.[26] Because if you argue, as I am, that restriction is bad because of the harms it causes, as opposed to the harms it is supposed to prevent, then you generate a positive need to extend viewpoint diversity as far as possible. The juridical relationship between freedom of expression and viewpoint diversity is well established in the US, where the Supreme Court's interpretation of the First Amendment has historically been based on a marketplace of ideas model: freedom of expression operates best in an unregulated marketplace, where opposing viewpoints can be aired, and the truth, or something approximating to it, can be discovered. Generally speaking, the more viewpoints that are allowed space in the market, the better. The idea of maximising viewpoint diversity can also, of course, be adduced in the other direction, namely as justifying regulations to prevent the dominance of one set of (politically powerful) viewpoints over more marginal ones. This, indeed, is the thrust behind Easton's critique of pornography, and it is one which has been particularly relevant to a medium like television, where the number of channels for communication has been severely limited and where entry costs for anyone wanting to start up their own station have been prohibitive, making it all the more important that regulations exist to ensure a plurality of viewpoints. In a world of spectrum scarcity, there is a role for government regulators in allocating access to a limited resource. That situation might well change with the advent of digital broadcasting. In any case, it is a situation that does not apply to the Internet. Despite some limitations to bandwidth on parts of the network, in theory the advent of a fibre optic information superhighway should provide all the capacity anyone needs to enable viewpoint plurality.

It is hardly a new thought, but even in its current form the Internet offers an excellent approximation to a genuine marketplace of ideas. Traditionally, thinkers on the left have tended to object to the marketplace of ideas model on the basis that the real marketplace always interposes between the viewer and listener or the writer and reader so as to skew the delivery of viewpoints in an unfair or unequal way. As we saw above, the economic structures of the media – ownership, production, management – are such that they inevitably give more space to some viewpoints (the mainstream, dominant, and saleable) at the expense of others (the marginal, 'difficult', or unpopular).[27] The great strength of the Internet, of course, has been that it offers a remarkably direct communication path: compared with traditional media, the route between writer and reader is wonderfully unmediated by editors, producers, marketing executives, proprietors, advertisers or politicians. The more people who use the Internet, the more it reflects the diversity of opinion and expression as it actually exists in society, and the greater the benefit for the health of our democracy.[28] On the Internet, the idea of restricting speech in order to increase viewpoint diversity really is the contradiction that it appears to be.

It will be argued that viewpoint diversity should never, under any circumstances, be extended to those who would themselves deliberately restrict freedom for others – a version of the old 'no platform' slogan. The question of whether to tolerate the intolerant is a classical dilemma for liberals, one which goes back at least to Locke (who thought that atheists could not be trusted and therefore should not be tolerated), and has been raised more recently by Karl Popper, who called it the 'paradox of toleration': in order to extend toleration as far as possible in society, we must in the last resort reserve the right to extinguish intolerant viewpoints, by force if necessary.[29] The fear with the Internet is that Popper's paradox is all the more applicable, because it gives an unprecedented platform and reach for intolerant viewpoints. However, this objection also, I think, fails for the same reasons that the harms justification fails, primarily because it targets the wrong thing: speech, rather than deed. There is simply no reason to believe that exposure to intolerant views is going to result in greater intolerance in society. If anything, the opposite should be expected: it is restriction that enables and fosters intolerance. And, as Anthony Skillen points out, 'The vision of a society in which only liberals have the right to liberty is conceptually, as well as actually, comic.'[30]

Be that as it may, there is still, as we noted at the outset, some outrageously offensive material online. Where does this leave my right, if such a right I have, not to be confronted by neo-Nazi propaganda, child pornography and the like? Might that not override – or at least have the same weight as – your right to freedom of expression? Further thought about how to deal with offensiveness depends on an appreciation of the context within which expression takes place. So: what kind of context does the Internet provide?

THE RULES OF THE ROAD

People sometimes talk about the Internet as if it were a different place, or existed in another dimension from the rest of the real world. This is partly because of the metaphors used to talk about it – 'cyberspace', 'the online world', and so forth – and partly because of the kind of difficulties we raised at the outset, about how community standards and laws as we have known them do not map easily onto the Internet. It is partly because of the blurring of geographies, which leads people to talk of virtual communities as distinct from real ones. And it also perhaps partly reflects a dissatisfaction with traditional modes of social interaction and with the media as they are currently constituted. The Internet offers an unparalleled degree of interactive communication and participation, which is sometimes represented in terms of escape from the real into the virtual.[31] That might, perhaps, also underlie the desire to keep cyberspace 'clean' by purging it of some of the nastier things we have come to accept as part and parcel of real life, like racism, sexism, abuse, intolerance and hatred.

But the distinction, in the end, is misguided. The Internet is as much a part of the real world as I am, or my local community is. Computer-mediated communities, after all, are real social entities. The network is rooted in a social context which, in the end, will determine the limits of acceptability. As one commentator has put it:

> We are living in a real world, and we must recognise that it is indeed the case that we cannot make of it whatever we wish. The institutions developing and promoting the new technologies exist solidly in this world ... Because it is a materially straitened and socially divided world, we should remember how much we remain in need of politics.[32]

The political character of the Internet is seen nowhere so clearly as in the vexed policy questions it raises. There is nothing so quintessentially political as the raging conflict between competing interests, rights, concerns and opinions to which the Internet gives direct expression. Nevertheless, having taken note of the need for scepticism, the concept of community still has a particular and important application with regard to the Internet and the expression of intolerant points of view.

In his analysis of the effects of hate speech, Kent Greenawalt raises a significant distinction between two different types of political community: one is the close-knit community of shared values, with a strong mutual regard between members and a collective sense of commitment; the other is a looser coalition designed mainly to enhance the individual or local group interests of participants. If, he argues, one thinks of society as a genuine community of shared values, the thought of restricting outright expressions of hatred becomes uncontroversial, because such expression is exactly in opposition to the core community values of equality and respect for all members. If, on the other hand, one thinks of society as more of a common enterprise, but one which makes no attempt to impose shared values, the question of suppression is much more difficult.[33]

The question for our purposes is: what kind of community is the Internet? The answer, I think, is straightforward: in so far as the Internet itself can be described as a community at all (as opposed to a lot of separate communities), it can only be a common enterprise. Given the extraordinary variety of expression, the diversity of uses and the differences among users, the idea of the Internet itself as forming a community of shared values is almost self-evidently wrong. Indeed, there is perhaps only one respect in which Internet users can be said to have a commonality of interest, and that is in keeping the channels of communication that they all use as open and as free from restriction as possible. And that interest arises directly as a result of their being involved in a common enterprise.

This is not to argue, however, that there are no rules of engagement in a common enterprise. Of course, if it is going to work at all, it is necessary that all involved agree to abide by certain standards of behaviour. At the simplest level, this is seen in terms of so-called 'netiquette', a series of behavioural norms aimed at encouraging consideration for other users by refraining from posting useless or irrelevant material to newsgroups, for example, or respecting other users' privacy. It might be possible to see different newsgroups as separate sub-communities, in which there are certain shared values which might affect the acceptability of certain kinds of behaviour. For instance, in her analysis of one newsgroup run by and for devotees of television soap operas, Nancy Baym[34] points out the specialised rules that evolve around the specific interests of those who use the group – not giving plot lines away in advance, for example – and the kinds of sanctions that are employed to punish transgressions.

At another level there are rules which are determined by commercial service providers, universities and so forth, the conditions of use that tell users what is acceptable conduct and what is not. These might or might not have the force of contract law behind them. The United Kingdom Education and Research Networking Association (UKERNA), which operates the academic network JANET, for instance, specifies various categories of unacceptable use, such as transmitting obscene or indecent images; transmitting defamatory material; infringing copyright; sending unsolicited commercial material; and so on.[35] A commercial server, such as America Online, also issues what it calls its 'Rules of the Road' to new subscribers, encouraging considerate, courteous and responsible use of their service. To this extent at least, the Internet can be seen as a successfully self-regulating community which encourages tolerance among its users. In which case, is there any need for further regulation from outside?

According to the Metropolitan Police, there is. In a letter to members of the UK's Internet Service Providers Association (ISPA) in August 1996, the Met sent out a list of about 130 Usenet groups which, they said, 'contain pornographic material', and asked ISPA members to monitor the newsgroups they carry. 'We trust that with your cooperation and self-regulation', said the Met, 'it will not be necessary for us to move to an enforcement policy'.[36] The ISPA had agreed, earlier in the month, to collaborate with the Met in removing obscene material from Usenet. At that meeting, ISPs had been told that either the UK industry must take action itself to deal with the issue of pornography on the Internet, or the police will be forced to intervene. A spokesperson for the ISPA said that it was only interested in restricting newsgroups which contained material which is illegal under existing regulations, namely child pornography and certain other kinds of obscenity, but acknowledged – as do the Met – that a complete ban on newsgroups is unworkable because there are always ways around it.[37] In that case, the Met's threat of 'enforcement' seems like an empty one, although as we shall see later, not entirely so.

The letter raises very serious concerns. It appears that the police regard ISPs as publishers of the material they carry and that the police expect ISPs continuously to monitor newsgroups and to remove those which contain illegal material. Illegal material can appear anywhere, in any newsgroup, at any time. The distribution of articles is not by any means random, of course – sexually explicit material tends to be concentrated in the alt.sex and alt.binaries hierarchies, for instance. But any attempt to control the news tends to cause articles to shift into different groups, as the Homolka case showed. Furthermore, sophisticated techniques for encrypting material and concealing messages within messages are in common use. The sheer volume of material would require a staff of thousands to review. ISPs simply do not have the resources to look at every file on their systems. Whereas a print publisher is completely aware of what it is publishing, to expect an ISP to know the content of every file passing through the server is to place an intolerable legal and commercial burden upon it. An ISP can no more be expected to eavesdrop on every Internet transaction than can BT monitor the content of every conversation taking place on the network.

Looked at another way, however, the implicit threats coming from the police could provide a very good argument for why we need a properly worked out system of regulation. The current situation, in which the police are having to interpret existing laws on permissible publication and apply them to the Internet, so that no one in the end knows where they stand, is clearly unsatisfactory. If regulation could establish the common-carrier status of ISPs and ward off the threat of arbitrary action by the police against those they believe to be carrying 'pornographic' or 'offensive' material, that would be an advance.[38] Clearly defined regulation also has the advantage of providing a mechanism for reviewing the scope and propriety of any restrictions.

The difficulty is that while the status of ISPs is so uncertain, no one is going to get what they want. One way of creating a balance between liberty and protection of the user from offence or obscenity lies in the creation of so-called 'walled gardens', in which ISPs offer partial or filtered Internet access. The user knows that there is no danger of accidentally stumbling on a pornographic newsgroup, for example. The current situation, however, could very easily work as a strong disincentive to ISPs to set up such 'walled gardens' because *any* attempt that an ISP makes to monitor the content of some or all of the material they carry could be held to trigger publisher-style liability and therefore lose common-carrier status. In other words, they must either monitor everything (impossible) or nothing (undesirable). Ideally, the market should be permitted to create a variety of online forums, some that provide only material appropriate for children, others that are designed for a wider audience, and others that are unfiltered. Anything else threatens a return to nineteenth-century standards of obscenity, by which the limits were drawn at anything which threatened to corrupt the morals of the most susceptible members of society. The Hicklin test, as established by Chief Justice Cockburn in 1868, was meant to judge 'whether the tendency of the matter charged as obscenity is to deprave and corrupt those whose minds are open to such immoral influences, and into whose hands a publication of this sort may fall'.[39] In other words, society could see and say no more than what was fit for children. And indeed, this was precisely one of the central objections of lawyers, ISPs and civil rights activists to the CDA.[40]

The case is stated by the advisory group to US Senator Patrick Leahy, who led the Congressional opposition to the CDA:

> Online service providers should not be forced to become private censors: If online services or individual system operators are held liable for all of their users' communications, the services will be forced to impose stringent censorship rules on their users in order to limit the corporate liability of the service provider. Such rules would create a chilling effect on users of interactive media ... Holding carriers responsible for the content of all information and communication on their systems is a grave policy error which will restrict the free flow of information and is contrary to First Amendment and personal privacy values.[41]

The drawback with this version of ISP liability, therefore, is twofold. Privatising censorship only so far as the ISP – making the ISP in effect take on the rôle of a regulatory agent of the state – would tend towards the imposition of stricter regulations as ISPs overcompensate in their efforts to cover their own liability; while users, for their part, would be discouraged from pushing the limits of acceptability, through fear of having their service cut off by the ISP. If ISPs are liable for the content of all material on their networks, they will have to try to screen all content before it is allowed to enter the system. Even where this is possible, such prior screening can severely limit the diversity and free flow of information in the online world. Of course, some ISPs will want to offer services that pre-screen content. The point is, though, that if all systems are forced to do so, the usefulness of digital media as communication and information dissemination systems will be drastically limited. It is vital, therefore, that regulations forcing those who merely carry messages to screen their content be avoided.

The alternative – treating ISPs as common carriers – puts responsibility firmly back in the hands of the Internet user. On this idea, censorship is privatised more completely, by cutting out the middleman and giving the responsibility for moral choices about what to read and what to avoid back to the individual. Relying on individuals rather than the government to make choices about the content that they and their families receive optimises the free speech rights of adults. Of course, ISPs have a vital part to play in this. A recent initiative in Israel has led to the setting up of Toranet, which is effectively a walled garden guaranteeing Orthodox Jewish subscribers protection from material that would offend their religious sensibilities.[42] The decision whether to subscribe to Toranet or to an unfiltered service, however, remains with the individual.

Reliance on user control is a genuine alternative to the draconian measures which were proposed under the Communications Decency Act. Indeed, the technology has begun to advance sufficiently to allow this model to be effective. Apart from the various screening packages that have existed for some time – Net Nanny, Surf Watch and Cyber Sitter, to name a few – the development of the Platform for Internet Content Selection (PICS) takes regulation at the point of delivery to a vastly higher plane of sophistication.[43]

PICS differs from the earlier screening programmes inasmuch as it is a meta-standard, that is, it provides a means for filtering material in line with a range of first-order standards, whether these are standards of decency, taste, ideology, or any other basis on which a user might wish to filter material. PICS itself is value-neutral. It simply provides a standard format with which anyone else might create such ratings, and will allow those ratings to be found and read by the standard browsing software. The browsing software can either accept or reject material based on individual users' standards and tastes, based on labels carried in the document's header. Parents, for example, could choose to rely on ratings provided by a commercial ratings company or by a local community group. Parents could then set up their Internet software so that it consulted this organisation's database before downloading the material onto the machine for viewing. Thus far only three major third-party rating systems have been developed for use with PICS: SafeSurf, Net Shepherd, and the Recreational Software Advisory Council's RSACi, which has become the de facto industry standard.

PICS gained instant approval from the Department of Trade and Industry as part of a wider strategy of self-regulation. 'The police already act where material available on the Internet is illegal', a DTI press release noted in 1996, 'but government will face increasingly strong calls for legislation to regulate all aspects of the Internet, unless and until service providers are seen wholeheartedly to embrace responsible self-regulation'. The problem remains, however: what kind of self-regulation will be both effective in protecting users from unwanted material while retaining the widest possible scope for free expression on the Internet?

The industry's first move towards self-regulation was contained in the Safety-Net proposals, drawn up jointly by the ISPA, the London Internet Exchange (LINX) and the Safety-Net Foundation in September 1996, after discussions with the Metropolitan Police and the Home Office.[45] This was avowedly an attempt to stamp out child pornography on the Internet once and for all. The aim was to encourage responsible behaviour by users and ISPs through rating material on the Web and on Usenet; and by setting up a free hotline to report the presence of illegal material online. A similar system was also set up in the Netherlands. At the time of writing, this model of self-regulation is being furthered at the European level through the Internet Content Rating for Europe project (INCORE), which brings together various industry and non-profit bodies, such as the Internet Watch Foundation in Britain and the German Electronic Commerce Forum.

There are, however, serious concerns about the effect that centralised rating might have on freedom of expression online. The American Civil Liberties Union has argued that the proliferation of such schemes represents an attempt at censorship by smothering controversial speech under the weight of cumbersome requirements upon Internet users to rate any material they publish.[46] Such requirements, says the ACLU, will bear more heavily on individual publishers than on well-resourced commercial organisations. The schemes will, in the end, only be workable if there are legal sanctions for those who misrate, or refuse to rate, their material. The inevitable result, the argument goes, will be to privilege bland, commercial speech over more robust, controversial material, with serious consequences for the nature of the medium as a whole. In the end, I believe, the nature of these consequences will come down to the degree of coercion that such systems employ. If they reduce the obligation for self-rating on providers of material, while extending choice to readers over what they see online in their homes, they will be relatively benign. If, however, they are backed up with a statutory requirement to self-rate, or are coupled with enforced blocking of 'objectionable' sites, the implications for freedom of expression become correspondingly severe.

Evidently, there is strong political pressure on ISPs and the industry as a whole to show willing to help keep their house in order. What is wrong with the current proposals is not that they concede too much to the media-driven stereotype of the corrupting Internet (although they do), or that they encourage vigilantism (they do that too); but that they fail to take seriously the distinction between self-regulation through filtering and rating (censorship at the point of delivery) and action by state agencies (in this case the Vice Squad) to persuade or compel users to restrict what they read or see online. The latter approach is, in the end, ineffective and doomed to failure. The former is empowering because it gives individuals, groups and communities the right and the ability effectively to regulate their own use of the online media. And, as we have seen, the European Commission's Green Paper, in attempting to combine the two approaches, runs the serious risk of paving the way for a much more stringent set of restrictions to freedom of expression based on a hazy notion of 'human dignity'.

CONCLUSION

No one can seriously deny that society as a whole has a compelling interest to prevent the wide circulation of child pornography. But for society to overplay that interest is to risk treating every Internet user as if they were a potential child pornographer. The advantage of filtering and rating technology is that it allows different degrees of access to coincide with the needs and values of different users, without simply setting the level of acceptability of content over the whole network at the very lowest threshold of tolerance. The Internet is extremely resistant to centralised regulation, and rating/filtering allows a decentralised form of self-regulation.

As we saw earlier, the frequency-scarcity justification for media regulation does not apply to the Internet. It may be the case with the Internet that an unregulated marketplace of ideas is the best way to produce the greatest possible diversity of viewpoints. This should be subject to empirical verification. For it to happen, of course, depends partly on ISPs offering a range of degrees of access to the Internet. In other words, it does not matter if most ISPs only offer filtered access as long as there are at least some ISPs offering unfiltered access at competitive rates. Viewpoint diversity is also enhanced by encouraging more users to get online. This is another good reason for treating ISPs as common carriers rather than publishers. With common-carrier status, ISPs would have a duty to make their services available to the public on a nondiscriminatory basis.

Is it not reasonable, however, to expect that ISPs will want to exercise some editorial control over the material they carry, over and above the usual conditions of service that subscribers accept? The answer, I think, is that ISPs must be encouraged to resist that temptation and to recognise that the Internet is altering the traditional editorial balance, away from the producer and towards the user. How and where we then strike the balance between the free expression rights of speakers and the privacy interests of listeners depends largely on how we think of the space in which the speech takes place. According to the *Harvard Law Review*, the situation in the US is such that:

> if the cyberspace in which the information superhighway operates is regarded as analogous to public space, then First Amendment principles evident outside of the electronic media suggest that the burden may be on users of the information superhighway to avoid unwanted messages by electronically averting their eyes. In other words, accessing the information superhighway may be like walking

> onto a city street, and users should be expected to cope with the wide array of entertainment, annoyance, and offense that normally takes place there.[47]

That is as it should be. Like any other kind of public space, the usual community standards apply. As users, we should get used to bearing the responsibility for what we choose to see and read online, because that is the only form of regulation which is going to have any real meaning. As the policy debate heats up, there are bound to be more calls for tighter restrictions; as with the European Commission, some of these calls will be well-intentioned appeals to values and rights other than freedom of expression, but they should be resisted nonetheless. Taking the responsibility for what we see out of the hands of self-appointed moral guardians, unaccountable quangos and industry watchdogs, and putting it back where it belongs, in the hands of the user, would be, for once, to treat us like adults, like citizens. If the Internet forces this on us, so much the better for us, and for it.

It should be remembered, nevertheless, that in the United Kingdom, at least, there is no shortage of legal means still available to the state against those who are thought to misuse their freedoms online. Apart from the statutory restrictions already mentioned – the Obscene Publications Acts, the Protection of Children Act, and so on – there is also the far hazier realm of the common law, where the niceties of statutory definition are not needed. Any ISP, and many users, for instance, could in theory find themselves up on charges of conspiracy to corrupt public morals, say, or conspiracy to outrage public decency. There is no legal definition for such offences, which means it is hard to know for sure whether one has committed one or not: it depends on what a jury decides. If the Safety-Net proposals fail to assuage the politicians' or the Met's desire for action, then we might well see one or two such prosecutions, if only to encourage the others. Without the countervailing presence of an enforceable right to freedom of expression, the insidious erosion of that liberty through misapplication of the common law, through veiled threats from the police and politicians, or through the kind of media scaremongering that hones a public appetite for scapegoats on which to pin the blame for society's problems, remains an ever-present threat to speech, both online and off. The Internet represents an extraordinarily important development in the field of social communications. To slam the brakes on before we even know where it might take us would be self-defeating in the extreme.

NOTES

1. The fact that the Internet has been described as a true marketplace of ideas is of particular relevance. The marketplace of ideas model, widely associated with John Stuart Mill's classic defence of freedom of expression in *On Liberty*, has become well established in this century in the First Amendment jurisprudence of the US Supreme Court. The marketplace of ideas model therefore underlies much of the debate (especially in the US) about access to and regulation of the Internet.
2. The European Commission delivered two important policy documents on 16 October 1996, in the wake of the Belgian child-sex scandal. The first, 'Illegal and Harmful Content on the Internet' (COM(96)487), deals specifically with preventing the circulation on the Internet of material whose content is in contravention of the laws of one or more Member States of the European Union. The second, a Green Paper on 'The Protection of Minors and Human Dignity in Audiovisual and Information Services' (COM(96) 483), is a more wide-ranging examination of the legal and policy implications of new communications media, including online services, with particular regard to the standards enshrined in the European Convention of Human Rights.
3. Clifford Stoll, one of the earliest, best-known and most enthusiastic exponents of the Internet, has done a dramatic turn around in his book *Silicon Snake Oil: Second Thoughts on the Information Superhighway* (Macmillan, 1995). In one of the book's harsher judgments he describes the Internet as a glorified form of CB radio.
4. Isabel Hilton, 'When Everything Has its Price', *Guardian*, 27 August 1996.
5. Some legal purists, who insist on reserving the use of the word 'censorship' specifically for restraints on publication imposed by the state or its agents, will find this idea contradictory, but I ask them to bear with me. Censorship is not easily comprehended by any one disciplinary approach, because it has several different dimensions – legal, ethical, philosophical, political, psychological. Accordingly, this chapter will not be limited to, or even primarily concerned with, judicial forms of restraint.
6. Ian J. Lloyd and Moira Simpson, *Law on the Electronic Frontier* (Edinburgh University Press, 1994), pp. 98–9.
7. For an extensive discussion of how existing laws regulating speech map onto the Internet, see Yaman Akdeniz's excellent Cyber-Rights and Cyber-Liberties site at http://www.leeds.ac.uk/law/pgs/yaman /yaman.htm
8. Paul F. Burton, 'Content on the Internet: Free or Fettered' at http://www.dis.strath.ac.uk/people/paul/CIL96.htm

9. Akdeniz, 'Pornography on the Internet' at Cyber-Rights and Cyber-Liberties site, see note 7.
10. Tolhurst et al., *Using the Internet: The Ultimate Guide to Getting Connected and Productive on the World's Largest Network* (Que, 1994).
11. In August 1996 the American neo-Nazi Gary Lauck was sentenced to two years in prison by a German court for sending neo-Nazi propaganda from the US to Germany through the mail. He was arrested in Denmark and extradited to Germany on the basis that his activities were also illegal in Denmark.
12. 'Internet Ethical Issues: Report from Ethics Collaborative Open Group', February 1995, at http://www.opengov/documents/cogs/ethics.htm
13. *Miller v. California* 413 US 15 (1973).
14. European Commission Green Paper COM(96) 483, Chapter II, 'Rules and Enforcement Measures Applicable to Protection of Minors and Human Dignity'.
15. Ibid.
16. For a good analysis of the jurisdictional problem generally see Anne Wells Branscomb, 'Jurisdictional Quandaries for Global Networks', in Linda M. Harasim (ed.), *Global Networks: Computers and International Communication* (MIT Press, 1993).
17. There is an excellent discussion of the Homolka case, and other Canadian attempts at regulating Usenet, in Lesley Regan Shade, 'Is There Free Speech on the Net?', in Rob Shields (ed.), *Cultures of Internet: Virtual Spaces, Real Histories, Living Bodies* (Sage, 1996).
18. The CDA sought to impose criminal sanctions on anyone who knowingly made available indecent material online so that it could be accessed by children. It was ruled unconstitutional by a federal court in June 1996, and is currently the subject of an appeal to the Supreme Court by the Department of Justice. The legal challenge to the Act is well documented by the Electronic Frontier Foundation, which spearheaded the battle, at http://www.eff.org/
19. A lawyer with the US National Security Agency, Stewart Baker ('The Net Escape Censorship? Ha!', *Wired*, September 1995), has argued that the willingness of countries such as Singapore, Malaysia, China and the Gulf States to attempt centralised control of the Internet shows that it is only a matter of policy that prevents Western governments attempting the same thing. This ignores the fact that for Western countries, where there is already a decentralised, independent telephone network, the means for central command and control do not currently exist.
20. Information Highway Advisory Council, 'Building the Information Society: Moving Canada into the 21st Century' at http://info.ic.gc.ca/info-highway/ih.html
21. Susan M. Easton, *The Problem of Pornography: Regulation and the Right to Free Speech* (Routledge, 1994), p. 108.
22. See, for instance, the Williams Committee report: *Report of the Committee on Obscenity and Film Censorship*, Cmnd 7772 (1979).
23. The argument in favour of establishing pornography – as distinct from obscenity – as a category for restriction is particularly associated with Andrea Dworkin, who first set out the issues in 'Against the Male Flood:

Censorship, Pornography and Equality', *Harvard Women's Law Journal*, 8 (1985). In *Butler v. the Queen* (ISCR 452 (1992)), Canada's High Court broadly followed Dworkin's recommendations by ruling that any material which is 'dehumanising' or 'degrading' to women should be banned. This approach is strongly echoed in the European Commission Green Paper on Protecting Minors and Human Dignity.

24. For an exhaustive analysis of the Supreme Court's approach to the harms justification for restricting speech see Kent Greenawalt, *Fighting Words* (Princeton University Press, 1995).
25. Nadine Strossen, *Defending Pornography: Free Speech, Sex, and the Fight for Women's Rights* (Scribner, 1995), p. 254.
26. Partly, of course, this comes down to questions of access, of how far the necessary equipment and knowledge for Internet use are available to less advantaged groups, and how differential access, can lead to social stratification on the basis of 'information wealth' or 'information poverty'. These questions, however, are beyond the scope of this essay.
27. See, for example, Anthony Skillen, 'Freedom of Speech', in Graham (ed.), *Contemporary Political Philosophy: Radical Studies* (Cambridge University Press, 1982), p. 145. Others, such as R.P. Wolff, have argued that even an internally free and fair market cannot circumvent broader societal constraints on viewpoint diversity. This is known as the 'market-failure model'.
28. Even the British government accepts that viewpoint diversity in the media is a good thing. The 1995 White Paper on media ownership says, 'A free and diverse media are an indispensable part of the democratic process. They provide the multiplicity of voices and opinions that informs the public, influences opinion and engenders political debate. They promote the culture of dissent which any healthy democracy must have' (*Media Ownership: The Government's Proposals*, CM 2872 (HMSO), para 1.4).
29. Karl Popper, *The Open Society and its Enemies*, vol. I (Routledge, 1966), p. 256.
30. Skillen, 'Freedom of Speech', p. 141.
31. Howard Rheingold is particularly associated with the idea of the virtual as compensating for the defects of the real, and as offering a return to a perceived golden age of communitarian living. In his book *The Virtual Community: Finding Connection in a Computerised World* (Secker and Warburg, 1994), he writes of cyberspace as 'one of the informal public spaces where people can rebuild the aspects of community that were lost when the malt shop became the mall' (pp. 25–6).
32. Kevin Robins, 'Cyberspace and the World We Live In', in Dovey (ed.), *Fractal Dreams* (Lawrence and Wishart, 1996).
33. Greenawalt, *Fighting Words*, p. 147. This distinction mirrors the long-standing disagreement between liberals and communitarians over the nature of political society.
34. Nancy K. Baym, 'The Emergence of Community in Computer-Mediated Communication', in Steven Jones (ed.), *CyberSociety: Computer-Mediated Communication and Community* (Sage Publications, 1995).
35. 'JANET Acceptable Use Policy' (UKERNA, 1995), at http://www.ja.net/documents/use.html

36. The text of the letter, dated 9 August 1996, and the list of newsgroups under suspicion are available at http://www.uk.vbc.net/censorship/theMet.html. Again, the irony in this is that the Met has provided a most convenient resource for anyone who wants to know where to find all kinds of 'cyberporn' from amputee fetishism to zoophilia.
37. Steve Gold, 'British Police Move to Stamp Out Internet Porn', Newsbytes News Network report, 16 August 1996. As with the Homolka case, cross-posting to several newsgroups is a simple way of circumventing any attempted ban. Since most effort is spent on identifying newsgroups with obviously pornographic names (alt.sex.fetish.tinygirls, for example), it is easy enough for anyone who is determined to make such material available to do so through more innocent-sounding newsgroups.
38. The Met's letter to the ISPA does not distinguish between offensive, pornographic and obscene material. Only the last category, of course, has any significance in statute law.
39. *R v. Hicklin* (1868), LR 3 QB 360, at p. 371.
40. See, for instance, Jonathan Rosenoer, 'Indecent Communication' which traces the development of obscenity standards from Hicklin onwards, at http://www.cyberlaw.com
41. 'Parental Empowerment, Child Protection, and Free Speech in Interactive Media: Interactive Working Group Report to Senator Leahy, 24 July 1995', available from the Center for Democracy and Technology at http://www.cdt.org/
42. 'Orthodox Jews go Surfing on the Kosher Internet', *The Times*, 21 October 1996.
43. The technological specifications are fully explained in James Miller and Paul Reznick, 'PICS: Internet Access Controls Without Censorship' at http://www.w3.org/pub/WWW/PICS/
44. 'DTI: Ian Taylor Challenges Internet Service Providers – Develop New Software to Come Clean', Hermes UK Government Press Release P/96/63, 14 August 1996.
45. R3 Safety-Net – Rating, Reporting, Responsibility for Child Pornography and Illegal Material on the Internet: an Industry Proposal, Adopted and Recommended by Executive Committee of ISPA, LINX and the Safety-Net Foundation, 23 September 1996.
46. 'Fahrenheit 451.2: Is Cyberspace Burning? How Rating and Blocking Proposals May Torch Free Speech on the Internet', American Civil Liberties Union, August 1997, at http://www.aclu.org/org/issues/cyber/burning.html
47. Harvard Law Review Association, 'The Message in the Medium: The First Amendment on the Information Superhighway', *Harvard Law Review*, March 1994.

2 Freedom of Information: an Electronic Window onto Government[1]

Andrew Ecclestone,
Campaign for Freedom of Information

> The people's enemies take care to represent government as a thing made up of mysteries, which only themselves understood; and they hid from the understanding of the nation, the only thing that was beneficial to know, namely, that government is nothing more than a national association acting on the principles of society.
>
> Thomas Paine, *The Rights of Man*, 1792 [2]

INTRODUCTION

Tom Paine saw clearly enough that people would only be free if they understood how their government worked, and for this to happen they needed information. The debate on civil liberties and the Internet has revealed that our lack of rights in the concrete world is allowing authorities to breach our civil liberties in the electronic sphere too. When we allow government to hide its inner workings, it behaves in an illiberal manner. We must establish our rights in the real world and then make them work for us electronically; this includes our right to information.

Britain does not yet have a Freedom of Information Act (FOIA),[3] but it is the policy of the Labour government to introduce one. The government also wishes to use information technology to revolutionise the public's dealings with it. However it needs to solve the problem, if it is to make substantial progress on this front, of persuading the public to trust government not to abuse the powers it will acquire to invade their privacy through such technologies as data-matching. One of the key elements of building and maintaining trust is openness. Easy access by people to government-held information, both about themselves and the functioning of government, will be essential if we are to start to rebuild our trust in government and, by extension, the political process.

With the introduction of a Freedom of Information Act the government has the opportunity, if it wishes to take it, to make transparency the foundation of the future electronic delivery of public services, as well as the means by which it is held accountable for the performance of its functions. Most overseas Freedom of Information (FOI) laws predate the electronic age. The long delayed British legislation will at least provide the opportunity to ensure the FOIA will take full account of modern information and communications technologies. If it does not address these issues, FOI will further complicate the administrative burden of carrying out government in the paper-based world.

Until an FOIA is introduced we have to rely on the Open Government code of practice when seeking information the government has not published.[4] This is a voluntary code introduced in 1994 and supervised by the Parliamentary Ombudsman. It has been used successfully to obtain previously unpublished information, but because it has no legal force the government is ultimately able, if it wishes, to withhold the requested information. The last Conservative government also took a number of positive steps to promote greater public access to information via the Internet and this has been continued by the present Labour government. But without the culture and structures of openness which could be fostered by a Freedom of Information Act, online information has developed in an ad hoc manner.

GOVERNMENT ON AND OFF THE INTERNET

The Internet has primarily been used by governments to improve access to information which, while publicly available, may be obscure or difficult to obtain. Only in a few instances has it been used as the main method of publication. A striking example of the latter is the US Department of Energy, which has a Website with a searchable database devoted to thousands of previously classified documents relating to American nuclear energy policy, including the deliberate exposure of military and other personnel to radiation, as well as details of enriched uranium unaccounted for after audits.[5] The then US Energy Secretary decided that instead of the previous policy of deliberately concealing these activities, they should be fully ventilated – and the Internet is used as a key tool for this release of information. The Department says that the site is intended to benefit a variety of 'stakeholders':

> Public interest organisations, historians, researchers, and scientists ... The public ... Concerned citizens will be able to investigate topics of interest and gain desired information ... The Department of Energy and the Government in general will benefit from database automation and access and reduced unnecessary repetition of document reviews.[6]

The Internet is now widely used by government departments in the UK, but it is still exceptional to find it being used as the primary publishing medium, although the BSE Inquiry provides such an example.[7] At most inquiries, the only way to find out what is happening is to rely on sketchy newspaper reports, or turn up in person day after day – something beyond all but the most dedicated observers. Some inquiries do produce a daily transcript but users have to buy these from the reporting company, usually at a cost of between £20 and £35 a day. A full set of transcripts for the Scott Inquiry on arms to Iraq would have cost over £2,000. Within two hours of an evidence session at the BSE Inquiry, a full transcript of every word that has been said can be read free of charge on the Inquiry's Website. All written statements are put online the week before the witness appears in person, and the Inquiry encourages anyone who thinks they have detected an error to notify the Inquiry – by e-mail if they wish. The Website also contains a detailed history of the BSE saga and a glossary of the technical and medical terms. It receives some 7,000 'hits' on hearing days, and has been accessed by Internet users from 64 different countries – particularly scientists. In the six weeks after the Inquiry opened at the beginning of March 1998, some 7,500 copies of witness statements and 14,000 copies of transcripts were downloaded onto visitors' own computers. The ease with which this information can be obtained contrasts markedly with the secrecy that has surrounded the BSE problem in the past.

Examples of the more conventional 'improvement of access' government Websites include:

- The publication of most government department press releases on a centralised Website.[8] These are not posted on the Net at the time they are published, since the Central Office of Information offers this as a commercially available service, but are put on by 10.30 the next morning.[9] People are able to read notices on subjects which the media judged to be too obscure to merit coverage, and to see what the government had to say unadorned by journalistic embellishment.

- The publication by the Inland Revenue of the directory of objects written off against inheritance tax.[10] It is a condition of this concession that the public can have access to them. It is possible to search this database by location, type of object and even maker, producing for example a list of where in London Chippendale chairs can be seen.

- Departmental sites such as the Treasury's, which in addition to the usual press releases, publishes speeches by ministers and senior officials, summaries of reports by independent forecasters, the National Asset Register, draft statutory instruments the Treasury will be promoting in Parliament, as well as the complete budget documentation.[11] Until the decision to transfer the setting of interest rates to the Bank of England it also published the minutes of the monthly meetings of the Chancellor and the Governor of the Bank of England. (The minutes of the Monetary Policy Committee are now available on the Bank's own Website.[12]) The publication in paper form alone of this level of policy advice is something which would have been considered unthinkable until relatively recently. The comprehensive nature of the Treasury's site is a big step towards the process of government being available to citizens online.

The government is increasingly using the Internet to publish many of the official forms needed by business.[13] One such example is a single form that can be used by people going into business for themselves to simultaneously notify the Inland Revenue, Customs and Excise and the Contributions Agency of the change in their affairs. At present the form must be printed out, completed and posted back manually, but a pilot scheme will encourage users to fill in and return the form electronically.[14] A more peculiar example of the same genre is a Home Office form for those wishing to import cocaine or opium into the country. The form's guidance notes ask potential importers to state the percentage of pure drug content in the raw drugs and to state the country of origin of the coca leaves or raw opium. [15]

Some departments put elements of their internal guidance on statutory requirements online, but at the moment this is mostly geared towards business regulation.[16] However it is just as important that the public should have access to internal departmental guidance relevant to the ordinary citizen. The Open Government code of practice commits the government to publishing such guidance – yet little attention is drawn by departments to those that appear on the Internet, a disappointing omission. There are two refreshing exceptions of practical use to people. The first is the publication of the guidance for adjudication officers who deal with appeals related to social security benefits.[17] Second is the publication – in an edited form so as not to aid illegal immigrants – of the Home Office Immigration Directorate's internal guidance to staff on the handling of immigration applications. Further guidance on processing of claims for asylum will appear on the Internet in due course.[18]

A number of government consultation papers are now published on the Internet, including some which are also sold by the Stationery Office as priced publications. These include the white papers on Freedom of Information,[19] the future of government in London,[20] integrated transport policy,[21] development and training for civil servants[22] and on the future of the NHS.[23] The *Government.Direct* green paper on the future use by government of IT is of course online.[24]

These are important developments which make it substantially easier for people to learn about and respond to government proposals. Some departments have been quick to adapt to rising expectations of the quantity and quality of information people expect to find on their Website. For example, in March 1997 under the last government the then Deputy Prime Minister announced the publication of the government's review of the Next Steps agencies stating that it 'makes a significant contribution towards opening up government to Parliament and the public by reporting in detail on the work of some 75 per cent of the Civil Service'.[25] Such was the government's commitment to making this 'significant contribution' available to the public that it sold copies of the Review for £56 and made no reference to it on its Website. A year made quite a difference, with the publication in March 1998 of the review in full on the Internet, in spite of the government charging £45 for paper copies.[26]

This has not been the case across government. The disparities between departments may be a sign that central guidance on publication of information on the Internet is lacking. In some ways this has been beneficial: departments seem to be competing to show off the best utilisation of the technology rather than merely complying with minimum standards. On the other hand without a centrally defined minimum, some departments have lagged far behind the best practice, while others have adopted esoteric methods of enabling access or unnecessarily overload their sites with superfluous gimmickry – the 10 Downing Street Website being the shining example of this.[27]

What else might be expected on government Internet sites, and what should the government be bearing in mind as it moves towards finally introducing freedom of information? The public is entitled to information under the Open Government code of practice, itself a little-known scheme, so an obvious starting point would be to publicise the Code. Yet although the text of the Code itself can be found on the Cabinet Office's site,[28] other government sites make only cursory reference to it. Those visiting departments' sites in order to seek specific information are therefore largely unaware of the fact that they have rights to information, and can enforce them by complaining to the Parliamentary Ombudsman. Since the Ombudsman has repeatedly pointed out that he receives few such complaints, and attributes this to the lack of public awareness of the code, this failure to emphasise the opportunities afforded by the Code on the Internet is regrettable.

The Code also commits departments to publishing the 'facts and analysis' relating to major policy proposals. Little of this seems to be done, although the Department of Trade and Industry has a specific page on this subject.[29] Indeed, the guidance on the Code actually warns departments that: 'It is not necessary to swamp Parliament and the public by an indiscriminate approach to this requirement.'[30] On the other hand, if this commitment were taken seriously one might expect to see a variety of important documents published, both on the Internet and on paper. These might include the detailed briefing that departments produce on government bills and amendments to bills as well as in-depth explanation of major decisions. A notable exception can be found on the Treasury's Website, where amongst the 'occasional papers' on various economic topics can be found the last government's thinking on issues relating to the convergence criteria and timing for European Monetary Union. The March 1997 paper has a foreword stating, 'The paper below has been made available under the Open Government Code of Practice on Access to Government Information in response to a request to see the "facts and analysis" behind the Cabinet decision of 23 January.'[31] The Treasury has also published explanatory notes on the government's draft proposals for new legislation on regulating the financial services industry.[32]

The government's white paper on freedom of information, 'Your Right to Know'[33] set out the 'Gateway' procedures people would have to pass through to have their access requests considered by public authorities. These are clearly meant to reduce the administrative burden which will fall on departments by filtering out what the departments consider to be frivolous or vexatious requests. However, little consideration is given in the white paper to the question of how IT and more specifically, the Internet, could help to ease this burden. By locating the documents released to requesters – such as the Treasury paper mentioned above – together in one section of the

Website, people will be able to see what types of information are likely to be released under FOIA requests. By seeing what types of information are commonly withheld under the Act's exemptions people are more likely to understand how these operate. Given the number of documents which will be released under a strong Freedom of Information Act it will quickly become necessary to organise these disclosed records in some form of database. The demands on civil servants' time can be further reduced by the government making its own internal filing indices and catalogues available online – except where this would in itself reveal information exempt under the scope of the Act. Almost nobody outside government understands the range and complexity of government's information holdings. By making these indices available people will be able to see which department has responsibility for what, what type of information a department is likely to hold on a subject, and therefore be able to target their requests much more accurately. This is not just a matter for Freedom of Information and the Internet but a key part of constructing 'joined up government' for the twenty-first century.

A good example of the beginnings of such a system can be found in the significant numbers of documents being declassified voluntarily by the government under the Open Government initiative, rather than being kept secret for 30 years or more under the Public Records Act. The Public Record Office 'Archives Direct 2001' Website gives online access to a catalogue describing records released by the government since 1916.[34]

Local authorities, who are already subject to legally enforceable public rights to information, are in some instances ahead of central government in using the Internet. The Local Government (Access to Information) Act 1985 obliges local authorities to make available the agenda and policy papers to be considered at public meetings of the authority three days before the event. Several local authorities have started publishing these materials on their Websites, which may be especially useful in rural areas – for example, Hampshire County Council provide the Director of Social Services' report on the implications of a Law Lords decision on the implementation of community care legislation.[35] Other local authorities are using the Internet to provide more information on the planning process. The London Borough of Wandsworth scans all planning applications and places them on their Website, allowing people to search for applications by address, and also to see officers' reports and the decisions of the Council's planning committee.[36] In effect, members of the public are able to read the civil servants' policy advice to councillors, something which we are a long way from being able to do with central government. Councils could, however, do much more, for example by putting registers of members' interests, details of safety and environmental enforcement notices served and council standing orders online. It is apparent that enhancement of public access via the Internet is, in the vast majority of cases, an extra bolted-on function to a pre-existing internal IT system. Public authorities will have the opportunity in the next few years when redesigning their systems to build in these 'accountability and transparency' functions from the start.

OTHER PUBLIC BODIES

Canada has both federal and provincial FOI laws. The Information Commissioner of British Columbia publishes on the Internet the full text of all his judgments relating to Provincial access to information laws.[37] The same is true of the Ombudsman in New Zealand, whose case notes on enforcement decisions are searchable by keyword,[38] and the Information Commissioner of Queensland.[39]

The Information Commissioner due to be appointed under the UK FOI proposals should make determined use of the Internet to fulfil the role of helping applicants and in publicising the Act. In any event the Commissioner's Internet presence will need to be more commanding than the site of the Parliamentary Ombudsman. Having only established a Website in 1998, four years after being given responsibility for supervising the Code of Practice on Access to Government Information, there is at present only one report available online summarising access to information cases in which the Ombudsman has been involved.[40]

Perhaps the best recent online development in this country is that *Hansard* is now available in full, the next day.[41] The high cost of *Hansard* has long been criticised as putting it beyond the reach of many. An annual subscription to the daily version, for both Houses of Parliament, costs £1,185. The annual fee for a commercial electronic version of *Hansard*, on CDs and through an online subscription, comes to £1,997. On the Internet though, all debates, questions, and answers in both Houses of Parliament can now be read free of charge. The site also provides access to the Bills before Parliament and to select committee reports. It is also possible to read statutory instruments, written evidence submitted to select committees and the transcripts of oral evidence. It is planned to include amendments to Bills currently before Parliament. There can be little doubt that the publication of parliamentary papers on the Internet has significantly enhanced public access to this material and has the potential to expand the dialogue between MPs and their constituents.

Missing from the Parliamentary Website (and its commercial counterparts) are the documents that in answers to parliamentary questions a minister will sometimes refer to as having been 'placed in the Library of the House'. For members of the public this is almost as good as not publishing the document, because the Library is inaccessible. To gain access to the document people have to write and ask the department concerned for a copy to be sent to them. The government should ensure that ministerial answers should in future include an Internet address at which any deposited documents in the Library can be found.

People ought to have online access to statistics and particulars of MPs' attendance and voting records in addition to an electronic Register of Members' Interests. By subscribing to an online mailing list it ought to be possible to notify people of new entries in the Register. This would prevent MPs from entering an interest on the temporary Register for a couple of weeks and then withdrawing it before it became incorporated in the annual version. This practice has been used in the past as a means of allowing an MP to say that he or she had registered an interest while at the same time ensuring that to all intents and purposes it was unknown to most people.

The rulings of the Law Lords are also on the Parliamentary site; judgments delivered since 14 November 1996 appear online free within two hours of delivery at the House of Lords, while paper copies cost £5 each.[42]

Perhaps more useful to people in their ordinary lives is the publication of information on the state of public services in their area. The NHS in Wales publishes details of waiting times for hospital operations on the Internet. They say that their research shows that 'most people put a reduction in waiting times as their top priority ... Central to this is providing real choice to GPs and patients whom they are referring to hospital for diagnosis and treatment. Regular information and advice on waiting times by procedure and speciality is therefore essential.'[43] In addition, parents can obtain OFSTED school inspection reports, indexed by type of school and education authority.[44]

New laws enacted since the beginning of 1996 are available online, being added by the Stationery Office as they are passed,[45] but statutes passed before then are not available on this site.[46] It is possible to have electronic access to these if you have the money, through a subscription to LEXIS–NEXIS. However for this you have to pay US$270 per hour of online time plus three cents for every line of text printed out. Older laws should be available for free on the Internet, particularly as the government acknowledged in 1995 that only a third of legislation is available on paper in its current amended form.[47] Every time an Act is amended a new version of the Act should in theory be produced, but in practice is not. The delay in producing these on paper is because not all the amendments to an Act will come into force at the same time and it would be misleading to produce a version which included sections which were not yet in effect. The Lord Chancellor's Department is developing a computer system to make all statutes accessible to the public in their current amended form and in the form in which they existed on any given date from 1 February 1991 onwards. The system has been designed to enable access using Web browsers, so it will technically be possible to allow Internet access. However, it will not be available until the end of 2000, and the decision as to whether to make it available free of charge or through a commercial service has not yet been taken. It would be highly regrettable if the government decided not to follow the precedent of the US House of Representatives, whose Website already contains the US Federal Code – the current public laws enacted by Congress.[48] Visitors to the site can search for a subject through the entire Code (and subsidiary Regulations). If instead they wanted to buy the Code on CD-ROM the price is $45 to those outside the US. The state government of Victoria in Australia has also introduced such a database, although only from July 1997 onwards.[49]

PUBLIC ABILITY TO INFLUENCE GOVERNMENT

The Internet is not a 'one way street' publishing medium. The government has already started to use the Internet as an additional location for publishing consultation papers, and the *Government.Direct* green paper proposes a far greater degree of electronic availability of government information:

> The strategy should rest on a clear commitment to make information of all kinds available electronically. This should cover the whole range of government information, barring that which needs to be withheld to protect personal or commercial confidentiality or in the public interest. Government should organise its information holding systematically so that publicly available data is readily accessible electronically, in forms which will assist the improvement of UK competitiveness and open government. [50]

The effect of such a strategy, were it to be implemented, would be to give instant electronic access to all information whose release would be incontestable under a Freedom of Information Act. Where a document contains information which may be exempt, delays would still occur – even under an electronic access regime – while departments consider whether or not it can be disclosed. The green paper also proposes that e-mail responses to consultation documents should be encouraged.[51] The Cabinet Office has led the way in this area by co-operating with a non-governmental organisation to run a Website to debate its proposals for a Freedom of Information Act and to collate online all the publishable responses to the white paper.[52] How successful it was in terms of allowing participants in the debate to access each others' responses in time to submit follow-up contributions is open to question. But there is little doubt that it stimulated some members of the public to respond to the government's proposals that otherwise would not have done.

But electronic communication between government and the public and business is unlikely to be limited to responding to consultation papers. First, the government is proposing that within the next few years people will be able to conduct 25 per cent of their transactions with public bodies online. They will be performing searches of government databases and other electronic information, and be able to do so far faster and more easily than if they had to search disparate specialist libraries for a range of journals and official publications. In the United States it is already possible to submit an online query to the Social Security Administration to find out what retirement or disability benefits one is entitled to on the basis of the amount of contributions so far paid.[53] The equivalent UK Department for Social Security scheme so far only provides access to a form which users must print out, complete and post back to the government. In this country a database on air quality is available from the Department of the Environment[54] and one of the *Government.Direct* pilot projects proposes to give access on a commercial basis to geographical and geological data supplied by Ordnance Survey, the British Geological Survey and the Land Registry.[55] The government suggests that this information will be of commercial use to the planning and construction industry.

The Data Protection Register is also available on the Internet, allowing people to see details of the types of personal information about individuals held by organisations.[56] The site provides access to the full register and is updated weekly.

The newsgroup part of the Internet ('Usenet') and the newly emerging 'push media' technologies are likely to be another way in which communication between government and the public is increased. In 1995 the G7 countries started work on the GovNews project to investigate how governments could use newsgroups to disseminate information:

> From the point of view of the government, Usenet news offers the possibility to dramatically cut current costs of information dissemination, while at the same time reaching orders of magnitude more people. From the point of view of the public, including schools, libraries, businesses, and local governments, huge quantities of information can be made available at very low cost.
>
> In addition to the ability to broadcast information inexpensively, Usenet provides a forum for discussions, which could be used to collect feedback from the public on policy issues, or to allow people within federal agencies, state, and local governments to discuss cross-agency issues.[57]

The use of such newsgroups will allow policy announcements to appear directly in open discussion groups not necessarily run by the government. In some ways the British government tentatively attempted to move in this direction with the creation of 'Collaborative Open Groups' (COGs) which discuss ideas and policy on various aspects of the Internet ranging from disability issues to ethics.[58] Unfortunately the COGs were hampered by the lack of use made of them by the government itself; they were not used for the purpose their name implied: the collaborative and open discussion between civil servants and public of the issues arising from new technologies. Civil servants seemed nervous about floating new ideas in public or publishing the results of research which may underpin the policies that are brought forward.

However 'push media' may supersede newsgroups in informing the public of government proposals. Whereas until now the World Wide Web – the most widely used part of the Internet – has been a medium where the user sought out the information she or he wanted, this new technology proposes to make it much more of a broadcasting mechanism, albeit one where users choose precisely what information is broadcast to them. The publication of information in this manner may be progress in some ways, but whether it will further enhance consultation and public involvement is open to question. As long as people are able to 'push' back their views to the information providers it should prove to be useful. This is an area where political will and a change of culture in policy making may well be more important than technological progress.

STATUTORY RESTRICTIONS

There are of course obstacles to be overcome if we are to gain free Internet access to official information. The most fundamental is the lack of a Freedom of Information Act. This lacuna in our civil rights means that the current presumption in law is that official information is unavailable to the public unless there is a statutory obligation or government decision to publish it. Under FOI laws this presumption is reversed. All information is available to the public on request, unless the government can show that it should not be disclosed because it falls into one of the categories of exemption under the Act. The 1993 Right to Know Bill[59] contained exemptions for information whose disclosure would cause significant harm to defence, national security, international relations, law enforcement, the authority's economic and commercial affairs, the competitive position of a third party or the authority's ability to obtain information. In addition the Bill contained exemptions for legal professional privilege, personal privacy and some policy advice. The factual element of this advice, the analysis, interpretation or projections based on them would not be exempt and nor would expert advice on a scientific, technical, medical, financial, statistical or legal matter.

Crucially, under FOI regimes around the world, the final decision as to whether the information would actually cause harm if disclosed does not rest with the government, but with an independent third party. In the US and Australia the courts decide, while in New Zealand it is the Ombudsman and in Canada an Information Commissioner or, on appeal, to the courts.

In Britain, the Labour government has published its proposals for a Freedom of Information Act, but has not given any firm timetable for introducing the legislation itself. In the meantime we continue with the Code of Practice on Access to Government Information which also presumes that information is disclosable unless it falls into a category of exemption, but although it has in some ways been a significant development – it is supervised by the Parliamentary Ombudsman – it is flawed in a number of serious aspects, many of which cannot be rectified without legislation. First, the Ombudsman's judgments are not legally binding. Government departments are free to ignore judgments if they choose, though this rarely happens. Second, the Ombudsman is statutorily prohibited from seeing some categories of information and from investigating complaints against bodies not explicitly listed as coming within his remit; this too would take legislation to correct. Third, some of the exemptions are either superfluous or unnecessarily broad; this could be corrected easily since it is an administrative document, but the former government amended the Code in February 1997 leaving some of the more objectionable exemptions in place. Finally, as an administrative code it is unable to override the 250 or so pre-existing statutory restrictions on the disclosure of official information.[60]

The main consequence of having a Code instead of a Freedom of Information Act is that Britain has no overarching framework of legal rights to information. A variety of laws give people rights to see some categories of information held on them by public bodies, while others grant access to some environmental, safety and local authority information. However there is no general right to the mass of information held by public bodies. In the case of central government this leaves ministers free to disclose this information if and when they choose. As elected politicians they are unlikely to be willing to disclose information which is capable of causing embarrassment to themselves. Those in public office have shown time and again that they are unwilling to trust people with information in these circumstances. A somewhat old but telling opinion poll finding showed that in 1993 only 14 per cent of people rated Conservative politicians as positively trustworthy, compared with 19 per cent for Liberal Democrats and 23 per cent for Labour politicians. In the same poll 43 per cent of people said they trusted no politicians of any party at all.[61]

This lack of trust by public bodies in people's ability to cope with 'difficult' information is demonstrated in a statutory restriction on disclosure from the Medicines Act 1968, the statute which governs the licensing of medicines. Pharmaceutical products must be evaluated by the Medicines Control Agency before they can be prescribed. However, the Medicines Act prohibits officials from disclosing 'any information with respect to any manufacturing process or trade secret ... or ... any information obtained by or furnished to him in pursuance of this Act'.[62] The penalty for disclosing safety information in contravention of this section is up to two years' imprisonment.

The Internet can sometimes help find a way round such blocks. The American Food and Drug Administration shows how much deeper rights of access go in the US, electronically as well as on paper. Its Website gives access to – amongst many other items – the transcripts of its expert drug advisory committee meetings. These include the presentations of pharmaceutical companies seeking approval for their products and the FDA's assessment of their claims.[63]

However, while it is possible to get information from American Websites on many British drugs – and on the results of hygiene inspections of British cruise liners[64] and on pesticides[65] used in both countries – the ability to do so is susceptible to government action of a different type.

Overseas governments have legislated to control Internet access. While it is unlikely that they would seek to block access to medicines or pesticides information, politically sensitive information is more likely to attract the beady eye of government censors. Access to the Internet in Singapore is filtered through government controlled computers which block access to Websites and newsgroups the government disapproves of. It would probably not be feasible for a government in this country to attempt something similar, given the large number of Internet service providers, universities and companies with their own links to the Internet. However, the government has shown in the past that it is prepared to go to great lengths in attempting to suppress publication of information which it finds embarrassing, the most commonly known examples being the government's prosecution of *Spycatcher* and a television documentary about the Zircon satellite. The difficulties faced by the government in trying to suppress the overseas publication of

Spycatcher in manual form would now be greatly magnified in any similar case by the ease of republication in other countries that the Internet offers.

CHARGING FOR INFORMATION

The cost of obtaining information can be just as much of a block on access in practical terms as a statute. The Internet provides not only access to a great volume of sometimes obscure information, but also *free* access to information that may otherwise be charged for. This has so far been perhaps its most significant contribution to the process of opening up government. The ability to read white papers, press releases, *Hansard*, statutes and other publications implies that public bodies have been willing to forego some sales income in the interests of making such materials more widely available, or alternatively that they assume that – at least at present – Internet access will not affect sales. For example, the white paper on the future of London government was published in its entirety on the Internet although paper copies remain on sale from the Stationery Office at £11.60. The fact that it is freely available over the Internet is promising both because more people will take the opportunity to read the document and because it improves public access to the policy-making process. Some departments are now putting their annual reports on the Internet thereby removing the cost barrier to information about departmental budgets and plans. The cost in 1994 of obtaining copies of the 18 central government departmental reports was over £250, so the more that do this the better.

However, there is a long way to go before all government information becomes freely available. The emphasis in recent years on government departments emulating private sector business practices has led to policies such as the Department of Trade and Industry's tradeable information initiative, whose 1990 guidelines state:

> Information is a particularly valuable commodity: almost uniquely it can be sold and retained at the same time ... As with most

> properties, information properties, whatever their inherent values, are only 'tradeable' if someone else wants them.

So if no one asks for a document, it may be available for free; but as soon as there is a demand, it has a value. *Government.Direct* appears to be a move in this direction as it envisages government 'encouraging the development of new, commercial, information products based on government information'.[66] There may be no objection to commercial products based on government information so long as this does not mean that information which the public presently receives, or would expect to receive, free of charge becomes available only at a price in future. Information used to hold public sector bodies accountable, or which gives details of rights, benefits and entitlements, should not be subject to charges. Regrettably the Labour government's FOI white paper proposes to exclude tradeable information from the FOI Act.[67]

PRIVACY/DATA PROTECTION

Until the problems of protection of personal data have been solved, public acceptance of the Internet for widespread online purchasing of good and services – and transactions with the government – will not really take off. Privacy concerns relate not only to interception and subsequent misuse of credit card or other personal data on the Internet but also extend to government use of information held on computers about individuals, such as health, tax and social security records, and to monitoring of what is downloaded from government sites and by whom.

If someone goes into a library the staff can record which books they are borrowing, but no one monitors their browsing, or the topics they look up in reference books. But on the Internet, the computers holding the Web pages log all comings and goings. The organisation running the site – in the case of official information, the government – has a complete record of everything they look at, their interests and concerns. Some parts of government at least warn users of this possibility. Thus CCTA, the Government Centre for Telecommunications, which runs the government's site gives FTP users the following warning:

> Hello and welcome to CCTA's anonymous FTP server. You should be aware that all access to this server is logged. If you do not like this policy, then please log off now.[68]

However, the government's Web pages provide no such warning. We know that CCTA monitors who is accessing government pages because they publish details of the most regular visitors, all of which are large institutions rather than identifiable individuals.[69] However it is clear that CCTA also retains the e-mail addresses of individuals who access their sites and the pages they have visited; CCTA have confirmed that such information is held and permanently stored for statistical and security purposes. It seems likely that the recording and retention of this information is a breach of the privacy people are entitled to under the Data Protection Act. The Act is based on the 'data protection principles', one of which is that people must be made aware that information which might personally identify them is being collected. If they are not told this at the time the information is collected, the Act's requirement that information be obtained 'fairly' is contravened,[70] and this appears to be happening at the government's site, as at many others.

Without the transparency afforded by building freedom of information and data protection principles into the systems which will deliver online government services, it is hard to see why people should trust government not to abuse the powers it will need to tie together the data from disparate sources. If the same 'smart' electronic card will in future be used for financial transactions, to hold medical records, criminal records, driving licence details and to authenticate my dealings with government departments, how can I be sure the government will not abuse the technology to track my movements, lifestyle, reading matter and so on? This gap in public trust is going to be one of the biggest problems facing the wiring up of public service delivery, and strong FOI and data protection laws are the absolute minimum requirements to bridge the divide.

THE CHANGING FACE OF GOVERNMENT – COMMERCIAL CONFIDENTIALITY

The changing make-up of government itself presents problems of access to information. Parts of government that were previously divisions of Whitehall departments are being hived off into the private sector, as the contracting out of Inland Revenue functions to the American firm EDS demonstrates. Where previously issues of accountability to the public were clearly defined, now functions of public administration are carried out by bodies which do not see themselves as accountable to the public, but to the government as customer. This process has led to significant amounts of information that would previously have been disclosed – for example on the cost or methodology of carrying out a specific administrative function – being withheld from the public on the grounds of commercial confidentiality since it is now sensitive information when the contract comes to be tendered. The same is true for local government where the process of compulsory competitive tendering means that authorities' departments must bid against outside companies to win the contract to do the job, whether it be refuse collection or management of the authority's housing stock. Such 'commercial confidentiality' has become a major obstacle to public accountability.

CONCLUSION: RIGHTS ENHANCE A CULTURE OF OPENNESS

While a great deal of government and other public sector information is available online in Britain it seems that the main reason why more use has been made of the Internet overseas than in the UK as a means of holding government to account is because most 'wired' democracies have a Freedom of Information Act. An Act does not create better use of the Internet in itself – although in the US recognition of the importance of the Internet in enhancing access to information has been acknowledged with the introduction in 1996 of the Electronic Freedom of Information Improvement Act. Countries with statutory FOI regimes tend to make greater use of the Internet for accountability reasons because experience has taught them the benefits of openness and transparency. More than that, it is accepted in these countries that their governments hold information in trust for the people and do not own it themselves.

The Labour government's policy is to introduce a Freedom of Information Act. Although its original proposals were widely welcomed,[71] subsequent reports suggest that the government is proposing to water down some key elements and that the legislation itself may be delayed.[72] It remains to be seen how far the mysteries of government so eloquently described by Tom Paine will be revealed to us.

NOTES

1. I am grateful for the guidance, assistance and patience of Maurice Frankel in producing this chapter.
2. *The Rights of Man*, Thomas Paine, Part Two, Chapter 1, 1792 reproduced in the *Thomas Paine Reader*, eds M.E. Foot and I. Kramnick, (Penguin, 1987).
3. This is legislation entitling people to access government held information on demand, subject to certain exemptions such as information whose release would cause harm to defence, national security, the effective management of the economy, prevention of crime or invade personal privacy. The crux of a Freedom of Information Act is that it takes the power to decide whether information is released away from government ministers and gives it to an independent appeals body.
4. *Code of Practice on Access to Government Information*, Cabinet Office, 1997, http://www.open.gov.uk/m-of-g/codete.htm
5. *Declassification of today's and historical inventory differences for highly enriched uranium at the Y-12 plant in Oak Ridge, Tennessee*; http://www.doe.gov/waisgate/opennet.new.html
6. http://www.doe.gov/html/osti/opennet/document/press/pc8.html
7. http://www.bse.org.uk
8. http://www.coi.gov.uk/coi/depts/today.html
9. There are plans to do so, including publication by e-mail, but it is not clear yet whether this will be a free or charged service, or when it will be introduced.
10. *The Register of Conditionally Exempt Works of Art*; http://www.cto.eds.co.uk/intro.htm
11. http://www.hm-treasury.gov.uk
12. http://www.bankofengland.co.uk/mpcmtg.htm

13. *Direct Access Government*; http://tap.ccta.gov.uk/dagii/welcome.nsf
14. http://www.open.gov.uk/dssca/pdfs/formcwf1.pdf and http://www.self-employment.direct.gov.uk/
15. http://www.open.gov.uk/home_off/drugsfor/md7.pdf
16. Department of Health, guidance on *The Food Safety (Temperature Control) Regulations 1995* and others can be found at http://www.open.gov.uk/doh/busguide.htm
17. http://www.cas.gov.uk/aogconts.htm
18. http://www.home-office.gov.uk/ind/idi/idiintro.htm
19. http://www.official-documents.co.uk/document/caboff/foi/contents.htm
20. http://www.london-decides.detr.gov.uk/page14.htm
21. http://www.detr.gov.uk/itwp/index.htm
22. Cabinet Office, Cm 3321 1996 http://www.official-documents.co.uk/document/caboff/dtcs/develtra.htm
23. Department of Health, Cm no.3807, 1997 http://www.official-documents.co.uk/document/doh/newnhs/newnhs.htm
24. Cabinet Office, Cm 3438 1996 http://www.open.gov.uk/citu/gdirect/greenpaper/index.htm
25. Cabinet Office press release OPS 24/97, 12/3/97; http://www.coi.gov.uk/coi/depts/GCO/coi7751c.ok
26. http://www.official-documents.co.uk/document/cm38/3889/contents.htm
27. http://www.number-10.gov.uk/index.html
28. http://www.open.gov.uk/m-of-g/codete.htm
29. http://www.dti.gov.uk/SMD3/OPEN/facts.html
30. *Code of Practice on Access to Government Information, Guidance on Interpretation*, Cabinet Office, 1997, para. 21.
31. http://www.hm-treasury.gov.uk/pub/html/top/emu/main.html
32. http://www.hm-treasury.gov.uk/pub/html/reg/fsmb3.pdf
33. http://www.official-documents.co.uk/document/caboff/foi/contents.htm
34. http://www.pro.gov.uk/finding/coreexec.htm
35. http://www.hants.gov.uk/scrmxn/c22220.html
36. http://www.wandsworth.gov.uk/tech/wandpl.htm
37. http://www.oipcbc.org/orders/
38. http://www.liinz.org.nz/liinz/other/ombudsmen/casenotes/
39. http://www.slq.qld.gov.au/infocomm
40. http://www.parliament.ombudsman.org.uk/pca/contents.htm
41. http://www.parliament.the-stationery-office.co.uk/pa/cm/cmhansrd.htm
42. http://www.parliament.the-stationery-office.co.uk/pa/ld199697/ldjudgmt/ld-judgmt.htm
43. http://www.open.gov.uk/hmis/intro.htm
44. http://www.open.gov.uk/ofsted/repdb3.htm
45. Acts can be found at http://www.hmso.gov.uk/acts.htm. Statutory Instruments can be found at http://www.hmso.gov.uk/stat.htm
46. With the exception of the Data Protection Act 1984 and the Disability Discrimination Act 1995
47. *Hansard*, 15 June 1995, col. 606 WA.
48. http://law.house.gov:80/usc.htm
49. http://www.dms.dpc.vic.gov.au/l2d/lthome.html

50. *Government.Direct*, Cm 3438 1996 para 5.7; http://www.open.gov.uk/citu/gdirect/greenpaper/chap5.htm
51. ibid, para 9.4; http://www.open.gov.uk/citu/gdirect/greenpaper/chap9.htm
52. http://foi.democracy.org.uk
53. http://s3abaca.ssa.gov/pro/batch-pebes/bp-7004home.shtml
54. http://www.aeat.co.uk/netcen/airqual/welcome.html
55. http://www.coi.gov.uk/coi/depts/GCO/coi7435c.ok Cabinet Office Press Release OPS 22/97, 5 March 1997
56. http://www.dpr.gov.uk/
57. http://www.govnews.org/govnews/
58. http://tap.ccta.gov.uk/cogs/cogdisc.nsf
59. Drafted by the Campaign for Freedom of Information and promoted as a private member's bill by Mark Fisher MP, the Bill received its second reading on 19 February 1993 and was talked out at Report Stage on 2 July 1993.
60. *Open Government*, Cabinet Office, Cm 2290 1993, Appendix B, page 80.
61. ICM/*Observer* opinion poll 19 December 1993.
62. Medicines Act 1968, section 118(1).
63. http://www.fda.gov/ohrms/dockets/ac/cder98t.htm
64. ftp://ftp.cdc.gov/pub/ship_inspections/shipscor.txt
65. http://www.epa.gov/pesticides/
66. *Government.Direct* para 6.16; http://www.open.gov.uk/citu/gdirect/greenpaper/chap6.htm
67. *Your Right to Know* paras 2.35 – 2.38, Cabinet Office, Cm 3818 1997.
68. ftp://ftp.open.gov.uk/
69. http://www.open.gov.uk/cctagis/usage.htm
70. Data Protection Act 1984, Schedule 1, Data Protection Principle No.1.
71. http://www.cfoi.org.uk/wpbriefings.html
72. http://www.cfoi.org.uk/july98debate.html

3 Privacy I: Liberty on the Line

Simon Davies and Ian Hosein

In early 1996 a trickle of countries began imposing wide-ranging regulation of Internet activities. By mid-1998, the trickle had become a torrent. In a notable reversal of stereotypes some developed countries led the third world on an assault against free speech, privacy and encryption. This chapter describes the efforts by governments to impose surveillance and curtail the Internet, and discusses the likely impact on human rights.

On 25 September 1996 some of the most influential figures from the arcane world of electronic communications privacy travelled to Paris to attend a conference on encryption. For three years the topic had fired the emotions and imagination of the Internet elite, but it had left politicians and editors unmoved and largely uninformed. The event was to be a test case to determine whether mainstream decision-makers could grasp this complex issue and its grave ramifications.

The 'International Symposium on the Public Voice and the Development of International Cryptography Policy' was organised by the Electronic Privacy Information Center (EPIC), a Washington-based public interest group. It was, in effect, an astutely timed 'summit' to coincide with the development of encryption guidelines by the Organisation for Economic Cooperation and Development (OECD). The US government had exerted strong pressure on the OECD to pass prescriptive guidelines that would limit the ability of people to use strong encryption. EPIC had fought to make the OECD aware that this would be a retrograde step for privacy and human rights.

The OECD was to hold a key meeting of its members on the following day to determine its encryption policy. EPIC had concluded that a non-government meeting on the doorstep of the OECD in Paris would be crucial to get the message across. According to one publication:

While EPIC had initially thought of staging a sort of anti-conference some smart lobbying enabled it to win recognition from the OECD. Held in the luxurious official setting of the International Conference Center on the Avenue Kleber, the OECD conclave was opened by the Australian magistrate Norman Reaburn, chairman of the OECD group of experts, and John Dryden of the OECD Science, Technologies and Communications division. The moderators of all the debates that followed were also members of the group of experts. Still, sitting side by side were four cryptographers who, between them, added up to a singular nightmare for western intelligence agencies.[1]

EPIC's task was by no means a simple one. While those involved in cyber-liberties had been working hard at the task of educating the law-makers about the importance of maintaining freedom on the Internet, the ground was rapidly being captured by the posturing of law enforcement agencies, religious crusading groups and a battalion of editors only too happy to promote horror stories about DIY terrorism and rampant pornography.

Such a polarisation is not unusual. Throughout recent history, all technologies that move into the mainstream have triggered a conflict between conservative campaigners and radical investors. Genetic engineering, nuclear power and information technology have inspired widespread action by groups concerned with the protection of the environment, peace, human rights and privacy. Such concerns are perceived by many to be at odds with the interests of the financial and investment industries.

The process of inculcating an interest within industry in such matters as health and safety, environmental protection and fundamental rights is often long and tortuous, and bound up in complex constitutional, legal, economic and cultural aspects. The Internet has not been around long enough for these aspects to become fully engaged.

Encryption on the Internet has emerged so recently as a public issue that existing institutions (security, law enforcement, commerce and media) have almost entirely captured the middle ground. During the consultation phase of the Department of Trade and Industry's 1997 and 1998 White Papers on encryption, law enforcement agencies were at no time called upon to quantify their case for key recovery. In the preceding year, restrictions on content imposed by police were implemented without even the slightest concession to due process.

On this theme, one important discussion swayed the delegates from the OECD: human rights. This topic was dissected with some passion from the outset by one eminent speaker, Justice Michael Kirby of the High Court of Australia. Kirby had chaired both the OECD's expert group on Transborder Data Barriers and the Protection of Privacy in the early 1980s, and its expert committee on the Security of Information Systems in the early 1990s. He therefore had good pedigree in this august gathering.

Kirby reminded the meeting that the OECD should regard human rights as a primary benchmark in all discussions. He said that the work of the OECD rested on three common principles: 'a commitment to the rule of law, an acceptance of the democratic system of government, and a respect for fundamental human rights'. He continued:

> It is important to remember these features of the OECD for they provide the milieu within which the cryptography policy guidelines must be fashioned ... [T]he issues of human rights have been assuming a higher agenda in the OECD, and rightly so. Not only do human rights have strong economic implications. They are the cement which binds together the Member States of the OECD, and provides the rationale for the existence of the organisation: by economic cooperation and development to strengthen the social and individual environment within which the citizens of the OECD countries live and work. After all, economics has no point in itself save as it serves and enriches the lives of individuals.

And, firing a shot across the bows of zealous law enforcement agencies and a contingent of US officials anxious to impose hasty controls on encryption, Kirby added:

> Patient consensus building rather than impatient demand for action is the way that the OECD operates ... It will be important that nothing be done in the preparation of the Cryptography Policy Guidelines which diminishes the high reputation which the OECD

Expert Groups enjoy in the field both for their product and for their methodology.

Kirby's words were carefully chosen. He was well aware that rights are compromised as much by carelessness as they are through tyranny. Without careful thought, a hastily drafted encryption policy designed to assist the detection of major crime might easily be hijacked to control basic freedoms. Widespread abuses of phone-tapping technology throughout the world provide a sombre reminder of this reality.

Most of the speakers at the EPIC Paris meeting concluded that systems based on Trusted Third Parties (one encryption key system favoured by the US) are pointless and ineffective. The implications on human rights and democratic development of a poor encryption policy were also systematically outlined. As a result, a new draft of the OECD guidelines was unexpectedly tabled before the group of experts the next day, this one stressing respect for individual freedoms.[2]

Beyond the themes which superficially influenced the OECD lay another idea which had always created some discomfort for intergovernmental organisations. Developed nations have a responsibility to set clear human rights benchmarks for developing nations. And in the field of information and communications technology, the speed of policy convergence is so compressed that this responsibility must be scrupulously observed. Regrettably, this is not the case. Across the surveillance spectrum – wiretapping, personal ID systems, datamining, censorship or encryption controls – it is the West which invariably sets a proscriptive pace.

Three days after the implementation of Compuserve's now infamous cutback on 'obscenity' on their sites, the Chinese government decided to do the same. However, obscenity is a culturally relative term, and thus goes beyond pornography to 'detrimental information'.[3] On 13 August 1996 the government of Singapore announced a plan to institute a draconian Internet censorship policy intended to 'focus on content which may undermine public morals, political stability and religious harmony'.[4] Three weeks later, on 4 September 1996, the ASEAN nations (Brunei, Malaysia, Singapore, Indonesia, Philippines,

Thailand and Vietnam) agreed to 'police the Internet and block off sites that run counter to Asian values'.[5]

The policy soon took effect. Later that year, Dr Prihadi Beny Waluyo, a lecturer at Indonesia's Duta Wacana Christian University, was arrested at his home by soldiers of the district military command. He was reportedly accused of distributing e-mail messages and also of sending messages relating to the 27 July riots to a destination in Holland. His arrest came after an unidentified person gave an officer photocopies of e-mail messages that were traced to Dr Waluyo. The person claimed the printouts came from a store in Kebumen, a district of Yogyakarta.

Following his arrest, Dr Waluyo was interrogated by the military about his connections with the People's Democratic Party (PRD), which the government has accused of masterminding the riots, but he denied any involvement with the PRD. He acknowledged that he had sent messages over the Internet. Following his questioning, he was reportedly ordered to go to his home and was told to report to the district military command on a regular basis. He is said to be under strict surveillance.

Technologies which are able to protect privacy and improve access to communications are routinely curtailed by all governments. The Pakistan government best exemplifies the notion of such control. In 1994 it closed down an entire cellular communications network until it was able to install sophisticated scanning equipment that would allow the government intelligence agencies to listen in.[6] Not content with this move, the Pakistan government then banned Internet telephony. According to the regulations binding all Internet service providers (ISPs) operating in the country, voice transmission of any sort is strictly prohibited. 'Violation of this clause shall lead to prosecution according to the Telephone and Telegraph Act of 1985.'[7]

Governments of developing nations also rely on first world countries to supply them with technologies of surveillance such as digital wiretapping equipment, deciphering equipment, scanners, bugs, tracking equipment and computer intercept systems. The transfer of surveillance technology from first to third world is now a lucrative sideline for the arms industry. A 1995 report,

'Big Brother Incorporated', by the watchdog organisation Privacy International highlighted the extent of this trade.

Western surveillance technology is providing invaluable support to military and totalitarian authorities throughout the world. However, the justification advanced by the companies involved in this trade is identical to the justification advanced in the arms trade, i.e. that the technology is neutral. Another view – certainly held by Privacy International – is that in the absence of legal protections, the technology can never be neutral. Even those technologies intended for 'benign' uses rapidly develop more sinister purposes.

ID card and 'smart' card systems have been marketed to more than three dozen developing countries. Without exception, they result in wholesale discrimination and hardship for vulnerable people. Such systems can adversely affect the delicate balance pursued by an emerging democracy. The adoption of information technology involves a change to the relationship between citizen and the state. The use of surveillance technologies vastly increases this change.

The emerging information superhighway also poses fundamental threats to developing countries. The 1995 summit of the G7 countries (the seven richest industrial powers) linked arms with some of the most dominant corporations in the technology industry to form a consensus about how the superhighway should be built. They agreed to a set of principles that would maximise growth, development and profit. Relatively little attention was paid to the negative impact of the superhighway on developing countries and on the rights and privacy of citizens of developed countries.

Martin Bangemann, Europe's Commissioner in charge of information technology, has remarked 'We will not achieve the information society unless we give the free market a free rein.' In the context of the trade in surveillance technologies to third world countries, this signals a 'hands off' policy. An unregulated superhighway is likely to maximise surveillance and increase the power of institutions in control of the technology.[8]

According to Privacy International, the unregulated development and export of these technologies creates grave and unnecessary threats to developing countries. According to human rights groups, the trade requires scrutiny and regulation to help minimise the fatal impact that it can cause. Whether this impact is intended or unforeseen, the surveillance industry has a responsibility to ensure that the export and development of its products conform to scrupulous ethical standards. Developed countries should ensure that the export industry is regulated. This might be achieved through a form of technological impact assessment.

Countries constantly lay precedence for others, but the process is not confined merely to the axis of the developed/developing world. South Africa justified its previous tyrannical practices, saying that there was little difference between apartheid and American practices in slavery and segregation, or Canadian treatment of their indigenous people. The refusal by successive New Zealand governments to honour Maori land claims was justified in part on the basis of successive Australian governments' refusal to acknowledge Aboriginal land claims.

In the absence of legal and cultural parallels, such international comparisons are often pointless. And the mere fact that two countries share the same region or economic status is insufficient. An 8–9 February editorial in the *International Herald Tribune* clearly outlined the differences between US and UK rights: 'The wide latitude enjoyed by the police is typical of the powers the British government holds over its citizens.'[9] As it is, the UK law enforcement agencies can wiretap without judicial approval and can stop and search anyone on the street at any time. In a Bill presented to Parliament in 1997, the police sought to make the planting of a covert bug easier than doing an open search, which at least requires a warrant. It is not unknown to hear of British ministers and civil servants publicly justifying the high extent of UK wiretapping on the basis of even higher French figures.

The UK situation is set within an environment of its Interception of Communications Act of 1985. Amongst other conditions, the Act allows for the interception of communications in obedience to a warrant, or by the consent of one of the parties. A Secretary of State grants the warrant under the conditions of the interest of national security, the purpose of preventing or detecting serious crime, or to safeguard the economic well-being of the

UK. The definition of 'serious crime' includes crime where there is 'a large number of persons in pursuit of a common purpose'.[10]

Meanwhile the encryption policy of the UK has been inconsistent, or perhaps better explained as 'a classic example of a 180-degree course change being adopted in the course of months of careful new management'.[11] At one point in 1994, the Prime Minister claimed in a parliamentary written reply to an MP that he envisaged no further restrictions on encryption in the UK. In 1995 there were indications of an escrow debate in Whitehall, but this debate was closed to the public.[12] In 1996 at a public meeting a government spokesperson said that escrowing of keys would be mandatory, and that an OECD expert group was working on global encryption guidelines. Previous movements of the OECD are a direct reaction to the US government lobbying them to install Key Escrow as a global initiative.[13]

France on the other hand has had a torrid recent history with wiretapping. In 1990 the European Court of Human Rights condemned France's government for illegal wiretapping. The Court found that 'French law, written and unwritten, did not provide the ... minimum degree of protection to which citizens were entitled under the rule of law in a democratic society'.[14] It has also been reported that the French government regularly wiretaps conversations of foreign companies for industrial information which they then pass on to French companies.[15] This all became known shortly after the wiretapping scandal that brought down the French Socialist Party in 1993.[16] Meanwhile, there has been word that the government is interested in lifting its complete ban on encryption only if the keys are escrowed. French authorities avoid the term 'mandatory', since using any other type of encryption is illegal.[17]

Germany's policy is rapidly approaching those of England and France. In the current mood of hypersensitivity to extremists and organised crime, the government has also placed a demand that all cryptographically protected traffic be licensed. Licensing requires that law enforcement agencies have access to the keys.

The differing degrees of acceptance of the Key Escrow scheme changes from country to country, but one can imagine a direct parallel between the extent of police power, the extent of demand for intrusion, and the simplicity of such implementation. Future global policy will ensure greater police powers, especially as the G7 announces its latest attempts at international cooperation on terrorism.

In the annual Country Reports on Human Rights Practices for 1996, the US Department of State reported that in more than 90 countries there is widespread, illegal or uncontrolled use of wiretaps by police, defence and intelligence agencies, despite controls.[18] Amongst the most common targets of these taps are human rights groups, reporters, and political opponents. In Mexico alone, it is estimated that 200,000 illegal wiretaps were in place in 1994.[19]

Consequently, human rights groups around the world, such as those in Central America, Ethiopia and China, use encryption to protect their communications and files. In a more popular case, the African National Congress developed and used encrypted e-mail for years without it being compromised by the South African government.[20]

Phil Zimmerman, developer of Pretty Good Privacy (PGP), has been told that Burmese freedom fighters learn to use PGP in jungle training camps, using it to keep documents hidden from the oppressive government.[21] He has also received e-mail from a human rights worker in Central Europe who explained how the police raided the office and confiscated computers in an attempt to discover the identity of the people who complained about government activities. PGP prevented that. The government-in-exile of Tibet uses PGP to mobilise demonstrators around the region. In Britain, the radical environmental group Reclaim the Streets uses PGP to protect its files.

Even if the American government succeeds in implementing Key Escrow on a voluntary basis, it will indeed set a precedent for the rest of the world. The 'voluntary' nature of Key Escrow (and previously the Clipper Chip) has always been an issue of contention, and an issue that raised much uncertainty as to the government's intentions. Groups opposing escrow often ask how a voluntary scheme can combat crime when criminals do not need to escrow their keys? Another argument is that if escrowed cryptography exists, only the dumb criminals will use it, when the smart ones will use proper, non-escrowed encryption.

This notion of 'dumb criminals' raises interesting questions. Many acts undertaken by criminal are in fact 'dumb' but not necessarily in the sense of IQ. Some criminals feel that they are invulnerable, and so do not need to worry about getting caught.[22] If criminals were not 'dumb', they would not leave fingerprints, make calls on any home telephone, or return a rental van that was heavily involved in a terrorist event.[23] Some argue that this is why the voluntary scheme will indeed work.

A much more pleasant picture is often painted of the American voluntary scheme in comparison with the European mandatory schemes, but this should not create any complacency about the American proposals. Numerous documents have been released to EPIC indicating that a voluntary scheme is not the end goal of the American government. Despite continual promises and rebuttals on this scheme,[24] formerly top secret documents released to EPIC suggest otherwise. These indicate that the FBI has been planning a strategy for a national policy that allows for strong cryptography that permits law enforcement interception and interference, and that prohibits cryptography that does not meet that standard.[25] All along the government was insisting that the Clipper Initiative was trying merely to offer another alternative: a trustworthy and powerful encryption scheme.

CONCLUSION

Trust and government should be synonymous. Government at one time was a human creation based theoretically on a social contract. It was set in place to provide order, to legislate for the good of the society, and to judge blindly to maintain the peace. Yet the Key Escrow initiative is as good an example as any of the dilemma facing current governments.

Trust in government has reached a level perhaps only slightly above the bare minimum necessary for government actually to function. Constant whittling away of core freedoms on the basis of deception or illusion does nothing to improve this dangerous state of affairs. The Clipper Chip fell through systematic and popular opposition, but was replaced with new initiatives that continued to regulate the export of cryptography, the escrowing of the keys, and the locations of the escrowed keys. What protected these initiatives from the same failure of trust? The claim of criminality is a powerful and supportive force in maintaining the Key Escrow initiative. Law enforcement agencies already have the right to search and seize in the case of criminal actions. The Fourth Amendment in the US limits them, but with legislation in 1968 under Title III, they were permitted to use secret searches under the form of wiretaps and bugging. Key Escrow is merely an extension of these powers in the light of new technologies.

The problem only seems to escalate on the global theatre. Other countries in the world do not enjoy the same strict controls on surveillance that the US government promises to practice. Whether they are allies or cold trading partners is irrelevant. The problem, on the one hand, is that the US is aiming to implement the Key Escrow scheme on an international level, and on the other hand, it is losing the higher moral ground for combating human rights breaches through precedence. Governments around the world do not practice the social contract in the same way as the Americans. They do not provide open and clear procedures for the scrutiny of their citizens. Corruption and power reign absolutely in some countries, and those who fight against this in the name of democracy and human rights are bound to fail because Key Escrow provides power to the government. As Anthony Giddens claimed, we should view surveillance not merely as a sort of reflex of capitalism, or of the nation-state, but as a power generator in itself.

Crime against society is indeed a problem. Key Escrow does provide a solution, undoubtedly to the problem of Title III interceptions in the future. However, the government has failed to promote this initiative on the grounds that are most endearing and important to the secondary holders of the contract on government: the people, and their trust. They have made mistakes in the past and that resulted in failure. Problems in trust have been outlined for the future with the sincerity of the government in question over the voluntary scheme. These are just two other nails in the coffin.

As Justice Michael Kirby observed during the EPIC meeting

in Paris, the responsibility of the West to promote democratic reform is compelling and clear. If developed countries were engaged in promoting and selling privacy-enhancing technologies rather than technologies of control, perhaps surveillance and control would more readily become a part of the matrix that binds global relationships.

NOTES

1. 'The World-Wide Encryption Battle', *Intelligence Newsletter*, 3 October 1996, Washington DC.
2. Ibid.
3. 'Silencing the Net – The Threat to Freedom of Expression Online', *Human Rights Watch*, 10 May 1996.
4. Letter to Minister for Information and the Arts, Singapore, *Human Rights Watch*, 13 August 1996.
5. Reuters, 4 September 1996.
6. 'Motorola Rolls Over Human Rights', *Wired*, June 1995; Wayne Madsen, 'Security Access and Privacy on the Internet', paper presented to the Compsec Computer Security Conference, London, 1995, pp. 45–72.
7. *Wired*, September 1996, newsbyte.
8. Privacy International, 'Big Brother Incorporated', report, November 1995.
9. 'Bugging the British', *International Herald and Tribune*, no. 35440, 8–9 February 1997.
10. Interception of Communications Act 1985, Chapter 56. HMSO, London.
11. Ross Anderson and Michael Roe, 'The GCHQ Protocol and its Problems', unpublished paper, Cambridge University Computer Laboratory, 1994.
12. Ibid.
13. 'The OECD Fails to Act on Key-Escrow Encryption: The US Accused of Policy Laundering', *Bulletin Lambda*, 2:8, 19 July 1996.
14. *Huvig v. France*, 12 EHRR 528 (24 April 1990).
15. Schweizer, 'Friendly Spies: How America's Allies are Using Economic Espionage to Steal our Secrets', *Atlantic Press Monthly* (1993).
16. David Banisar, 'French Wiretapping Scandal Leads to Electorial Defeat', *Privacy Times*, 7 September 1996.
17. 'A Letter Reveals French Key-Escrow Scheme', *Bulletin Lambda*, 2:12, 5 December 1996.
18. *EPIC Alert*, 4:3, 27 February 1997.
19. David Banisar, 'BUG OFF! – A Primer for Human Rights Groups on Wiretapping', *International Privacy Bulletin*, October 1995.
20. Ibid.
21. Steven Levy, 'The Cypherpunks vs. Uncle Sam', *New York Times Magazine*, 12 June 1994, Section 6.
22. Stewart A. Baker, 'Don't Worry Be Happy', White House, Office of the Press Secretary, 'Statement by the Press Secretary: Announcement of the Clipper Initiative', for Immediate Release, 16 April 1993. *Wired*, June 1994.

23. David Gelertner, 'Wiretaps for a Wireless Age', *New York Times*, 8 May 1994, Section 4.
24. Dorothy E. Denning, 'International Key Escrow Encryption: Proposed Objectives and Options', paper presented to the International Cryptography Institute Conference 1994: Global Challenges, National Intellectual Property Law Institute, Washington DC, 22–23 September 1994.
25. EPIC, *1996 EPIC Cryptography and Privacy Source Book* (EPIC, 1996).

4 Privacy II: Cryptography and Democracy – Dilemmas of Freedom

Caspar Bowden and Yaman Akdeniz

INTRODUCTION

'As we prepare to enter a new century, our society stands on the threshold of a revolution as profound as that brought about by the invention of the printing press half a millennium ago.'[1] The revolution is the creation of a global infrastructure that can transmit voice, video and text in a single inter-operable medium. Confidential messages may be sent without prior arrangement between parties, and public directories used to authenticate authorship with digital signatures that cannot be forged. Digitised intellectual property can be marked by electronic copyright management systems to identify owners or consumers. The ubiquitous new medium could in time become the primary means of mass communication, subsuming the marketing of and payment for general goods and services.

The technologies for protection of confidentiality, digital payment, authentication of identity, and ownership of intellectual property are all based on the science of cryptography. In the past 20 years, a variety of elaborate (but mathematically precise) protocols for cryptographic transactions have been invented with properties that are bewilderingly counter-intuitive. Perhaps because of popularisation of the ULTRA story,[2] there is a common lay assumption that fast computers can crack any code. This is false – the policy dilemmas arise from the brute fact that computers cannot prise open the strong encryption now possible.

While professionals are baffled by contemplation of the social consequences of the interaction of these technologies, public opinion remains almost entirely uninformed about the nature, imminence, or *finality* of the decisions to be made. The finality arises from the inter-penetration of the new medium with every aspect of society. The new communications infrastructure will not be an isolated technology (say like nuclear power) which can be substituted or dispensed with, or a treaty obligation from which a sovereign state can withdraw. Basic technical choices affecting the degree of anonymity and confidentiality possible in mass-market systems, may actually determine (albeit in ways hard to predict) the evolution of democratic political culture.

Policy-makers know that the Information Society will be built on these foundations. Governments may attempt to change policy in the future by legislation, but paradigmatic reform may be unenforceable, once a commercial and political grid, supporting an enormous weight of economic activity, is established internationally.

The growth of the information economy will be built on the regulated issue of 'digital passports' by 'Certification Authorities' and 'Trusted Third Parties' (see below). Market forces will enforce a convergence towards inter-operability of signatures, encryption, electronic cash, and electronic copyright management systems (ECMS), that will occur in leaps and bounds as markets for new digital services are established.

The uniform technical standards of the new networks will be intrinsically capable of supporting computer-automated mass surveillance and traffic-analysis of all digital communications. The potential scope and efficiency of feasible surveillance apparatus is without precedent – conventional techniques are limited by practical constraints. Should the cryptographic infrastructure be designed so that future implementation of mass or even selective surveillance is either possible, or impossible?

Inter-operable electronic copyright, payment, and signature systems could create cradle-to-grave personal audit trails of all transactions, and such information could be used for targeted micro-marketing, credit and insurance, copyright enforcement, and tax/benefit data matching.[3] Can abstract principles of Data Protection provide an effective check on abuse, or should these systems be designed with Privacy Enhancing Technologies, which could prevent data integration not authorised by the individual?

Attitudes to these questions often cut across orthodox left/right political allegiances. Cryptography offers the possibility of erecting strong bulwarks to privacy, if we so choose. Although Big Brother has entered the language as a reference point, an unfortunate codicil to Orwell's legacy is the common assumption and a resigned acceptance that the computer abolished privacy long ago.

This chapter seeks to explore the civil liberties and human rights issues raised by these developments. As the book is written for the lay reader, we have provided a primer on cryptography and a brief summary of surveillance issues before going on to examine the implications for individual rights and freedoms which arise from attempts to regulate the use of encryption, whether escrow would actually work, and the UK government's proposals as they stand at the time of going to press. The chapter concludes with an overview of recent developments, both domestic and international.

Who Needs Cryptography?

Banks presently use encryption all around the world to process financial transactions. For example, the US Department of the Treasury requires encryption of all US electronic funds transfer messages.[4] Banks also use encryption to protect their customers' PIN numbers at bank automated teller machines.

> As the economy continues to move away from cash transactions towards 'digital cash', both customers and merchants will need the authentication provided by unforgeable digital signatures in order to prevent forgery and transact with confidence.[5]

The security of electronic commerce is already an important issue for Internet users. Companies selling anything from flowers to books rely on credit card transactions (and increasingly electronic cash) secured by Internet browsers incorporating encryption techniques. However, because of US controls on the strength of encryption software that can be exported, browser versions for non-US use have designedly weak security which can be broken easily. These transactions remain vulnerable not only to isolated attack by hackers, but also to systematic compromise by well-resourced criminal organisations (or intelligence agencies mandated to engage in economic intelligence gathering).

Cryptography can also provide anonymity as well as confidentiality, essential for certain special interest groups, and was used on the Websites of the Critical Path AIDS Project in the US and the Samaritans in the UK. Internet anonymous remailers allow human rights monitors in repressive regimes to communicate without fear of persecution or reprisals.

CRYPTOGRAPHY: A PRIMER

The word cryptography[6] comes from the Greek word *kryptos* which means hidden while *graphia* stands for writing. Cryptography concerns ways in which the meaning of messages may be concealed so that only certain people can understand them, and methods of ensuring that the content of messages remains unaltered.

David Kahn traces the history of cryptography from ancient Egypt to the computer age.[7] During the Second World War, the first electro-mechanical computers were built for the ULTRA project, which allowed the British to read German communications enciphered with the Enigma machine.[8] They were specially designed to automate the task of exhaustively searching for the correct Enigma settings, assisted by various 'cribs' (short-cuts deduced from previous analysis or lapses in security). An organisation was created to decrypt large volumes of intercepted traffic, and distribute the intelligence securely for operational use.

Codes

A code is the correspondence of a fixed repertoire of messages to a set of previously agreed symbols. In a computer, the alphabetic, numeric and punctuation characters comprising a message are each assigned a number between zero and 255 according to a conventional code (such as ASCII). A message can thus be represented as bytes – groups of eight binary digits (bits – 1s and 0s).[9] The ASCII representation of a message is not encrypted, because the code is well known. Even if a code is secret, it cannot encrypt a message that falls outside the agreed repertoire.

Ciphers

A cipher allows encryption of an *arbitrary* message using a general rule or scheme (algorithm) together with a key, to turn plaintext into ciphertext. The most secure cipher is the 'one-time pad'. This uses a random binary number as the key, and the algorithm acts on plaintext by flipping the bits ('exclusive-or') in positions where the one-time pad key is 1. Decryption applies the same rule to key and ciphertext, producing plaintext. Without the key, no information can be gleaned about the plaintext. The disadvantage of this method is that it requires a key (which must not be re-used hence 'one-time') as long as the message itself.

More complex ciphers may involve complicated sequences of substitutions and transpositions. In Julius Caesar's substitution cipher each letter of the original message is replaced with the letter three places beyond it in the alphabet. Transposition ciphers rearrange the order of characters. In these symmetric ciphers both sender and receiver use the same key to scramble and unscramble the message.

If a key is reused, there is a risk that it may be deduced through statistical analysis of intercepted samples of ciphertext. This is much easier if a cryptanalyst (code-breaker) can arrange for a hapless opponent to encrypt chosen plaintext messages that systematically divulge clues. More elaborate cipher algorithms recycle a conveniently short key, but successively chain the output with the preceding block of ciphertext, to scramble any regularity. Nevertheless, various kinds of mathematical short-cut have been discovered to crack apparently robust algorithms, and ciphers may have certain weak keys or even an intentional back-door which makes cryptanalysis easy.

Ciphers for which the algorithm is known can in principle be broken by a brute-force attack, in which every possible key is tried – if the key is n-bits long, then there are 2^n possible key values. But however fast computers become, quite short keys can generate a number of combinations[10] astronomically beyond their reach. A cipher that cannot be broken by the brute-force or cunning (of a particular adversary) is termed 'strong'.

Public Key Cryptography

All ciphers seem to suffer from the same drawback. Trusted couriers are needed to deliver keys to those wishing to send encrypted messages to each other. The key cannot be sent over the same channel as the message, because that channel is presumed insecure – otherwise why bother to encrypt? This difficulty is so obvious, and so apparently insurmountable, that when Whitfield Diffie and Martin Hellman solved the key distribution problem in 1976,[11] it completely revolutionised cryptography. Instead of using a single key that could both encrypt and decrypt a message, they proposed a scheme in which every individual has both a public key (which can be published in a directory) and a private key (which is kept secret).

If Alice wants to send a confidential message to Bob, she looks up Bob in a directory and encrypts her message with his *public key* contained there, and sends it. When Bob receives the encrypted message, he decrypts it into plaintext with his *private* key. This is bafflingly simple – how is it done? How are the public and private key related? Why can't anyone else just look up Bob's public key as well, and use that to decrypt the (intercepted) message?

The trick is to use a mathematical one-way function: once a message is encrypted with such a function, it cannot be decrypted with the same key used to encrypt. There is however a corresponding key (the private key), which will decrypt the message – but the calculation of the private key from the public key can be made arbitrarily time-consuming by sufficiently lengthening the keys.

This is a completely counter-intuitive notion, understandably alien to common-sense ideas of how codes and ciphers work. Nevertheless it means that completely secure communication can occur between two parties without prior negotiation of a shared secret key.

RSA

The system first used for public key (or asymmetric) cryptography is called RSA (after the inventors Rivest, Shamir and Adleman)[12] and was developed in 1977.[13] Two very long prime numbers are chosen at random, and these generate (but are not the same as) the public and private keys. It turns out that showing that a certain number is prime (that is, has no smaller divisors) is much easier than actually finding the factors of a number which is not prime. The cryptanalyst's problem of finding the private key from the public key can be solved by factoring the product of the two primes (without knowing either – which would be trivial). The best-known methods would take current computers millions of years for keys several hundred digits long.

If the invention of public key cryptography was indeed so revolutionary, why has it taken 20 years for these issues to come to a head? The reasons are various: the patenting (in the US) of the RSA algorithm, strict US export controls on cryptography and the strivings of intelligence agencies to preserve their national security interception capabilities.

DIGITAL SIGNATURES

Public key cryptography can also *authenticate* that a message originates (and has not been altered en route) from a person using a kind of signature. To send a signed message, Alice encrypts with *her private* key, before sending to Bob. This time Bob can only decrypt the message using Alice's *public* key (it works this way round as well), which he has to look up in a directory. If Bob can do this, it verifies Alice's signature, because the message must have been sent using her private key (which only she should know).

Note that in this example, anyone else can look up Alice's public key to decrypt the message (and thus verify the signature) as well, so the message is not confidential. A signed and secret message can be sent by layering the encryption protocol for signature inside that for confidentiality, however using the same public/private key-pair for both (only possible with the RSA system) has practical and regulatory disadvantages (see 'Self-certification' below).

CERTIFICATION AUTHORITIES

Although trusted couriers are no longer needed for key delivery, a new type of key distribution problem arises with public key cryptography. If Alice looks up Bob's public key in a directory, how does she know that that key really belongs to Bob? An impostor might have published a phoney public key under Bob's name, hoping either to intercept messages sent to him (if it was a confidentiality key), or convince the unwary to accept forged documents (if it was a signature key).

The solution is for Bob to present his public key to someone who can reputably vouch for his identity – a Certification Authority (CA) – and get them to (digitally) sign a key certificate which can be then be published. Anyone can verify that the public key attached to a certificate can safely be used, by validating the signature of the CA. The public signature key of the CA thus becomes the 'gold standard' for routine checking of certificates issued, and may itself be certified in a 'hierarchy of trust' of ever more unimpeachable authorities. Certificates could equally be signed by (many different) individuals, on the basis of personal acquaintance, in a 'web-of-trust'. However, vouching for someone's identity is not the same as vouching for their honesty or diligence in performing identifications, so in a web or a hierarchy, a 'chain' of certification is only as strong as the weakest link. Note that the private key of the end user is nowhere required or involved in the certification process.

SELF-CERTIFICATION

The risks associated with compromise of a private key used for signature are substantially different from those for a key used for message secrecy. A person may therefore have two different pairs of keys (private/public), for separate confidentiality and signature use. In this case, there is actually no need for a CA to be involved in certifying the public key used for encryption. A user may 'self-certify' their public encryption key by signing it with their own digital signature. If their signature is trusted (because the signature is certified by a CA and can thus be verified) then their self-signed encryption key should be trustworthy to the same extent.

REVOCATION

All certificates should be stamped with an expiry date, and new keys must be generated and re-certified before this date to prevent disruption of service. In fact any certification system must provide for the case of a private key becoming compromised, and propogate revocation of invalid certificates through the directories used to verify signatures. Should revocation be under the control of the key owner or the certifier? If certification occurs through a hierarchy of trust, entire branches of the hierarchy could be disabled by revocation of a high-order certificate, which could be regarded either as a vulnerability, or a strategic lever of control. In contrast, a web-of-trust (in which a certificate is validated by multiple signatories) is immunised against single-points of attack or failure. In trust networks, the structure of revocation is a political issue.

SESSION KEYS

Software implementations of public key cryptography, involving operations on very large numbers, are relatively slow. Although chips to speed up the necessary mathematical operations are available, software running on todays PCs would take an inconveniently long time to prepare long messages. To get around this, hybrid cryptography uses a combination of conventional cipher and public key systems to get the best of both worlds. The idea is to choose a conventional cipher with a key-length resistant to brute-force attack, and encipher with a key *randomly chosen for each message* (a session key). The session key (for example, 128 bits) is then itself encrypted with public key cryptography (which can be done quickly because the key is much smaller than a typical message), and then attached to the end of the ciphertext. In other words, the receiver's public key is being used as a key encryption key. To decrypt the message, the receiver's software first detaches and then decrypts the session key with her private key, and then uses the session key to decipher the actual (long) message. Although seemingly a gratuitous complication (in an already complicated process) this works well, and allows messages to be encrypted and decrypted quickly, with the full strength and benefits of public key cryptography.

Pretty Good Privacy

In 1992 Phil Zimmerman, a US computer security consultant, created a complete implementation of RSA public key cryptography which could run on most computers, using a strong session key cipher. It allowed users to generate their own public and private keys, maintain a 'key-ring' of signed certificates in a web-of-trust, and certify the keys of other users. Any Internet user could now send and receive electronic mail that could not be decrypted (as far as anyone knows) by the most skilled cryptanalysts using the most powerful computers. It was called Pretty Good Privacy (PGP).[14]

Phil Zimmerman's motive for creating the program was political and not for profit.[15] Zimmerman believes that the intrinsic susceptibility of digital communications to automated mass surveillance is an unprecedented threat to civil liberties[16] and wishes to provide the public with a secure means of communication. The program has been used by human rights monitors inside countries with repressive political regimes, but also by criminals to conceal evidence.[17]

The disclosure or transfer of cryptographic software to a foreigner is illegal under the US ITAR[18] export regulations. Zimmerman never personally exported PGP, he created it, encouraged its use and distributed it to friends and colleagues, one of whom posted it to an Internet Usenet discussion group.[19] Later, improved and extended versions were collaboratively produced by other programmers around the world.[20] Zimmerman was put under investigation, with a grand jury hearing evidence for about 28 months. A campaign was established for his defence, and the civil liberties issues achieved wide publicity on the Internet. After acquiring folk-hero status, the prosecution was finally dropped[21] by the Federal Government in January 1996 without explanation. These disputes are now moot, and PGP has become an international de facto standard for Internet public key cryptography. In 1997, the source program of the latest version was published in the form of a book, constitutionally protected under the First Amendment. The book was then scanned outside the US, and the program re-compiled, which allowed distribution of a free version on the Internet, and a 'shrink-wrap' version for commercial use.

US Clipper Chip Proposals

In 1993, the Clinton administration announced the Clipper chip initiative (which is also known as the Escrowed Encryption Standard – EES). In response to concerns expressed by law enforcement and national security bodies that uncontrolled use of strong encryption for voice telephony and computer data could threaten the ability to intercept and monitor communications, the plan called for the incorporation of a hardware encryption chip into every telephone, fax machine, modem and computer (the chips for the latter actually called Capstone/Fortezza, although based on the same technology).

The concept was that a copy of the individual cipher key embedded in a tamper-proof chip (manufactured under government licence), would be held in a database by a new independent judicial 'escrow' agency[22] (a legal term for an honest broker), which would release the key copy to law enforcement agencies on presentation of a valid warrant. This would then enable decryption of intercepted traffic generated by the device containing the chip.

The encryption algorithm (Skipjack), designed by the National Security Agency, was to remain secret,[23] which raised concerns that it might contain an intentional or unintentional back-door that could be exploited by government or others to achieve unauthorised decryption. The history of cryptography contains several examples of algorithms that were believed to be strong for many years, before finally yielding to attacks from academic cryptanalysts (for example, the Knapsack system of Diffie–Merkle–Hellman).

The policy was severely criticised on civil liberties, technical, and economic grounds.[24] There was a general objection that a future government might engage in Big Brother mass surveillance, a technical flaw was discovered in the design which could enable circumvention of escrow (i.e. communication could take place which the escrowed key could not decrypt), and industry objected that Clipper products would be unsaleable abroad.

The US Government in December 1995 presented a revised version of their Clipper Chip proposal which introduced the notion of key escrow achieved through software.[25] This idea was expanded in May 1996, in the document *Achieving Privacy, Commerce, Security and Public Safety in the Global Information Infrastructure.*[26] A new public key infrastructure (PKI) would enable users of encryption clearly to identify the people they communicate with, and export restrictions would be lifted on cryptographic software which properly escrowed confidentiality keys with an approved agent,[27] where the underlying cipher system employs keys of no more than 56 bits. This is a belt-and-braces approach, since it is generally believed that specially designed cipher-cracking computers, which may be available to governments (or other large organisations), can crack 56-bit ciphers in days.[28]

Finding a foreign market for encryption products with key escrow under US control will be difficult, whatever the length of keys.[29] Political and commercial organisations might reasonably believe that US authorities would intercept their communications.[30]

Trusted Third Party

The term 'Trusted Third Party' is unfortunately ambiguous. It originally meant merely a Certification Authority (which has no technical or commercial need to escrow private keys) however the term is now usually synonymous with software escrow, for the simple reason it is a mandatory requirement of government proposals for regulation of TTPs.[31]

The role of a TTP/CA is to provide (for a fee) a certificate that authenticates (on the authority of the TTP organisation) that a public encryption key or a public digital signature key actually belongs to the named owner. TTPs can function as 'escrow' agencies, by insisting that the private decryption key is surrendered to (or generated by) the TTP, and held in a database for safe-keeping. If a key owner loses her private key, she can apply for a replacement copy from the TTP. A law enforcement agency could also apply for a copy of the private key with a warrant, without the knowledge of the key owner.

Financial and legal institutions, telecommunications companies, Internet content vendors, and network service providers could all act as TTPs, although there is little consensus about how many a regulated market could support, the tariff structure, or the degree of vertical integration and conflict of interest which should be permitted. The Data Protection Registrars Twelfth Annual Report stated that there are several problems to be resolved before setting up a TTP system:

> Who would supervise it; who would the TTPs be; what products be used; how could you stop users from bypassing the system ... would a TTP be able to offer services on a European or even a global basis?[32]

TWO KINDS OF TRUST

The meaning of 'trust' is radically different for a CA and an escrowing TTP. The CA must take appropriate care before certifying identity, to guarantee that only the named key holder can decrypt messages (in the case of confidentiality keys), or that the key holder has signed a document (in the case of signature keys). Thus the legal liability of a CA can be controlled by a clear statement of the reliance to be placed on its procedures for ascertaining identity, and its demonstrable conformance to those procedures. The key holder's privacy is never at risk. In contrast, if a TTP holds private confidentiality keys, immeasurable damage can be caused to the key owner – privacy can be compromised.

The provision of certified keys for confidentiality and digital signatures are separable problems – indeed there is a compelling reason why they should be accomplished separately under any putative escrow regime. If a government were able to obtain access to a private key used for signatures, documents and transactions purportedly originating from the key owner could be forged. There is general agreement that this possibility would fatally discredit judicial and public confidence in digital signatures.[33]

KEY RECOVERY

If messages are sent outside the jurisdiction covering the TTP, a foreign territory must apply for extradition of an escrowed key. This may make either side uncomfortable. Schemes have been proposed allowing recovery of the plaintext of individual messages without escrow, by attaching a Law Enforcement Access Field ('LEAF' – effectively the session key encrypted under a recovery agents public key), but these do not address civil liberties concerns any better, and are difficult to make tamper-proof in software.

'ROYAL HOLLOWAY' TTP

If however there is a TTP in each jurisdiction, then keys can be recovered without the involvement of foreign jurisprudence. However, this requires both TTPs to remain synchronised, with identical databases of escrowed keys, which would involve frequent updating (as keys change), over an ultra-secure channel.

Cryptologists at Royal Holloway College (RHC) have proposed a TTP design[34] which obviates this awkward operational requirement. Instead of keeping an escrow database of (randomly generated) individual keys, the two RHC TTPs employ a *single* 'shared secret key' (like a master-key) and a key-generating function, from which each users individual keys are generated (taking the key holder's name as parameter). There is therefore no need to keep an escrow database at all, and thus no synchronisation problem. If a private key needs to be recovered, it can be regenerated at will by either TTP. Provided only the two TTPs know the secret master-key, this arrangement is as secure as maintaining a groaning database full of individual keys.

This cuts both ways however. If there is concern that keys might leak (to intelligence agencies, corporate spies or criminals), the shared secret key is a jackpot (which would fit on the back of a lottery ticket), allowing decryption of all traffic between all patrons of that pair of TTPs. Perhaps the inconvenience of dual escrow databases is to be preferred.

The RHC system has been adopted as the basis for the Cloud Cover scheme advocated by CESG (the Communications Electronics Security Group – the defence division of GCHQ) for the protection of UK Government communications. The scheme has been severely criticised[35] for its signature-key escrow design (which could permit centralised alteration of official document records) and its rigidly hierarchical approach to key distribution (making major departmental reorganisation very costly). CESG has been inviting private companies to produce implementations of Cloud Cover 'on spec', with a view to their wider use in quasi-government organisations (without offering explicit guarantees about its official adoption).

KEY-SPLITTING

It is possible to divide the escrow of keys between more than one TTP. This provides some security against the malfeasance of a single individual or agency. It is also possible to produce split keys with any desired degree of redundancy, so that possession of a threshold number of fragments permits reconstruction of the entire key.

SURVEILLANCE, ANONYMITY AND TRAFFIC ANALYSIS

> There was of course no way of knowing whether you were being watched at any given moment. How often, or on what system, the Thought Police plugged in on any individual wire was guesswork. It was even conceivable that they watched everybody all the time. But at any rate they could plug into your wire whenever they wanted to. You had to live – did live, from habit that became instinct – in the assumption that every sound you made was overheard, and, except in darkness, every movement scrutinised.[36]

What use is a morass of raw digital intercepts? Why should anyone believe that a government could marshall the resources for their analysis, or that the products of that analysis could be useful?

Traffic Analysis

Traffic analysis refers to the study of the who-is-talking-to-whom, rather than what-they-are-saying. By analysing call-signs, frequencies, flurries of activity, military signals intelligence (SIGINT) can deduce a great deal about order of battle and movements, without any ability to decipher message content. Civil law enforcement also relies on traffic analysis, for example to trace a drug-dealers contacts (and their contacts) from a telephone log.[37] Computerised analysis of traffic associations is a potent weapon in the law-enforcement armoury, but is prejudicial to civil liberties unless carefully targeted.

MASS SURVEILLANCE

> Mass surveillance is the surveillance of groups of people, usually large groups. In general, the reason for investigation or monitoring is to identify individuals who belong to some particular class of interest to the surveillance organizations.[38]

The public key infrastructure will tag every message and transaction with a digital signature. Specialised programs for investigating relationships latent in large volumes of unstructured text are already widely used by intelligence agencies.[39] Should any government ever have the possibility of trawling through and automatically analysing the national telephone log of the Superhighway?

COMPUTER PROFILING

> This technique [computer profiling] is used primarily for law enforcement purposes to locate potential violators when there is a general idea about the characteristics of offending behaviour, but no precise information on the violators ... Profiling involves the correlation of information to determine how closely persons or events fit previously determined violation prototypes. Statistical

> selection methods and inductive logic are used to determine indicators of behaviour patterns related to the occurrence of a certain activity (for example, persons most likely to under-report taxable income or persons most likely to engage in illegal drug activity).[40]

This is a powerful shortcut to compiling a list of suspects – profiling can be combined with traffic analysis and ad hoc rules (heuristics) to list individuals deemed suspicious by association, without any capability for decrypting intercepted messages.

PERSONAL SURVEILLANCE

> Personal surveillance is the surveillance of an identified person. In general, a specific reason exists for the investigation or monitoring.[41]

Heuristic profiling could be the basis for selecting *which* subjects were promising targets, and constitute prima facie evidence for a key-recovery warrant to be granted.

Anonymous Mail

Internet privacy activists have developed experimental anonymous remailer programs which circumvent traffic analysis. An anonymous remailer is simply a computer service that forwards e-mails or files to other addresses over the Internet. But the remailer also strips off the header part of the message, which shows where it came from and who sent it. All a traffic analyst can tell is that the sender has sent a message to a remailer, and that (perhaps another) remailer has sent a message to someone else. Sender and receiver cannot be connected (assuming a reasonable throughput of messages).

The most untraceable implementations (for example, MixMaster)[42] use public key cryptography to chain together several remailers, which allows unprecedented anonymity both to groups who wish to communicate in complete privacy[43] and to 'whistle-blowers' who have reason to fear persecution if their ame known.[44] According to Raymond Wacks, 'it rticipation in the political process which an indi- therwise wish to spurn'.[45]

best-known anonymous remailers on the Internet (anon.penet.fi) run for more than three years by Johann Helsingius was closed in August 1996 following allegations by the UK *Observer* newspaper that it contributed to the distribution of child pornography.[46] Among its users were Amnesty International and the Samaritans. West Mercia Police also used it as the basis of their 'Crimestoppers' scheme.[47] Contrary to the newspapers allegations, the sending of pictures through the remailer had been disabled for two years.[48]

In the US, the Supreme Court[49] recently stated that 'an author's decision to remain anonymous, like other decisions concerning omissions or additions to the content of a publication, is an aspect of the freedom of speech protected by the First Amendment' and 'the anonymity of an author is not ordinarily a sufficient reason to exclude her work product from the protections of the First Amendment'.

Anonymity is important both to free speech and privacy.[50] A public key infrastructure would identify the nominal source and destination of messages. The Internet Watch Foundation (formerly known as Safety-Net),[51] recently endorsed by the UK Government, sees anonymity on the Internet as a danger, stating:

> ... [A]nonymous servers that operate in the UK [should] record details of identity and make this available to the Police, when needed, under Section 28 (3) of the Data Protection Act (which deals with the disclosure of information for the purpose of prevention of crime).[52]

A key aspect of the Safety-Net approach is that users take responsibility for material they post on the Internet; it is important to be able to trace the originators of child pornography and other illegal material. But on the other hand, groups such as the Critical Path AIDS Project, the Samaritans, and Stop Prisoner Rape depend on anonymity for the avoidance of social stigma. Dissident political movements may also need to access and supply sensitive information without risking identification.

Privacy Enhancing Technologies

Absolute anonymity may create unacceptable possibilities for criminal abuse for some types of transaction (for example, e-cash ransom payments); on the other hand, universal traceability of all messages creates Big Brother traffic analysis risks, even if the content of messages is encrypted. Privacy Enhancing Technologies may provide a combination of last-resort traceability, whilst protecting against intrusive traffic analysis. In many cases, the identity of a data subject need not be known at all (except when suspected of crime), or only by a restricted number of people, but information from different records belonging to the same individual needs to be matched – for example medical records passing through a number of hands in the course of treatment. In these cases an alias or pseudonym can be used. The pseudonym is bound to the true identity through an identity protector, with access cryptographically limited to those with proper authorisation.

CIVIL LIBERTIES

Since the Clipper initiative, there has been vigorous debate on escrow in the US by non-governmental organisations such as Computer Professionals for Social Responsibility (CPSR), the Electronic Frontier Foundation (EFF), and the Electronic Privacy Information Centre (EPIC). Although most of the Internet community are by now to some degree aware of the issues (for example via campaign banners on many World Wide Web pages), there is scant understanding of these issues amongst the general public, especially outside the US. The general position of non-governmental organisations has been to oppose escrow. It should be noted that Cyber-Rights & Cyber-Liberties (UK) has led opposition to the UK governments TTP escrow proposals since its announcement and its response to the DTI consultation paper was endorsed by 15 organisations including the CPSR, EFF and the American Civil Liberties Union.[53]

Chilling Effects

Most people would accept the need for democratic governments to intercept communications on a limited scale, for detection and investigation of crime, and for defence of the realm. According to the FBI, wiretapping is crucial to effective law enforcement:

> If the FBI and local police were to lose the ability to tap telephones because of the widespread use of strong-cryptography, the country would be unable to protect itself against terrorism, violent crime, foreign threats, drug trafficking, espionage, kidnapping, and other crimes.[54]

Without this capability, governments would be less able to protect the safety of the public, and this in itself would constitute an infringement of civil liberties. The question is not whether any such interception is wrong, but whether it is safe to entrust all future governments in perpetuity with an unprecedented technical capability for mass surveillance. The state strategy seems naive as it assumes that criminals will use encryption tools that can be decrypted by law enforcement bodies. But government capabilities for automated (and archived) large-scale surveillance could have a chilling effect on the private expression of political opinions by the law-abiding. Although the Internet community is presently a politically negligible minority, as the convergence of electronic media proceeds, there are plausible scenarios for serious and cumulative erosion of the democratic process. It is a sea-change in the relationship of the citizen to the state.

The Slippery Slope

> Domestic espionage is the hidden underside of political history. It may be immensely important. It is possible that without it we would be a very different country from what we are today. We might have a different religion, a different queen, or a different political system.

> We might be a satellite of a French or German or Russian empire. We could even have a Labour government.[55]

The case for stringent technical limits on surveillance is essentially a slippery slope argument. In one sense, this argument is not new: civil liberties campaigners have always argued that interception of mail and telephone communications carries a risk of escalating abuse. However, the scale of such interception is intrinsically limited: the bureaucracy and expense of opening letters and transcribing conversations ensures that any abuse can only occur on a small scale. Large-scale domestic surveillance has hitherto been impractical. In contrast, the ECHELON[56] system can trawl digital communications secretly, centrally, to an increasing degree automatically, at feasible operational cost. The present coverage of ECHELON is unknown, but the EU and US have harmonised arrangements for direct government access to public telecommunications networks.[58]

David Herson, the ex-GCHQ official from DGXIII of the European Commission, with responsibility for piloting TTP systems to create standards for European Trusted Services (ETS), expresses justifiable and implicit faith in the reasonable behaviour of the law enforcement and national security authorities in democratic societies. Further, according to Herson, 'occasional lapses ... will ... eventually come to light'. However these remarks sit uneasily with his remarkably candid view of policy motivations, given in an unofficial interview: 'Law enforcement is a protective shield for all the other governmental activities ... we are talking about foreign intelligence ... Law enforcement is a smoke screen'.[60]

Security authorities argue that flexible options for large-scale surveillance are needed for intelligence-led operations to counter organised crime, or proliferation of weapons of mass destruction. But if the design of the new communications infrastructure is predicated on an absolute capability to counter such threats, the resulting apparatus is indistinguishable from that required to anticipate, subvert, and neutralise political dissent. Economic upheaval and social unrest, shocking terrorist incidents, or national emergency could progressively or suddenly widen the use of such capabilities, either with Parliamentary consent or covertly authorised under Crown Prerogative. At what point does the qualitative efficiency of surveillance invalidate the democratic legitimacy it is used to protect?

Therefore the crux of the argument is that the *new* slippery slope is not only much *steeper* (because analysis of digital intercepts can be automated), but it does not *flatten out*, in fact there would actually be economies of scale with increasing coverage. Whether this is perceived as a categorical difference, or one of degree, will sharply affect opinions about whether procedural and legal safeguards are adequate to prevent abuse in the indefinite future, or whether the infrastructure itself should be designed to be technically incapable of mass monitoring.

Are there alternatives to escrow?

Is it possible to design an infrastructure that only has the technical capacity for surveillance on a limited scale, comparable with present arrangements? If not, should we simply accept the introduction of surveillance architecture as necessary, and trust that democratic continuity will never allow its abuse? What are the precise risks, technical and political, in doing so? If technical safeguards cannot be found, but granting governments a mass-surveillance capability is deemed too dangerous, can and should judicial and law-enforcement procedures be revised to compensate for loss of existing means of interception? Alternatives to escrow might include:

- Covert installation of software or hardware bugging devices in a suspect's computer which capture passwords and keys – such technologies will in any case be needed to intercept Mafia and terrorist communications that are not key-escrowed, and for military 'InfoWar' purposes.

- Making failure to comply with a judicial decryption warrant (requiring disclosure of a private key) a specific offence.

- Legal admissibility of intercepted communications as evidence in court proceedings, already widely used in the US. Currently intercepts can only be used for intelligence purposes in the UK.

This combination of measures could be reasonably effective, and formulated with civil liberties safeguards, but could not be abused to achieve large-scale surveillance.

WOULD ESCROW WORK?

Steganography

The concept of randomness is subtly connected with cryptography. When analog signals (for example, sound samples, photographs) are converted to a digital code, the numbers representing the properties of the real world contain a degree of *noise* (imprecision about the particular loudness, pitch, shade of colour) which is random. Without a key to make sense of it, an encrypted message also looks like a random number or noise. This means that it is possible to camouflage an encrypted message by distributing it in the noise of the digital representation of a sound or picture.

This technique of camouflage is known as steganography,[61] and it means that a hidden message can be concealed in any digital data that contains noise. The consequence is that escrow of encryption keys can be circumvented by sending sound, pictures or video, with a hidden message sprinkled into the noisy cracks created by digitisation. Done properly, this cannot be detected or proven.[62]

The policy implication for law enforcement is that serious 'bad hats' will escape any escrow net. Escrow cannot be justified on the grounds that it will enable interception of the internal communications of the Mafia, or professional terrorists. Any competent and well-funded organisation can easily establish secure, hidden channels.

Both pro- and anti-escrow advocates recognise that circumvention of any escrow regime is technically possible, and will become easier as strong encryption tools inevitably proliferate. Nothing can technically prevent data being encrypted against an unescrowed key, concealed with steganography, and sent via anonymous remailers.

Advocates of escrow point out that even if Mafia and terrorist organisations are able to circumvent escrow in their internal communications, they must still communicate externally with law-abiding organisations. However, the permanent records and co-operation of legitimate organisations are already available to investigators – the argument is about whether near real-time traffic-analysis/interception/decryption is justifiable, given the dangers for civil liberties. Both sides agree what is important is whether the majority of communication systems become escrowed, and (remarkably) foresee a similar conclusion: if the most important criminals will escape the escrow net, then eventually a ban on unescrowed strong encryption must follow. Official statements[63] support this reasoning.

A Strategically Destabilising Initiative?

> ... no administration can bind future administrations, and Congress can change a law at any time. More importantly, widespread acceptance of escrowed encryption, even if voluntary, would put into place an infrastructure that would support such a policy change. Thus, the possibility that a future administration and/or Congress might support prohibitions on unescrowed encryption cannot be dismissed.[65]

With an escrow infrastructure in place, compliance with a ban on unauthorised double-encryption could at least be partially enforced by the deterrent effect of random sampling, to see if decryption with escrowed keys produced plaintext (this process could be automated). Although steganography could circumvent a ban (unless transmission of all material not susceptible to unambiguous interpretation – for example, poetry, painting, and journals of the *Society for the Exchange of Random Numbers* were also banned) this logical absurdity has not inhibited at least one Western European government from banning unauthorised encryption.[66]

Inter-operability

If TTPs or CAs are licensed, the exact specification of the protocols permitted will determine whether the ultimate infrastructure leans toward facilitation of surveillance, or protection of privacy. A huge range exists between, on the one hand, Certification Authorities that only serve to authenticate digital signatures and encryption keys, and at the other extreme single-master-key (RHC) escrow TTPs. The jurisdictional problems presented by international access to escrowed keys also add immense complications. If escrow is to work, standards must be created for sharing directories, excluding or barring access to non-escrowed certificates, and searching and linking directories on a global scale.[67] Law enforcement and intelligence agencies will advocate rigid controls to maximise their operational capability. Civil libertarians will argue against any escrow, or many safeguards for access, to ensure that abuse is difficult, isolated, and hard to conceal.

Electronic Warrants

The DTI envisages a system of electronic warrants to authorise lawful access. The warrant would be e-mailed to the desk of a Secretary of State, approved with a digital signature, and forwarded to the correct Trusted Third Party via a central repository (see DTI Proposals below). The TTP must respond with the key within one hour to meet its licensing obligations (insufficient time to challenge a warrant in court). GCHQ presently intercepts under non-specific warrants,[68] which permit unlimited trawling of foreign communications.[69] Domestic communications may also be intercepted in support of the security and intelligence services. Warranted interception with technical safeguards to prevent abuse including key-splitting, time-bounding, and technically robust audit trails on escrow access might preclude real-time interception, and may therefore be resisted by intelligence and law-enforcement agencies.

Costs and Risks

In May 1997, a group of independent experts released a report that examined the risks and implications of government proposals for key-recovery systems. The authors of the report are recognised authorities in the fields of cryptography and computer security, including Ross Anderson, Matt Blaze, Whitfield Diffie, John Gilmore, Peter G. Neumann, Ronald L. Rivest, Jeffrey I. Schiller, and Bruce Schneier. The report, entitled 'The Risks of Key Recovery, Key Escrow, and Trusted Third-Party Encryption',[70] cautions that 'the deployment of a general key-recovery-based encryption infrastructure to meet law enforcements stated requirements will result in substantial sacrifices in security and cost to the end user. Building a secure infrastructure of the breathtaking scale and complexity demanded by these requirements is far beyond the experience and current competency of the field.'

Drawing a sharp distinction between government requirements for key recovery and the types of recovery systems users want, the report found that government key recovery systems will produce:[71]

- *New Vulnerabilities and Risks* – Key recovery systems make encryption systems less secure by adding a new and vulnerable path to the unauthorised recovery of data where one need never exist. Such backdoor paths remove the guaranteed security of encryption systems and create new high-value targets for attack in key recovery centres.

- *New Complexities* – Key recovery will require a vast infrastructure of recovery agents and government oversight bodies to manage access to the billions of keys that must be recoverable. The field of cryptography has no experience in deploying secure systems of this scope and complexity.

- *New Costs* – Key recovery will cost billions of dollars to deploy, making encryption security both expensive and inconvenient.

- *New Targets for Attack* – Key recovery agents will maintain databases that hold, in centralised collections, the keys to the information and communications their customers most value. In many systems, the theft of a single private key (or small set of keys) could unlock much or all of the data of a company or individual.

UK POLICY

Since 1994, a committee of permanent officials[72] has formulated UK encryption policy, providing unified advice to Ministers. Since 1995, the consistent aim of UK and US policy has been to introduce systems for ubiquitous 'key recovery', intended to maintain covert access to electronic communications. The policy has never been debated by Parliament, or scrutinised by any Select Committee. After unsuccessful attempts by representatives of GCHQ to persuade the OECD to adopt Royal Holloway TTPs as an international standard,[73] the Department of Trade and Industry was assigned the lead role, and announced in June 1996 its intention to regulate the provision of encryption services to the public,[74] stating that:

> It is not the intention of the Government to regulate the private use of encryption. It will, however, ensure that organisations and bodies wishing to provide encryption services to the public will be appropriately licensed.[75]

Labour Party Policy

Communicating Britain's Future set out the pre-election policy of the Labour Party on encryption:[76]

> We do not accept the 'Clipper chip' argument developed in the United States for the authorities to be able to swoop down on any encrypted message at will and unscramble it. The only power we would wish to give to the authorities, in order to pursue a defined legitimate anti-criminal purpose, would be to enable decryption to be demanded under judicial warrant.

If this amounts to a generic rejection of escrow, it appears that the Labour Party intended solely to penalise a refusal to comply with a demand to decrypt under judicial warrant. The Labour Party further argued that attempts to control the use of encryption technology were 'wrong in principle, unworkable in practice, and damaging to the long-term economic value of the information networks .... It is not necessary to criminalise a large section of the network-using public to control the activities of a very small minority of law-breakers.'[77]

Mandatory Licensing – DTI Consultation

The DTI published the Consultation Paper[78] *Licensing of Trusted Third Parties for the Provision of Encryption Services* on 19 March 1997 (two days before a General Election was called). The paper was a detailed proposal for legislation in the first session[79] of a new Parliament, with a consultation period overlapping the election campaign, and expiring at the end of May. The timing of the announcement might uncharitably be construed as an attempt to present a new government with a policy *fait accompli,*[80] but not apparently through the political direction of the previous administration.[81]

The preamble to the Consultation Paper introduced the proposals in the context of the Government's Information Society Initiative, with laudable aims for the promotion of electronic commerce, educational networks, and better delivery of government services. However the subsequent exposition of the linkage between these goals and regulation of encryption services is parochial and deftly obscure. The US is only mentioned twice and the Clipper Chip not at all, nor is there any reference to the four years of vigorous controversy that it ignited. There is no acknowledgement of the tremendous outcry against escrow from the Internet community, and the overwhelming opposition of academic cryptographers, the business sector, and civil liberties groups.[82] The exclusion of human rights organisations from the deliberations[83] of the OECD 'Ad-Hoc Group of Experts' is also passed by. The inference to be drawn from the drafting is that the DTI attached little weight to the views of the broad coalition opposed to escrow.

The proposals are formulated in such a way that the most significant condition is only implicitly stated. Public 'encryption services' would be *prohibited*, unless they incorporated key escrow (or key recovery),

> ... whether provided free or not, which involves any or all of the following cryptographic functionality – key management, key recovery, key certification, key storage, message integrity (through the use of digital signatures), key generation, time stamping, or key revocation services (whether for integrity or confidentiality), which are offered in a manner which allows a client to determine a choice of cryptographic key or allows the client a choice of recipient/s.

The DTI (initially) described their framework as *voluntary* because 'those wishing to use any other cryptographic solutions can continue to do so, but they will not be able to benefit from the convenience, and interoperability of licensed TTPs'. Without mechanisms to establish trust, this is analogous to saying that friends may freely converse in private, but public meetings can only be arranged in venues wired for eavesdropping.

The key owner would thus be obliged indirectly to pay the costs of the TTP meeting much more stringent licensing criteria, and the TTPs insurance against negligent disclosure or employee malfeasance. Moreover the absolute amount of any damages claim will be limited by statute, and the TTP indemnified against claims arising from government access. The DTI also suggested that contracts made with digital signatures might only be presumed valid if certified by licensed TTPs.[84]

Without compulsory key escrow, competition between CAs will ensure that basic certification is available, from a plurality of organisations, for low cost. With key escrow, the choice of TTPs will be limited to those able to apply economies of scale (or cross-subsidise) the costs of licensing, perhaps a handful (after market shakeouts) of large financial, telecommunications, or publishing organisations.

The natural model for certification services is that users will select as CAs (for particular purposes) organisations with which they have a pre-existing affiliation or fiduciary relationship (solicitors, accountants, political or professional associations, trade unions). Such organisations would benefit from the goodwill established by long-standing trust relationships with their clients or members. This commercial franchise would be expropriated by mandatory TTP licensing with escrow, as the marketing of value-added services is skewed in favour of larger combines. In the Information Society should government, or the public, decide who is to be trusted?

The paper also states that 'encryption services by unlicensed TTPs outside the UK will be prohibited', without suggesting how this extra-territoriality could be enforced. Section VI stated that legislation similar to the Interception of Communications Act (IOCA) will be introduced for the recovery of keys. But the intended scope is much wider than IOCA because it will cover not only information in transit, but also 'lawful access to data stored and encrypted by the clients of the licensed TTPs'.

For the purposes of legal access, the paper proposes that a 'central repository' be established to 'act as a single point of contact for interfacing between a licensed TTP and the security, intelligence and law enforcement agencies who have obtained a warrant requiring access to a client's private encryption keys'. The report 'The Risks of Key Recovery, Key Escrow, and Trusted Third-Party Encryption' expressly warns of the hazards[85] of concentrating keys in centralised repositories. They present an irresistible target for penetration, and there are documented instances of unauthorised access to every kind of military, police and corporate system gained through lax security or suborned employees.

RECENT DEVELOPMENTS

OECD

In March 1997, while not taking sides on the benefits or drawbacks of key escrow, the OECD issued cryptography recommendations that warn against 'unjustified obstacles to international trade and the development of information and communications networks (8th principle)' and 'legislation which limits user choice (2nd principle)'.[86] The 5th principle stated that:

> The fundamental rights of individuals to privacy, including secrecy of communications and protection of personal data, should be respected in national cryptography policies and in the implementation and use of cryptographic methods.

The 6th principle refrained from recommending government access to keys, allowing only that 'national cryptography policies *may* allow access to cryptographic keys or encrypted data'. The 6th OECD principle concludes that 'these policies must respect the other principles contained in the guidelines to the greatest extent possible'.

United States

Several bills have been stalled in Congress for more than a year, undergoing contradictory revisions from various sub-committees. There are three major encryption-related bills currently pending through the US Congress:

- The Security and Freedom Through Encryption Act (SAFE, HR 695), which rejects both domestic controls on strong encryption, and regulatory inducements to use trusted third-parties or key-recovery agents, while liberalising export controls.
- The E-Privacy Act (S. 2067), provides that personal confidential information, such as health and financial data, should be securely encrypted, intends to liberalise export controls, and establishes a 'NET Center' to develop computer penetration techniques for eavesdropping to assist Federal, State and local law enforcement authorities.
- The Secure Public Networks Act (S.909, also known as 'McCain-Kerrey'), coerces domestic use of 'third party' key-recovery agents through voluntary licensing linked to

> regulatory incentives and liabilities, and stipulates key-recovery as a requirement for all government financed research into future Internet architectures.

If UK policy continues to shadow that of the US, S.909 may prove to be a model for the forthcoming Secure Electronic Commerce Bill through the UK Parliament (below).

The FBI continues vigorously to assert an absolute requirement for law-enforcement to have covert access to private keys. Diffie and Landau offer critical scrutiny of their arguments,[87] suggesting that the FBI has expediently confounded statistics on the efficacy of microphone versus wiretap surveillance, to extrapolate a stronger case.

European Commission

In October 1997, the European Commission published *Towards a European Framework for Digital Signatures and Encryption*.[88] The Commissions communication paper, 'in contrast to the UK initiatives and despite years of US attempts to push the "government access to keys" idea overseas, finds key escrow and key recovery systems to be inefficient and ineffective'. According to the Communication paper:

> nobody can be effectively prevented from encrypting data ... by simply downloading strong encryption software from the Internet. As a result restricting the use of encryption could well prevent law-abiding companies and citizens from protecting themselves against criminal attacks. It would not however prevent totally criminals from using these technologies.[89]

The European Commission further called on the Member States to avoid disproportionate national restrictions, 'to ensure that the development of electronic commerce in the Internal Market is not hindered and to facilitate the free circulation and use of encryption products and services'.

This communication was followed by a May 1998 'Directive on a Common Framework for Electronic Signatures'.[90] The directive highlights the problem that:

> … different initiatives in the Member States lead to a divergent legal situation ... the relevant regulations, or the lack of them, will be different to the extent that the functioning of the Internal Market in the field of electronic signatures is going to be endangered … Further uncertainty results from different liability rules and the risk of uncertain jurisdiction concerning liability where services are provided among different Member States.

The proposed solution of the European Commission is that 'the legal recognition of electronic signatures should be based upon objective, transparent, non-discriminatory and proportional criteria and not to be linked to any authorisation or accreditation of the service provider involved'. Therefore, according to the European Commission: 'Common requirements for certification service providers would support the cross-border recognition of signatures and certificates within the European Community.'

The proposals of the Commission have direct consequence for the suggestion in para. 53 of the DTI Consultation paper that a presumption of legal validity be accorded to signatures certified by a licensed TTP/CA. If the onus of proof were on the signer to rebut validity, rather than on the counter-party to establish it, this would provide a powerful incentive in commercial transactions to prefer signatures made with licensed certificates. Even if the acceptability of unlicensed signature certificates could be established through a test case in common law, would legislation granting a preferred status to licensed certificates be regarded as 'discriminatory', and therefore in breach of the Directive?

The Directive only addresses certification of keys used for signature. In the early phases of e-commerce, it may be anticipated that for convenience, the public will prefer to obtain signature and encryption technology from a 'one-stop shop'. If licenses to certify digital signatures were only available to organisations that operated key-escrow/recovery for their encryption services, and signature certificates were only presumed valid if licensed, market forces would strongly coerce adoption of the 'voluntary' regime.

Responses to DTI Consultation

An official 'Summary of Responses' to the March 1997 consultation paper was published by the DTI in April 1998, at the same time as the 'Secure Electronic Commerce' statement (below). The summary tabulated responses to the specific questions asked in the consultation. However, since many responses disagreed with the basic premise that facilitating e-commerce requires access to private keys under third-party control, on which views were not sought, it would be unreliable to infer any consensus on dependent issues. The summary acknowledged that:

> The issue of access to keys for law enforcement purposes attracted by far the most comment – particularly from individuals. Much of it was fundamentally opposed to the whole concept of lawful access.
>
> Many of the more technical responses questioned the effectiveness, or even the feasibility, of the key escrow proposals in the paper.

Voluntary Licensing – 'Secure Electronic Commerce'[91]

The Labour Government on 27 April 1998 announced its intention to 'introduce legislation to license Trusted Third Parties, Certification Authorities and Key Recovery Agents' and 'such licensing arrangements will be voluntary, as business has requested'. Organisations facilitating encryption services will be 'encouraged' to seek licences, but can only do so if they 'make recovery of keys' (or other information protecting the secrecy of the information) possible.

The statement refers to a 'clear policy differentiation between digital signatures and encryption', but whether an organisation can get a license to issue signature certificates, if it also wishes to offer encryption services without key-recovery, remains inscrutable. Pressed on this point, the DTI has said that the issue raises 'consumer protection' concerns which may require 'Chinese walls'.[92]

The Home Office will introduce legislation to enable law enforcement agencies 'to obtain a warrant for lawful access to information necessary to decrypt the content of communications or stored data (in effect, the encryption key)'. The new powers will apply to anybody holding this information, including the user.

Strategic Export Controls

Cryptographic research and development, whether academic or commercial, requires frequent exchanges of source code, compiled code, abstract discussion, and mathematical analysis. This is commonly done via e-mail or the World Wide Web. Cryptographic methods (and research into 'attacks' on such methods) are intrinsic to the protection of intellectual property, securing the cyber-infrastructure, privacy and protection of personal data, and the enabling of electronic commerce.

A DTI White Paper on Strategic Export Controls[93] was published in July 1998, primarily dealing with Scott Report[94] recommendations concerning proliferation of technologies for weapons of mass destruction. However, the DTI paper also contains proposals for extending export controls to 'intangibles', that is information carried electronically, rather than on physical media. Section 3.2.1 proposes that: 'new legislation should provide it with the power to control the transfer of technology, whatever the means of transfer'. This power would cover transmission by fax, and e-mail over the Internet (or organisations' intranets). 'Documents transferred abroad containing controlled technology should be subject to export licensing requirements, whether exported physically or in electronic form.'

The reference to 'controlled technology', in contrast to other sections of the White Paper, is not qualified or related to weapons of mass destruction, and therefore applies to cryptography.[95] Hypothetically, a researcher e-mailing a colleague abroad with implementations of (or even mathematical remarks bearing on) cryptography would be in legal jeopardy, unless they obtained export license approval to do so.

The secondary powers created under 3.2.1 would also allow the Government to ban oral discussions and dissemination of abstract mathematical research, without further primary legislation, although the paper incongruously acknowledged that:

> ... it is right that controls on the transfer of information orally or through personal demonstration should be limited to the areas of greatest concern, in view of the difficulties of licensing such transfers, both for applicants and for the licensing authority, and given also that there are sensitivities in relation to free speech and academic freedom.

Elsewhere there is reference to Government support for parallel measures at EU and Wassenaar level.[96] The intention is to put the encryption 'genie back in the bottle', by criminalising international development and electronic dissemination of non-approved encryption software (presumably that which lacks key-recovery), and thus contravenes Labour's pre-election policy. The combined effect would be to deter world-class researchers from working in Britain, inhibit innovation and dissemination of knowledge necessary to secure the cyber-infrastructure, and create sweeping powers to limit academic freedom of expression, leading to a predictable decline in a strategic economic sector. Moreover the policy is unenforceable as encryption and steganography could be used to distribute intangible 'controlled technology' undetectably. It would be a tragic irony if enforcement of a ban on the dissemination of cryptography became the *raison-d'être* for the kind of Internet surveillance apparatus which motivated Phil Zimmerman to create PGP in the first place.

CONCLUSION

The central difficulty underlying the manoeuvres of the pro- and anti-escrow lobbies is that there is a genuine dilemma: current technology really *does not admit striking a balance*; voluntary measures only make sense as a prelude to later prohibitions. The *realpolitik* view of the Internet community is that the DTI proposals are the product of a joint UK and US strategy: voluntary escrow is *designed* to be unstable, and squeeze out non-escrowed systems competing outside the legal protection of a regulatory umbrella. It places Britain at the sharp end of promoting US policy in Europe.

The forthcoming Secure Electronic Commerce legislation will only bestow a 'safe and secure' licence of government approval on those TTPs that can recover the decryption key of their subscribers. The supposed attraction depends on the canard that organisations or individuals who lose their keys need the service provider to retrieve a copy. But everyone can – and should – backup their key (good software insists on it), and keep a copy in a safe place anyway, just as everyone should keep a backup copy of the data itself. Key recovery is a useful facility, but there is no need for the end-user to forfeit custody.

If a critical mass of the infrastructure adopts licensing, a future government could claw its way to a position of blanket key recovery later: keys expire or can be instantly revoked, and government could insist on recovery compliance for renewal. It remains to be seen how many players in the nascent information economy opt for licensing, or whether they will allow their customers custody of their own keys and the responsibility of keeping a backup.

The new policy statement contains enough ambiguity for the DTI to gauge the degree of dissent before defining carrots-and-sticks in the licensing restrictions, or possibly to defer questions of detail to a regulator created by primary legislation. Despite several years of UK lobbying at the OECD and European Commission, few democratic countries appear keen to have strong limits on the domestic use of strong encryption. Only Belarus, China, France, Israel, Pakistan, Russia and Singapore currently restrict domestic use of cryptography.[97]

The Home Office plans to introduce legislation to allow keys to be subpoenaed under warrant, whether covertly from a service provider operating key-recovery, or from the end-user, which will raise difficult questions. What will constitute prima facie grounds for issue of a warrant, to recover evidence that by definition is unknown? Will a judge be able to draw adverse inference from a suspect's refusal (or inability) to produce a key to unlock information which the prosecution believes to be incriminating? Suppose a suspect has genuinely lost their key? In any event, given the likely proliferation of steganography techniques, the prosecution may be unable to demonstrate the existence of any encrypted data at all. The new legislation will be introduced at a time of renewed unease about oversight and safeguards governing conventional forms of surveillance.[98]

In the US, the current two-year relaxation on export of 56-bit non-escrowed encryption expires this year, and key-recovery systems that can feasibly be deployed globally and interoperably are no nearer realisation. Proposals for a 'NET Center', a national facility to develop software bugging devices which can be inserted (possibly remotely) into targeted computers to defeat encryption, may be seen to offer a better solution.

The fork in the road is clear. One path leads to an infrastructure capable of an unprecedented degree of state surveillance limited only by perpetual government self-restraint; the other leads to a dilution of power and strengthening of privacy, but with compensatory reforms to assist law-enforcement. Without independent expert scrutiny and public debate of the law-enforcement case, escrow may happen by default.

STOP PRESS

As this book went to press the DTI previewed details of a new consultation on encryption regulation. The proposals provide certain recognition of digital signatures only for certificates issued by licensed CAs, coupled with a prohibition on licensed CAs offering unescrowed encryption services. The effect may therefore be similar to the mandatory licensing proposals but 'voluntarily' imposed by market forces.

NOTES

1. 'Communicating Britain's Future', (The Labour Party, 1995).
2. Gordon Welchman, *The Hut Six Story* (McGraw-Hill, 1982).
3. Social Security Administration (Fraud) Bill, London: HMSO, 1996. Under section 1.[116A](4)(b) 'amended or supplemented information' can be fed back to the original department, for purposes other than SS and HB enforcement. Section 2.(2) [116B].(1)(b)) creates secondary powers for data to be requested from any government department.
4. See Gerald Murphy, US Department of Treasury, Directive: Electronic Funds and Securities Transfer Policy – Message Authentication and Enhanced Security, No. 16-02, section 3 (21 December 1992).
5. A. Michael Froomkin, 'The Metaphor is the Key: Cryptography, the Clipper Chip and the Constitution', *University of Pennsylvania Law Review* 143 (1995), 709–897 at p. 720.
6. Bruce Schneier, *Applied Cryptography* (John Wiley, 1996) is an excellent practical introduction to computer implementations.
7. See David Kahn, *The Codebreakers* (Macmillan, 1972).
8. See David Kahn, *Seizing the Enigma* (Houghton Mifflin, 1991).
9. For example, 'Myrmidon' in ASCII is '01001101 01111001 01110010 01101101 01101001 01100100 01101111 01101110'.

10. A 128-bit key has 2^{128} = 340282366920938463463374607431768211456 possibilities.
11. W. Diffie and M.E. Hellman, 'New Directions in Cryptography', Institute of Electric and Electronic Engineers Transactions on Information Theory, 22:6 (November 1976).
12. R. Rivest, A. Shamir and L. Adleman, 'A Method for Obtaining Digital Signatures and Public Key Cryptosystems', *Communication of the Association of Computing Machines*, 21:2 (February 1978).
13. In fact GCHQ invented both RSA and Diffie-Hellman around 1971, but it was not disclosed until 1997. See 'The History of Non-Secret Encryption', http://www.cesg.gov.uk/storynse/htm
14. Philip R. Zimmerman, *The Official PGP User's Guide* (MIT Press, 1995).
15. The program is now also available as a commercial product http://www.pgp.com
16. Philip R. Zimmerman, Testimony to the Subcommittee on Science, Technology, and Space of the US Senate Committee on Commerce, Science, and Transportation, 26 June 1996 http://www.pgp.com/phil/phil-quotes.cgi
17. 'The Mob gets Wired – Crime Online', *Time* 23 September 1996.
18. See US International Traffic in Arms Regulation, 22 CFR ss. 120–130.
19. See Jonathan Wallace and Mark Mangan, *Sex, Laws, and Cyberspace* (Henry Holt, 1996), p. 42.
20. Ståle Schumacher, The International PGP Home Page http://www.pgpi.com/
21. See the CDT Policy Post No. 34, 12 January 1996 at http://www.cdt.org. See also [1996] CUD 8, 5 at http://www.soci.niu.edu/~cudigest
22. The two government agencies, the National Institute of Standards and Technology (NIST) and the Department of Treasury, would each hold half of the encryption key.
23. The original Clipper project is now defunct, and the SKIPJACK algorithm has recently been published http://csrc.nist.gov/encryption/skipjack-kea.htm
24. See generally B. Schneier and D. Banisar, *The Electronic Privacy Papers: Documents on the Battle for Privacy in the Age of Surveillance* (John Wiley & Sons, 1997).
25. See Center for Democracy and Technology, 'Clinton Administration Continues to Push For Flawed Crypto Export Policy' from the Clipper II Archives at http://www.cdt.org
26. See the proposal at http://www.epic.org/crypto/key_escrow/white_paper.html
27. See the CDT Preliminary Analysis of 'Clipper III' Encryption Proposal, 21 May 1996 at http://www.cdt.org
See also Senator Conrad Burn's Response to the proposal, 'Burns: Clipper III Strikes Out' at
http://www.epic.org/crypto/key_escrow/burns_on_white_paper.html
28. The weakness of DES, a standard 56-bit commercial cipher, was recently demonstrated when hardware costing $250,000 cracked it in three days. See Electronic Frontier Foundation, 'EFF Builds DES Cracker that proves that Data Encryption Standard is insecure', 17 July 1998 at

http://www.eff.org/descracker.html
See also EFF, *Cracking DES: Secrets of Encryption Research, Wiretap Politics & Chip Design* (O'Reilly & Associates, July 1998).

29. Leonard Doyle, 'Spooks All Set to Hack it on the Superhighway' *Independent*, 2 May 1994 reports that: 'The US plan for a Clipper Chip has raised fears among European businesses that sensitive information would no longer be secret if it were vetted by the CIA or the FBI.'
30. Michael Froomkin, 'The Metaphor is the Key: Cryptography, the Clipper Chip and the Constitution', at p. 817.
31. Paper On Regulatory Intent Concerning Use Of Encryption On Public Networks, DTI, 10 June 1996, http://dtiinfo1.dti.gov.uk/cii/encrypt/
32. Data Protection Registrar, Twelfth Annual Report, HC 574, (HMSO, June 1996) p. 52.
33. 'On Solutions to the Key Escrow Problem', Mark P. Hoyle and Chris J. Mitchell, Information Security Group, Royal Holloway University, London (pre-print).
34. C.J. Mitchell, 'The Royal Holloway TTP-based key escrow scheme', *Information Security Technical Report*, 1:1, Elsevier/Zergo, ftp.dcs.rhbnc.ac.uk /pub/Chris.Mitchell istr_a2.ps
35. 'The GCHQ Protocol and its Problems', Ross Anderson and Michael Rowe, Cambridge Computer Laboratory http://www.cl.cam.ac.uk/users/mrr/casm/casm.html
36. George Orwell, *Nineteen Eighty-Four*, (Secker & Warburg, 1949). The FSB (successors to the KGB) have proposed that all Internet Service Providers in Russia install high-capacity tapping lines from their equipment direct to a monitoring centre, allowing immediate access to all Internet traffic of subscribers. See J. Meek, 'Big Brother is kind enough to collect – and read – your e-mail for you', *Sydney Morning Herald*, 25 July 1998.
37. *The Sci Files*, BBC2 transmitted 3 March 1997.
38. Roger A. Clarke, 'Information Technology and Dataveillance', in Charles Dunlop and Rob Kling (eds) *Computerization and Controversy: Value Conflicts and Social Choices* (Academic Press, Inc., 1991), p. 498.
39. See http://www.ptizan.com.au/memex-tx.html
40. Office of Information and Privacy Commissioner/Ontario. 'An Overview of Computer Matching, Its Privacy Implications, and the Regulatory Schemes of Select Jurisdictions'. *Government Information Quarterly* 9:1 (1992) p. 38.
41. Roger A. Clarke, 'Information Technology and Dataveillance', in *Computerization and Controversy*, p. 498.
42. Lance Cottrel, Mixmaster FAQ, http://www.obscura.com/~loki/remailer/mixmaster-faq.html
43. Froomkin, 'The Metaphor is the Key', at p. 818.
44. See the written evidence submitted by the Christian Action Research and Education (CARE) to the House of Lords, Select Committee on Science and Technology, 'Information Society: Agenda for Action in the UK', Session 1995–96, 5th Report, London: HMSO, 31 March 1996, p. 187.
45. Raymond Wacks, 'Privacy in Cyberspace' presented at the Society of Public Teachers of Law (SPTL) Seminars for 1996 – Pressing Problems in the Law: Privacy, 29 June 1996.

46. Another reason was a Finnish court's recent decision in favour of the Scientologists that Helsingus had to provide some of the users' names. See for more information and the full press release on http://www.penet.fi/
47. See 'Dirty Anoraks 2' from *Private Eye*, 20 September 1996, No. 907, at p. 6.
48. *Ibid.*
49. *McIntyre* v. *Ohio Elections Commission* 115 S.Ct. 1511, (1995).
50. See the ACLU challenge in *ACLU* v. *Miller* to a Georgia law restricting free speech on the Internet. ACLU and others successfully argued that the law is unconstitutionally vague and overbroad because it bars online users from using pseudonyms or communicating anonymously over the Internet. See the ACLU Website for more details at http://www.aclu.org
51. Safety-Net, supported by the UK Government was announced on 23 September 1996. Safety-Net has an e-mail, telephone and fax hot-line from 1 October 1996 and online users will be able to report materials related to child pornography and other obscene materials. See the Safety-Net proposal, 'Rating, Reporting, Responsibility, For Child Pornography and Illegal Material on the Internet' adopted and recommended by the Executive Committee of ISPA – Internet Services Providers Association, LINX – London Internet Exchange and The Internet Watch Foundation at http://dtiinfo1.dti.gov.uk/safety-net/r3.htm
52. Safety-Net proposal 1996, para. 30.
53. See Ashley Craddock, 'Rights Groups Denounce UK Crypto Paper', *Wired*, 30 May 1997, at http://www.wired.com/news/politics/story/4175.html
54. FBI Director Louis Freeh, Address at the Executives' Club of Chicago, February 17, 1994, at p.13.
55. Bernard Porter, *Plots and Paranoia: A History of Political Espionage in Britain 1790–1988*, (Unwin, 1989).
56. See European Parliament Scientific and Technological Options Assessment (STOA) Report, 'An Appraisal of the Technologies of Political Control: A Consultation Document' (PE 166 499/Final), 6 January 1998, written by S. Wright (Omega Foundation, Manchester). An online copy is available at http://jya.com/stoa-atpc.htm
57. Nicky Hager, *Secret Power* (Craig Potton Publishing, 1996).
58. Resolution of the Council of the European Union, 17 January 1995, published 4 November 1996 (C 329/1-6) in the *Official Journal of the European Communities.*
59. David Herson, European Commission DGXIII, 'Ethical TTPs – a New Security Approach', *Information Security Technical Report*, 1:1, Elsevier/Zergo.
60. David Herson – Head of SOGIS, Senior Officers' Group on Information Security (EU): Interview in Paris, 25 September 1996, Kurt Westh Nielsen (*Engineering Weekly*) and Jérôme Thorel http://www.cs.berkeley.edu/~daw/GCHQ/herson.htm
61. Johannes Trimethius (Abbot of Sponheim), Steganographia. See also Information Hiding, First International Workshop, Cambridge UK May/June 1996, ed. Ross Anderson, *Springer Lecture Notes in Computer Science* 1174.
62. See also 'The Steganographic File System' for stored data, in which the

existence of a particular file cannot be proven unless both the filename and password are known. http://www.cl.cam.ac.uk/ftp/users/rja14/sfs3.ps.gz

63. 'Technical solutions, such as they are, will only work if they are incorporated into all encryption products. To ensure that this occurs, legislation mandating the use of Government-approved encryption products or adherence to Government encryption criteria is required.' See 'Encryption: The Threat, Applications and Potential Solutions' FBI briefing document to National Security Council, February 1993 (obtained by EPIC under FOI).
64. 'Empirical testing against small-scale threats is a testing scenario more similar to defending the US against Soviet retaliation after a largely successful American first strike than it is to defending against a Soviet first strike'. Herbert Lin, *Software for Ballistic Missile Defence*, p.68, Centre for International Studies, MIT 1985.
65. Kenneth Dam and Herbert Lin (eds), *Cryptography's Role in Securing the Information Society*, National Research Council, Washington, DC 1996. http://www.replay.com/mirror/nrc/
66. 'loi 90-1170 du 29 Decembre 1990': export or use of encryption equipment must be previously declared when used only for authentication, and previously authorised by the Prime Minister in all other cases, with penalties of fines of up to 500,000F and three months in jail.
67. Internet Engineering Task Force, Architecture for Public-Key Infrastructure Working Group, Draft November 1996, pki-tg@opengroup.org
68. Intelligence Services Act 1994, Section 5.
69. See Nick Taylor and Clive Walker, 'Bugs in the System', *Journal of Civil Liberties* 2, (1996) 105–124 at p. 112.
70. See the updated version of A Report by an Ad Hoc Group of Cryptographers and Computer Scientists, 'The Risks of Key Recovery, Key Escrow, and Trusted Third-Party Encryption', *CDT Digital Issues* No. 3, Washington, June 1998, at http://www.cdt.org/crypto/risks98
71. See for a summary of the 'The Risks of Key Recovery, Key Escrow, and Trusted Third-Party Encryption' Report in *Centre for Democracy and Technology Policy Post*, 3:6, (21 May 1997) at http://www.cdt.org/
72. The committee is chaired by the Cabinet Office, with representatives from the DTI, Home Office, Foreign Office, Treasury, GCHQ/CESG, Security Service and SIS.
73. Private information from those present at OECD meetings.
74. See Yaman Akdeniz, 'UK Government Policy on Encryption' *Web Journal of Current Legal Issues* 1 (1997).
75. See paper On Regulatory Intent Concerning Use Of Encryption On Public Networks, DTI, 10 June 1996 at para. 8.
76. 'Communicating Britain's Future', (The Labour Party 1995) was removed in June 98 from its official Website
http://www.labour.org.uk/views/info-highway/content.html
but is now available at
http://www.liberty.org.uk/cacib/legal/crypto/labour2.html
77. The policy document, available on the Labour Party Website since 1995, was removed in June 1998. It has since been re-posted on other sites. For example see the Campaign Against Censorship of the Internet in Britain at http://www.liberty.org.uk/cacib/legal/crypto/labour2.html

78. See Cyber-Rights & Cyber-Liberties (UK) below for further information and for a critique of the DTI Consultation Paper. See also Dr Brian Gladman's home page at http://www.seven77.demon.co.uk See also Y. Akdeniz et al., 'Cryptography and Liberty: Can the Trusted Third Parties be Trusted? A Critique of the Recent UK Proposals', *The Journal of Information, Law and Technology* (JILT) 2 (1997), at http://elj.warwick.ac.uk/jilt/cryptog/97_2akdz/default.htm
79. DTI Consultation paper, Annex F.
80. The Conservative Party would also face political difficulties questioning the proposals in opposition.
81. Conversation between one of the authors (CB) and a Labour spokesperson, 27 March 1997.
82. See Cyber-Rights & Cyber-Liberties (UK) 'First Report on UK Encryption Policy: Response to the DTI Consultation Paper', Comment, *The Journal of Information, Law and Technology* (JILT) 2 (1997).
83. Organisations opposed to escrow arranged a parallel conference http://www.epic.org/events/crypto_paris/ and eventually secured a hearing.
84. See the DTI Consultation paper, paras 52, 53.
85. See 'The Risks of Key Recovery, Key Escrow, and Trusted Third-Party Encryption' Report mentioned above.
86. See OECD Cryptography Policy Guidelines: Recommendation of the Council Concerning Guidelines for Cryptography Policy, 27 March 1997, at http://www.oecd.org/dsti/iccp/crypto_e.html
87. W. Diffie and S. Landau, *Privacy on the Line: The Politics of Wiretapping and Encryption*, (MIT Press, 1998).
88. European Commission Communication, *Towards a European Framework for Digital Signatures and Encryption*, Communication from the Commission to the European Parliament, the Council, the Economic and Social Committee and the Committee of the Regions ensuring Security and Trust in Electronic Communication, COM (97) 503, October 1997, at http://www.ispo.cec.be/eif/policy/97503toc.html
89. Y. Akdeniz, 'No Chance for Key Recovery: Encryption and International Principles of Human and Political Rights', *Web Journal of Current Legal Issues* 1 (1998).
90. Proposal for a European Parliament and Council Directive on a common framework for electronic signatures (European Commission) – Communication from the Commission to the European Parliament, the Council, the Economic and Social Committee and the Committee of the Regions: Proposal for a European Parliament and Council Directive on a common framework for electronic signatures COM(1998) 297, Final, 13 May 1998. See http://www.ispo.cec.be/eif/policy/com98297.html
91. Department of Trade and Industry, Secure Electronic Commerce Statement, 27 April 1998 is available at http://www.dti.gov.uk/CII/ana27p.html See for a critique of the new proposals in Y. Akdeniz and C.P. Walker, 'UK Government Policy on Encryption: Trust is the Key?' *Journal of Civil Liberties* (1998) pp. 110–16.
92. Nigel Hickson, DTI, 'Scrambling for Safety', conference, 29 May 1998.
93. DTI, White Paper: Strategic Export Controls, July 1998, http://www.dti.gov.uk/export.control/

94. See Sir Richard Scott, *Report of the Inquiry into the Export of Defence Equipment and Dual-Use Goods to Iraq and Related Prosecutions*, London: HMSO, July 1996, HC 115 (95/96).
95. Current Export Control Lists is available at http://www.dti.gov.uk/export.control/
96. See the Wassenaar Arrangement on Export Controls for Conventional Arms and Dual-Use Goods and Technologies at http://www.wassenaar.org/
97. See GILC, 'Cryptography and Liberty: An International Survey of Encryption Policy', Washington DC, February 1998, at http://www.gilc.org/crypto/crypto-survey.html
98. JUSTICE, 'Under Surveillance: Covert Policing and Human Rights Standards', July 1998.

5 Copyright I: Copyright, Civil Rights and the Internet

Nick Braithwaite, Bindman and Partners

> If we do not find the right balance between the legitimate interests of rightholders in a fair exploitation of their works and other protected material and the interest of consumers in freedom of access to 'everything of interest', the viability of the Information Society may be at stake.
>
> Paul Vandoren, European Commission

The freewheeling culture of the Internet poses a threat to the vested interests of intellectual property rights owners. Its origins in academe meant that scientists and other Net users, who had traditionally been prepared to make their work available to the rest of the Net community for the greater good of mankind, expected the same approach from all future users. Indeed, the hallmark of the Internet is still a readiness to make information available freely for scientific, political, cultural or humanistic purposes as well as for publicity and marketing reasons.

This has not happened in several important areas. There are frequent complaints that the material found on the Net is of poor quality, the main deficiencies being:

- lack of organisation;
- lack of authority;
- lack of entertainment value.

The reason for lack of authority and entertainment value has to do with the fact that so much of the material is 'unmediated', i.e. not subjected to editorial controls. Professional content providers such as book authors and TV programme makers still largely shun the Net as a distribution vehicle, and not just for technical reasons. There have been legitimate, although perhaps exaggerated, fears that if piracy is discovered, no legal remedy will be available against those who merely transmitted a work digitally, since an exclusive right to transmit digitally is not expressly granted by the current copyright legislation in the UK.

So as the Internet moves from wacky cyberspace towards mainstream commerce, legislators have, in recognition of their concerns, agreed internationally to tweak copyright laws to bring them into line with digital developments. It will soon be easier for rights owners to enforce copyright, at least when they know there has been infringement.

The difficulty with the Net, however, is knowing when infringement has occurred. Owners of some kinds of high quality content will still not distribute their works on the Net without comfort that their revenue streams will not dwindle through piracy, whatever the state of the law.[1] The problem is one of detection and enforcement.

Much of the original anarchic criticism directed at rights owners by the Net community was unhelpful – it showed little effort to understand rights owners' reasonable concerns. This dialogue of the deaf has now subsided a little. It is fair to ask a question, as we stand at the threshold of the information age: will the continuance of copyright in its present form enable us to capitalise on the huge opportunities available, or will it blight the development of the gathering revolution?

This chapter suggests (without any claim to originality) that we are in danger of tilting the balance too far in favour of vested interests. Unless that balance is redressed, civil rights of access to information and of the right to use it may progressively be eroded. Copyright as an approach to information policy needs to be pushed progressively into the background if the true value of information is to be unlocked.

WHERE IS COPYRIGHT NOW?

Copyright in the UK is essentially a statutory monopoly stretching back nearly 300 years. Prior to that it was a Crown monopoly used primarily as an instrument of censorship. The

Statute of Anne granted an exclusive right lasting 28 years. With successive Copyright Acts until the latest in 1988, copyright law has become a veritable Leviathan.

Copyright law protects the right to exploit the form in which information is expressed rather than the information itself. In that sense, it protects the 'envelope' rather than the contents. Although there is little to prevent a person from reusing the underlying information, this can only be done where the original form is not subjected to copying or any of the other acts which are exclusively the preserve of the copyright owner.

In the European Union (EU) copyright protection for the majority of works now lasts (in general) from the death of the author for a period of 70 years. The comparison with patent law is instructive, where economic arguments for encouraging investment are probably at least as strong:

- There is no requirement of any creativity in a copyright work, only the minimal requirement of 'originality' that the work should not itself have been copied (in the UK at least, although this threshold varies around the world), whereas under patent law any invention must be 'novel' in order to be patentable.

- There is no requirement of registration in any of the countries adhering to the Berne Convention, including the UK and the US. Patents are protected for a period of 20 years from registration, compared with up to 150 years or so in Europe from the date of creation.

- Finally, potent criminal sanctions are available under the UK copyright legislation to punish what is essentially an infringement of a commercial right.

Why, then, does the subject-matter of copyright merit this extraordinary legislative attention? In a nutshell, because the economic interests protected are of enormous importance in the information economy. In particular, the computer software industry has grown to rely upon copyright law rather than patent law primarily to protect its investment in product development, and copyright law has been amended to that end. Yet it is difficult to see why software requires protection for 150 years. In reality, 10 or 15 years' protection from publication probably would be adequate given the pace of change in the industry.

DANGERS OF THE DIGITAL AGE

What has changed in the digital age that poses a new threat to the civil rights of information users? One major danger is posed by the advent of digital technology: it is the fact that for the first time in history it may be possible to incur liability simply by reading.

The interests of the software industry were largely responsible for this. In the early days of the industry, it was far from clear that computer programs were protected by copyright law in many countries. The industry lobbied hard to improve its position in the face of threats from software piracy and misuse. The EU legislated to harmonise the copyright protection of software in Europe, making it an infringing act to load the software, as a 'literary work', into computer memory. In the context of the Internet, or any other method of electronic distribution, this had the presumably unintended effect that you cannot now even look at a genuine 'literary work' electronically to decide whether you want to acquire it because you will already have infringed copyright in the work by loading it into your computer's memory.

This is not far short of outlawing reading, since unless you keep your computer permanently loaded with the same information you will constantly be infringing copyright afresh. This type of legal environment is inimical to the sharing, discussion and manipulation of information which are essential to learning and the growth of knowledge. The negative impact of such restrictions is likely to grow with the importance of the electronic networks comprising the information superhighway. At the same time, there is a danger that those who cannot pay to participate in the exchange of ideas will be further excluded as digital media become more mainstream.

EXCEPTIONS TO COPYRIGHT PROTECTION

Because of the harshness of the strict application of copyright law, exceptions have grown up over the years, to permit what are considered to be legitimate uses of copyright works. Thus, for example, under UK law the exceptions include the following:

> Fair dealing with a literary, dramatic, musical or artistic work for the purposes of research or private study does not infringe any copyright in the work, or, in the case of a published edition, in the typographical arrangement.[2]
>
> Fair dealing with a work for the purpose of criticism or review, of that or another work or of a performance of a work, does not infringe any copyright in the work provided that it is accompanied by a sufficient acknowledgement.[3]
>
> Fair dealing with a work (other than a photograph) for the purpose of reporting current events does not infringe any copyright in the work provided that ... it is accompanied by a sufficient acknowledgement.[4]

These exceptions are quite narrow and specific, although nowadays the courts seem to apply them in a liberal spirit. Preferable is the US 'fair use' exception,[5] which gives the court considerable latitude to deal leniently with uses it considers legitimate. The section says that fair use of a copyright work for purposes such as criticism, comment, news reporting, teaching, scholarship or research is not an infringement. The factors to be taken into account are:

- the purpose and character of the use, including whether such use is of a commercial nature or is for non-profit educational purposes;
- the nature of the copyright work;
- the amount and substantiality of the portion used in relation to the copyright work as a whole;

- the effect of the use upon the potential market for or value of the copyrighted work.

Continental jurisprudences have 'private use' exceptions which in a different way permit non-commercial user. Similar flexible provisions will be a stimulus to the growth of the information society. It is no blank cheque for pirates or cheapskates, but creates a margin of comfort for bona fide users of information.

Prominent amongst these users will be librarians, teachers and other information mediators. Far from being rendered redundant by the Internet, the importance of their role as organisers, sifters and validators of information is likely to grow exponentially. Yet they are not even permitted by the current fair dealing exceptions to organise databases of copyright information or distribute copies to students electronically. Serious thought needs to be given to improving their position. Amongst the uses which currently receive scant protection are parodic and satirical use, historical analysis, bona fide discussion of matters of public concern, and archival use.

INTERNATIONAL INITIATIVES

In December 1996 two World Intellectual Property Organisation (WIPO) Treaties were concluded. This was an important step forward for rights owners in providing a framework for protecting digital transmissions of copyright material.

Meanwhile, in November 1996, the Commission published a follow-up paper to the July 1995 Green Paper. This identified a need for further harmonisation in a number of areas, including in particular the scope and limitation of the reproduction right in the electronic environment, i.e. the extent to which the full rigour of copyright protection may be softened by legitimate uses of various kinds.

Because the WIPO diplomatic conference failed to agree on the scope of exceptions, it appears likely that the European Commission will forge ahead of the rest of the world copyright community on this issue. The Commission has proposed 'a differentiated legal approach' under which private copying may be permitted in some circumstances. It remains to be seen what progress will be made.

COPYRIGHT MANAGEMENT SYSTEMS

A big issue for the future is the interaction of the law of copyright and the development of copyright management systems using encryption technology. Various systems are currently under development, but they have in common the use of encryption to enable, in effect, 'pay per view' access. They can, equally, ensure that it is difficult or impossible for the user to transmit the material onward as would be the case with unencrypted information.

If such systems are successfully introduced, some of the consequences will be straightforward. For example, you may only want to read once one chapter of a reference book. Currently you have a choice between buying the whole book, photocopying the relevant pages (copyright permitting) or borrowing the book from a public library. In future, electronic 'pay per view' may be quicker, cheaper, and more convenient to the user.

Certainly, such systems give publishers the opportunity to move into a more direct relationship with their public. The print-based industries currently have an indirect commercial relationship with their readers – although of course a fairly direct editorial one – whereas the Web cuts out the distribution chain. This opens up important possibilities, including a better understanding of the end-user's needs.

But there is a worrying possibility – leaving aside privacy issues – that copyright management systems will enable rights owners to ride roughshod over the carefully carved out exceptions to copyright law such as fair dealing, and even the existence of the public domain (works falling out of copyright protection after 50 or 70 years from specified events such as death of author).[6] Because copyright management systems give rights owners absolute de facto control over access to the material, they permit rights owners to exercise absolute control over the use made of the work.

Unfortunately, the WIPO Treaties and the follow-up paper to the EU Green Paper have paved the way for such developments apparently without detailed consideration of the potential impact on the flow of information in society at large, and the availability of information to those who can ill afford it.

SUMMARY

The traditional balance struck between the commercial interests of rights owners and the needs of society at large has handed too much power to rights owners. Digital technology, far from threatening the position of rights owners, may actually in the longer term make their position stronger by giving them the physical ability to control access to their works.

Whilst this may be a suitable mechanism for establishing a market value for particular works, it neglects civil rights of equal access to information, and threatens the interests of the underprivileged. It also enables – and this is a potentially sinister element – a rights owner to become an information owner, by controlling the uses to which information is put. This has always been true between rights owners and licensees but it has been difficult to achieve against third party users.

In the face of the 1996 WIPO Treaties, the (so far) voiceless majority needs to organise effectively so that the interests of information users are taken into account to a greater extent. The agreements in Geneva bear testimony to the power of lobbying by industry, but it is not too late for information users to affect the position at EU level. Information may be the capital of the twenty-first century, but it belongs to us all.

NOTES

1. The issue is particularly acute in relation to book publishers, hardly any of whom currently publish on the Web, because their business is founded upon the long-term exploitation of rights. Conversely the newspaper and magazine publishing industries, who have typically survived on a mixture of advertising, sales and subscription revenues from the efficient distribution of relatively ephemeral material, have ventured onto the Net.
2. Copyright Design and Patent Act (CDPA) Section 29(1).

3. CDPA Section 30(1).
4. CDPA Section 30(2).
5. Copyright Act 1976 S.107.
6. The Legal Advisory Board to the EU Commission noted in its comments on the relevant EU Green Paper that 'the widespread use of technical protection devices might result in the de facto creation of new information monopolies, [and] this would be especially problematic in regard of public domain materials'.

6 Copyright II: Copyright and the Internet

Charles Oppenheim

Once upon a time, there were authors, there were publishers, and there were users. The authors created good things like works of fiction, scholarly research, artistic works, photographs, films and so on. The publishers and distributors took over the responsibility of selling these artefacts, and shared the income with the creators. The users willingly paid to buy the items. A few naughty people did make illicit copies, but because it was tedious, expensive, and time-consuming to make copies, and because the quality of the copies was not as good as the original, the problem was largely controlled. So everyone was living happily ever after. Then along came those wicked witches, the Personal Computer and the Internet, and suddenly people could make copies quickly, cheaply, reliably and the copies they made were perfect. Now some were not living happily ever after. The creators were worried, the publishers and distributors were panic-ridden. Why? Because the users were now copying and forwarding material to their hearts' content to all their friends all over the world, either deliberately ignoring copyright law or unaware that material on the Internet was copyright at all. Observers split into two camps. One camp said copyright is obviously dead, so let's abolish it anyway. The other camp said, not at all, what is required is that copyright law needs to be strengthened and we need technical solutions to police what people are reading and copying to ensure that they do not infringe.

No doubt you'd like to know the end of the story. No doubt you'd like a happy ending. Before I give you that, let me put a little bit of flesh on the fairy story.

WHAT IS COPYRIGHT?

Very briefly, copyright is, as its name implies, all about the right to copy items. In very general terms, anyone who creates something original and new is automatically entitled to copyright and gets it without any formality, payment of fees, etc. Copyright arises as soon as something new is created. The copyright belongs to the creator unless that creator is an employee paid by his or her employer to do the creating – someone paid to write press releases for example – when the copyright automatically belongs to the employer.

Having gained copyright, the copyright owner can exercise it him- or herself, or, very commonly, assigns it to some third party, such as a publisher, film distributor, etc. in return for money, and then that publisher owns the copyright instead. Whoever owns the copyright, the lifetime is linked to the lifetime of the author – it lasts until the author dies, and another 70 years thereafter.

FAIR DEALING

Copyright gives its owner the right to prevent others from making copies of, or doing certain other things to, all or a substantial part of their work without permission. 'Substantial', incidentally, can mean quite a small proportion of length – it all depends on individual circumstances whether it is considered substantial or not. If you do copy without permission, you are deemed to have infringed and can be sued for financial damage caused, or if what you have done is piracy to make money illegally or has been done with deliberate criminal intent, you can be subject to criminal proceedings. However, there is an important exception to this right to stop third parties copying, called 'fair dealing'. This is a defence against an infringement action. It relies on the argument that although the individual made the copy (or under certain circumstances, even multiple copies) of all or part of the work, the copying was done for one of a list of specified purposes and the copying did not damage the legitimate interests of the copyright owner. In the UK, you can fair deal for: private research; commercial research;

private study; criticism or reviewing; or reporting current events. 'Fair dealing' does not apply to all types of copyright works, but applies to most of those that are relevant to the Internet.

Whilst it is reassuring (for those who wish to copy) to know that fair dealing applies to most copyright works, the copyright owners (particularly publishers) are deeply suspicious of its application in the electronic environment. They believe, with justification, that once an electronic copy has been made and is on a network, it is enormously difficult to police any further copying.

Therefore, even the taking of one copy might not be fair dealing as it implies an invitation to take multiple copies, which certainly would damage legitimate commercial interests. Therefore, some publishers have attempted to restrict users' rights to make any copy at all electronically. Let me explain their argument in a bit more detail.

The traditional rights of authors and publishers must be maintained, but as the attributes of digital use are quite different from those of the print environment, the application of those rights must be carefully protected. Respect for copyright and compliance with the copyright law is not an obstacle for the information society; it is a necessary building block without which no meaningful content will be available.

The new electronic environment is very different from the analog print environment. To 'browse' in the print world conjures the vision of flipping through pages of a book on a bookstore or library shelf.

In the electronic world, however, browsing involves making a temporary copy on your hard disk, and it is trivially easy to download the material into permanent storage for subsequent redissemination. Electronic versions can be replicated an infinite number of times with no degradation. They can be distributed electronically, world-wide, in an instant. Unauthorised digital uses can destroy the sales of a copyrighted work.

Digital uses are not equivalent to non-digital uses, and, when undertaken without regard for copyright, can have harmful consequences. Many users are digitising their print collections to facilitate a virtual library that can provide service to patrons at remote locations and facilitate resource sharing. Such a concept will destroy not only the incentive to create new copyrighted works, but the revenue from existing works that provides the investment in new works by authors and publishers.

Copyright holders and creators must retain the rights provided by copyright law to determine how to exploit their copyrights and to be able thereby to treat different types of works differently: for example, to provide some works direct to consumers and other works to intermediaries; to package some works as collections of items and others as individual works; to provide some products in encrypted form for a limited audience and others more broadly. A highly specialised work with a limited audience cannot withstand copyright infringement even if another type of published product has some level of tolerance for minimal abuse.

The publishers also argue that the lending of electronic products causes problems. They say the marketplace is a powerful incentive for creators. However, because electronic products are easily copied they are far more vulnerable to copyright abuse if they are lent. Therefore, publishers should be entitled to stop people lending electronic materials.

At the same time, some publishers' associations are lobbying government to make explicit in law that fair dealing does not apply to machine readable data, and/or to introduce new monopoly rights, such as a so-called 'browsing right', that states it shall be an infringement to simply browse, or read the material electronically without permission, and/or a so-called 'transmission right' that makes it an infringement to send material down a network without permission.

Deep issues are raised by these ideas from the publishers. The idea that publishers should be able to police what you do with an electronic work has obvious civil liberties implications – do you want publishers knowing your reading habits?

INTERNET AND COPYRIGHT

So, with that as background, let us look at the question of copyright on the Internet.

E-mail messages, material loaded onto FTP sites or World Wide Web servers, and anything else put up on the Internet is copyright. Just because it is widely available free of charge does not change the situation. Most authors of such materials are probably only too happy for their material to be reproduced and disseminated; nonetheless, the material is still copyright and should be respected as such. Therefore one should be careful about copying such material, or forwarding it to someone else. Such copying is only a problem if the person who owns the copyright loses income as a result of the infringement.

Remember, unless you do the copying with criminal intent, all you can be sued for is the financial damage caused to the copyright owner.

THE FUTURE OF COPYRIGHT IN A NETWORKED ENVIRONMENT

Copyright has always been about the tension between access and ownership. However, the ease with which people can copy and forward electronic data puts traditional copyright law under new strain. The owners have responded to these problems with a two-pronged attack. On the one hand, they are relying on technical mechanisms, such as encryption (described in detail by others in this book) or ECMS (Electronic Copyright Management Systems), to log people's use of copyrighted material and to control what they can or cannot do with it in terms of viewing it, printing it, downloading it or forwarding it. On the other hand, they are pressing governments around the world to tighten up and update copyright law to make browsing on screen and transmitting over a network without permission infringement, and to abolish fair dealing in a networked environment.

No ECMS exists yet, but they will soon be on the market. They also may soon have the backing of the law in the US. There is a Bill before the US Congress to change the US's copyright law to include a provision to prohibit the importation, manufacture or distribution of any device, the primary purpose or effect of which is to avoid, bypass, remove, deactivate, or otherwise circumvent, without authority of the copyright owner or the law, any ECMS.

CONCLUSIONS

There is little point in the law being strengthened if all that results is greater violation of, and contempt for, the law than at present. A law that is regarded as unfair, is widely flouted and that cannot be policed effectively is probably not worth being on the statute book, as the developers of the Poll Tax discovered. Nonetheless, although very few copyright infringement cases ever get heard, and despite the widespread infringement and piracy that occurs world-wide, copyright provides the legal bedrock upon which the many licences that abound are based.

Without the ultimate legal basis, and the threat in law to sue for infringement, I cannot see how such licences could be negotiated. Without such licences, and in the present and probable future absence of any foolproof, tamperproof technical method of metering use, establishing ownership and establishing where the data has been, the selling of electronic information would not be possible.

The people who think copyright is dead point out, rightly, that digital materials are incredibly easy to amend, and it is incredibly difficult to prove where you got the material from. Whilst I agree that it is difficult, and will get even harder in the future, for people to enforce their rights, I do not think this is an argument to abolish copyright. My own hope is that copyright, the bedrock for the publishing and electronic information industry, will, despite its many faults, continue.

What about my fairy story? I think that people will rather live rather happily kind of ever after, and the wicked witches will turn out to be not so wicked after all. In other words, much more like real life, with all its compromises and fudges, and nothing like a fairy story at all.

7 European Policy on Regulation of Content on the Internet

Penny Campbell and Emmanuelle Machet

During 1996, an explosion of interest took place in the use of the Internet for illegal activities. Governments all over the world started to think about, and in some cases enacted, legislation on different aspects of the Internet. Most of this interest, in Europe, has focused on the use of the Internet for the exchange of information and photographs between paedophiles. The high-profile paedophile case in Charleroi in Belgium in August 1996 involving the deaths of four girls and young women focused European Union (EU) attention on paedophilia generally. This case had a particularly significant impact, not only because of the gruesome nature of the deaths and allegations of police corruption and political protection, but by being so close to the heart of EU government in Brussels. It sparked action at EU level to combat paedophilia in general, and the subsequent discovery in several European countries of paedophile networks using the Internet for the transmission of information about and actual child pornography brought the spotlight onto the potential misuse of the Internet.

Although the Charleroi case proved a catalyst for action at EU level, there was already concern within the EU about the use of the Internet. 1997 had been designated Europe's Year against Racism, which had focused concerns on the use of the Internet for disseminating racist material. The proposal for the designation of the Year against Racism, made in December 1995, specifically referred to problems with the Internet and the use of bulletin boards to distribute prohibited material.[1] The European Commission therefore started at the beginning of 1997 to put together proposals for controlling content on the Internet and preventing its use for illegal activities. Since then, extensive work in this area has been carried out by the European institutions.

The EU is widely perceived as an excessively bureaucratic organisation whose main aim is to extend its own powers through the adoption of legislation in an ever-widening area. The idea of such an organisation addressing the issue of Internet regulation is therefore potentially a worrying one, conjuring up visions of a Big Brother censoring our e-mail messages and the imposition of a European-style Communications Decency Act. This does not seem to be the case, however, and the approach likely to be taken is a light-handed one based principally on greater cooperation between Member States, self-regulation by the industry and the use of filtering systems to control access. The main focus is on content, the objective of the proposals under discussion being to limit the presence of illegal content, such as racist material and child pornography, and to prevent children from accessing unsuitable material.

The Commission even argues 'Over-hasty legislation should be avoided until it is clear where and what type of intervention is required',[2] in stark contrast to the approach taken in the US (although it should be noted that the US Communications Decency Act has not been enacted and has been successfully challenged in the Supreme Court as an infringement of the constitutional right of free speech[3]). There are several key factors that explain why such an approach has been taken, the most important of which stem from the legal basis or constitution of the EU. In particular this sets out the areas of competence in which the European Community has powers to enact legislation, and the fundamental rights, such as the right to freedom of expression, which the EU institutions are obliged to protect.

REGULATING NEW SERVICES

In addressing the Internet, the European Community must therefore first establish what powers it has to act under the Treaty. It must also bear in mind the rights and freedoms it has to uphold. In addition, the emergence of new audio-visual services such as the Internet raises specific regulatory problems.

These services have arisen because of the convergence of different media brought about by digitalisation. The convergent sectors involved – telecommunications, information technology and the audio-visual media, are normally subject to different regulatory regimes.

Telecommunications has traditionally been a heavily regulated monopoly service in EU countries. Key objectives have been to provide universal service (access to a basic telephone service at a reasonable cost), encouraged through tariff adjustment (where connection and local call charges are cross-subsidised by higher charges for long distance and international calls), and to raise revenue for government. Since the late 1980s, the sector has gradually been liberalised, and recent EU legislation[4] fully opened it to competition from the beginning of 1998. However, a degree of 're-regulation' is taking place in order to ensure fair competition and to guarantee universal service in such a competitive environment. Telecommunications operators are not normally held responsible for the content of messages or services that they carry across their networks.

In the audio-visual sector, broadcasting has also been traditionally highly regulated. The objective of legislation has been to protect the public interest, for example by guaranteeing pluralism and universal access. Content is also normally stringently regulated. Current broadcasting legislation evolved in a situation where the number of possible channels was limited by the scarcity of terrestrial frequencies, but the advent of cable, satellite and digital television is making many more channels available, which challenges some of the principles underlying existing legislation and poses new problems in protecting the public interest. At European level, the 'Television without frontiers' Directive[5] provides for cross-border provision of broadcast services and defines responsibilities in the sending and receiving countries. The situation in the telecommunications and audio-visual sectors contrasts with that of the information technology sector which has largely been unregulated.

One of the main problems in considering regulation of the new services is that no one yet knows what they will be. However, while those such as interactive television and video on demand are not yet commercially available (and might not be for some time), the explosion of the Internet over the last six years, and in particular the World Wide Web, has made it the focus of attention. The European Commission has described it as 'the most visible part of the information society'.[6] The Internet illustrates well the regulatory problems posed by convergence, combining publishing (of text and pictures) and private communications (e-mail, newsgroups) and beginning to encompass broadcasting.

The question for regulators is which regulatory regime, if any, to apply to new services which are developing. At European level such new services are considered in the context of the European information society, a concept which was first officially promoted in the work of a task force under the leadership of member of the Commission Martin Bangemann. The task force became known as the 'Bangemann Group' and its recommendations were published in May 1994 as the 'Bangemann Report'.[7] The report was endorsed by the European Council in June 1994, which invited the Commission to produce an Action Plan, which was published as the 1994 Action Plan for the Information Society.[8] The Action Plan presented an overview of the Commission's activities in this area, principally existing proposals and some new measures to complete the programme in the light of the Bangemann Report.

The report's key point was that the information society should be market driven. The role of the Community is to create the necessary regulatory framework that will encourage private sector investment, particularly in infrastructure, and to act as a catalyst by promoting the development of new applications and demonstration projects, and targeting Community-funded research. A key element of this framework, and one of the few really new elements of the Action Plan, was the full liberalisation of the telecommunications sector, on the basis that this would reduce the costs of telecommunications and so promote the market for new services. The message of both the Bangemann Report and the Action Plan is that the growth of the information society will bring economic benefits in terms of increased growth, competitiveness and employment. It is these perceived economic benefits that motivate much of the EU interest in the development of the information society.

The Action Plan also covered a whole range of areas seen as necessary for promoting the growth of the information society, such as privacy, information security and electronic protection, legal protection, intellectual property, standardisation, interconnection and interoperability, tariff adjustment, financing of universal service, the world-wide dimension, media ownership, and competition. It also stressed the importance of avoiding the creation of a society of information 'haves' and 'have nots'. The only specific reference to the Internet in the Action Plan is in the context of standardisation policy, although several of the measures proposed would clearly address issues related to the Internet. The Communication on the implications for EU policies makes specific reference to the distribution of unwanted or offensive content over the Internet and the need to protect minors, but does not make specific proposals.

The Action Plan was reviewed in July 1996 in the form of two Communications looking at the new priorities of the information society[9] and the implications for EU policies.[10] The first of these identified four 'new' priority areas: improving the business environment (telecommunications liberalisation, internal market); investing in the future (research, education and training); people at the centre (cohesion, social and societal aspects, consumer interests, culture, pluralism); and meeting the global challenge. The second summarises the activities of the EU to date in meeting these priorities. There is more emphasis on the social and societal aspects of the information society and the need for global coordination, but otherwise the measures proposed are similar to the first Action Plan. These new priorities were subsequently endorsed in a Council Resolution in November 1996[11] and a new 'Rolling Action Plan'[12] reflecting these new priorities was produced by the Commission.

The principal discussion document concerning new audiovisual services is the Green Paper on the convergence of telecommunications, media and information technology sectors and the implications for regulation.[13] This paper addresses the regulatory aspects of new services in the broadest sense and will lead to proposals for actions, including possible legislative proposals, to be published in Autumn 1998.

In terms of competence, criminal law, and the definition and restriction of obscene or otherwise offensive material, is a matter for the Member States and the Commission has no power to propose criminal law Directives. These definitions – and so the definition of what is illegal content – vary between Member States. However, in general child pornography, trafficking in human beings, dissemination of racist material or incitement to racial hatred, terrorism and fraud are considered criminal in most or all Member States. Even if no specific laws have been passed relating to it, the Internet is not unregulated, but is covered by existing national legislation and definitions of criminality in the Member States, the principle being 'what is illegal off-line remains illegal on-line'.[14]

Justification for EU involvement is based on two principles, the first of which is the international or trans-frontier nature of the Internet. Material that is illegal in one country might be located on a server in another country where it is legal. It is very easy to move material from server to server and almost impossible for national authorities acting alone to ensure that harmful or illegal material is not available. Pillar 3 of the Maastricht Treaty, allowing for cooperation in the field of justice and home affairs, provides a basis for national law enforcement bodies to coordinate their efforts and for the Commission to make proposals in this area.

Secondly, because the definition of illegal content varies between Member States, there are implications for the development of the single market as it might hamper the free circulation of services. The potential adoption by Member States of disparate legislation directly targeted at the Internet could exacerbate this. For this reason the Commission has made a proposal for a transparency mechanism regarding proposals for national legislation relating to new services,[15] which is intended to ensure that Member States do not introduce conflicting regulation.

The Commission is an enthusiastic promoter of the benefits of the Internet, describing it as an 'essential enabler of the Information Society in Europe'.[16] Many of the Commission's initiatives, such as in the areas of intellectual property and data protection, are intended to promote confidence in the use of electronic networks from both the security and moral point of view, because of concern that lack of such confidence on the part of consumers could adversely affect the growth of the information society.

In addressing Internet regulation, the EU is behind the US, principally because it is a more developed phenomenon and has far more subscribers in the US than in Europe. The US experience is illustrative as it has focused attention on the two main issues from the perspective of human rights: content and privacy. From the content point of view the question is how to control illegal or harmful/offensive material without unduly impinging on the right to freedom of speech. There are two strands to the privacy issue. The first is ensuring the privacy of personal data, and the second, which has assumed more importance at the current time in the context of the Internet, is ensuring the privacy of personal communications while still empowering law enforcement agencies to intercept and if necessary decrypt electronic communications. The two issues overlap because controlling illegal content will at some time involve the monitoring of personal communications.

In Europe the debate is focusing principally on the content issue but is taking place from a slightly different perspective from that in the US, where the now infamous Communications Decency Act (CDA) has floundered because of the restrictions it imposes on free speech. This is partly because there is no absolute principle of free speech as there is in the US through the First Amendment, and partly perhaps because with the benefits of hindsight the problems of adopting a strategy such as the CDA are more apparent. In contrast to the US, there is more apparent public interest in protecting against illegal and harmful content than in protecting free speech.

Individual Member States' governments have begun to consider national legislation, in response to public concern. Some governments have tried to censor content on the Internet, for example in Germany where the service provider Compuserve was obliged to prevent access to a number of newsgroups that were deemed to contain illegal material. As it was unable initially to block access only to German subscribers, it had to block access to all subscribers world-wide, though access was subsequently restored to most of the newsgroups to non-German subscribers. However, the threat of prosecution by the German authorities was only lifted in early 1997. This case illustrates the technical difficulties of censoring the Internet, because the newsgroups in question continued to be accessible by other routes. Some countries – Austria, France, Germany, the Netherlands and the UK – have adopted or proposed legislation defining the legal responsibilities of access providers so that they are only liable for content where they can reasonably be expected to know that it is illegal or fail to remove it once it has been pointed out to them. A number of countries have also encouraged the setting up of self-regulation systems by the industry, including Belgium, Germany and the UK. Discussions are at an advanced stage in France, Greece and Italy, and working parties have been formed in Denmark, Ireland and Sweden. In Belgium access providers set up research units in order to be able to prevent access to paedophile groups after the Charleroi case. The French government also proposed in October 1996 the development of a charter for international cooperation on the Internet within the OECD.

The EU first formally started to address Internet regulation during 1996, at an informal joint Council meeting of the Telecommunications Ministers and the Culture and Audio-visual Ministers in Bologna on 24 April, which, whilst recognising the applicability of national law, asked the Commission to produce a summary of the problems posed by the rapid development of the Internet and to assess the desirability of European Community or international action. A Commission working group was set up to respond to this request.

At the UN World Congress against sexual exploitation of children in Stockholm in August 1996 the European Commission expressed concern about the use of networks such as the Internet for the distribution of child pornography and for paedophile networks. In the aftermath of the Charleroi case, this was also discussed at an informal meeting of the Justice and Home Affairs Ministers on 26 September 1996 and at a meeting of the Culture and Audio-visual Ministers on 25 and 26 September 1996.

The Telecommunications Council of 27 September 1996 discussed the question of paedophilia and the Internet specifically at the request of the Belgian delegation. The Council decided to extend the working group set up after the Bologna meeting to include representatives of the Ministers of Telecommunications, access and service providers, content industries and users, with a view to presenting concrete proposals at the following Telecommunications Council of 28 November 1996. At an Industry Council meeting on 8 October the greater need for international coöperation and coordination on information society policy, and a proposal from the German government to host an international conference on this subject and to address the possibility of an international convention on illegal and harmful content, was accepted.

In October 1996 the Commission produced the first document specifically addressing regulatory issues and the Internet, in the form of a Communication on illegal and harmful content on the Internet.[17] In the Communication, the Commission argues that it is crucial to differentiate between illegal content, such as child pornography, and other harmful content such as adult pornography accessed by children. It also argues for the need to take into account the different ethical standards in different countries.

The Communication points out that it is the responsibility of Member States (i.e. national governments) to enforce existing laws which may make some content illegal (i.e. in the UK, the Obscene Publications Act 1959 and the Protection of Children Act 1978). However, it argues that coordinated action is necessary at EU level to ensure the proper functioning of the internal market and the free flow of services between Member States. The Communication also points out the difficulties of applying such laws to a network such as the Internet with its world-wide reach and unlimited accessibility, therefore questioning whether the application of existing or creation of new legislation is appropriate.

In respect of illegal content, the Commission proposes greater cooperation between Member States both to ensure the enforcement of criminal law and for the definition of minimum European standards on criminal content. It calls for the development of a common European framework for the definition of the liability of access providers and host service providers, and the encouragement of self-regulation.

The issue of harmful content is more complicated because of the balance which must be struck between protecting freedom of speech and ensuring that harmful content is not for example made available to children. The Commission refers to the European Convention on Human Rights and says 'it is recognised that fundamental rights, especially the right of freedom of expression, have to be fully respected'. One of the Commission's main arguments is that restrictions should not be placed on the Internet simply because of its wide potential reach. So, material such as adult pornography that is widely available in other media should not be prohibited on the Internet solely on the grounds that it might be accessed by children. Rather, existing rules should be examined to see if they can be applied by analogy.

The Commission's preferred method for dealing with harmful content is again self-regulation. It identifies two basic technical means of protecting children from accessing harmful content: 'upstream control', which means preventing illegal content from being published, and 'downstream control', which means preventing harmful content from reaching minors, for example through the use of a filtering device. This is a pragmatic rather than a legal response and puts the emphasis on parental control rather than government intervention, in contrast to the Communications Decency Act.

Three models of filtering are identified: blacklisting, where certain sites are vetoed; whitelisting, where only specific sites are allowed; and neutral labelling, where sites are categorised and parents can choose which categories they allow their children access to. PICS (the Platform for Internet Content Selection) is cited as a global industry standard which has the advantage of separating the rating and filtering functions. Labelling is seen as particularly advantageous because it can be used to take account of different national sensibilities.

The Commission has called on industry to form a common platform enabling the use of filtering systems Community-wide based on common standards, and proposes that the Council of

Ministers adopt a Recommendation encouraging the use of filtering software such as PICS and the development of a European rating system. It also argues that European content providers should be encouraged to cooperate in this system by adopting their own Code of Conduct for content published on the Internet, including systematic self-rating of content.

At the same time as this Communication, the Commission also produced another document on harmful content – a Green Paper on the protection of minors and human dignity in audiovisual and information services.[18] This encompasses the Internet in the context of online services and again argues in favour of a labelling system, stating that 'only the generalised introduction of the neutral labelling filtering system would make it possible to regulate the question comprehensively'. It also stresses the fact that the protection of minors from harmful content is in principle a matter for the Member States. The justification for the Commission's involvement is the international aspect of online services, the free movement of services within the single market, and the Treaty provision for cooperation in the field of justice and home affairs. An open consultation process on the Green Paper produced a set of conclusions which were submitted to the council on 30 June 1997 as a working document.[19]

The Commission working party on illegal and harmful content on the Internet also produced a report, taking into account the Communication and Green Paper and concentrating more on practical proposals. The report reflects the views of all participants in the working party and so can be said to have the support of a wide spectrum of interested parties. It concluded that 'information on the Internet should be allowed the same free flow as paper-based information',[20] and that any restrictions should respect the fundamental rights to freedom of expression and privacy. It also argues in favour of a system of self-regulation, which should include a Code of Conduct for service providers, based on common standards across Europe, and a hotline for complaints. It calls for the establishment of representative bodies in all Member States to enable industry and users to participate in the system and an independent self-regulatory body, and proposes that all of these bodies should be coordinated at European level. It also proposes that the self-regulation system should be supported by the legal system so that action could be taken if it does not work. Regarding the question of liability, the working party argues that service providers and network operators should only be liable for illegal content if they have been informed of its existence by the relevant body and they are able to remove it.

It emphasises that the use of anonymity is legal in accordance with the principle of freedom of expression and the right to privacy, and argues that a user should not be required to justify anonymous use, but that further consideration should be given to how criminals might be identified for the purposes of law enforcement. It does, however, agree with the Communication on the need to promote rating and filtering systems such as PICS. It proposes that the EU target some of its research activities to develop third party rating systems and improved privacy-enhancing and tracing mechanisms, so that users can, for example, refuse to receive anonymous e-mails. It also recognises the need for an international framework and the need for further police and judicial cooperation.

An attempt within the European Parliament on 12 November 1996 to extend the broadcasting regulations in the 'TV without frontiers' Directive to cover new services including the Internet failed because it did not receive a sufficient majority.

The Commission's Legal Advisory Board (LAB), which addresses legal issues and the European information market, discussed the Communication on 25 November 1996. Although generally supportive there was some criticism of the reliance on self-regulation, on the basis that self-regulation could in fact lead to more onerous controls.

The Telecommunications Council of 28 November 1996 discussed the report and the Communication and passed a resolution endorsing them. This was formally adopted at a further Council meeting on 17 February 1996.[21] It called on Member States to encourage and facilitate self-regulatory systems, encourage the provision to users of filtering mechanisms (mentioning PICS in particular), and to participate in the proposed International Ministerial Conference in Germany. A further Council meeting on 17 February 1996 called on the Commission to foster coordination at Community level of self-regulatory and representative bodies, facilitate the exchange of information on best practice, foster research into technical issues and consider further the legal liability for Internet content. It also called on the Commission to work on the follow-up to the Green Paper.

The follow-up to the Green Paper was produced by the Commission in November 1997 in the form of a Communication including Proposal for a Recommendation.[22] The Commission stated in this document that the role of the EU is to improve the effectiveness of national measures by ensuring a minimum level of coherence in the development of national self-regulatory frameworks and by encouraging cooperation at European level. To this purpose, the included Proposal for Recommendation sets out a common reference framework at EU level. This includes the adoption of a specific methodology for dealing with questions on the drafting of common guidelines for the implementation of a self-regulatory framework at national level and the development of initiatives, for example, relating to new means of parental control. The Council adopted the slightly modified Recommendation on 28 May 1998.[23]

As a follow-up to its Communication on illegal and harmful content on the Internet and building in the findings of the Internet Working Party and the political consensus that had emerged throughout 1997, the Commission also published, in November 1997, an Action Plan on promoting safe use of the Internet.[24] Even though the above mentioned Recommendation and the Action Plan are two independent documents, they are complementary. The Recommendation is a legal act which aims to provide guidelines for national legislation, whereas the Action Plan aims to provide impetus for market adoption in improving financial support. The Action Plan is aimed especially at actions where financial support from the Community is necessary and covers the years 1998 to 2001. It identifies the following main areas within which concrete measures are needed and could be supported by the EU: creating a safe environment through hotlines and industry self-regulation, developing filtering and rating systems and encouraging awareness actions.

In the area of privacy, the US has also in some respects addressed regulation in advance of the EU. This can principally be seen in the 'Clipper Chip' saga, where the US government has tried to limit the use of encryption technology by imposing the use of a government-sponsored encryption algorithm (the original proposal was for a hardware, i.e. chip-based, solution; this was rejected by industry, but all subsequent initiatives have been described under the (now) generic term 'Clipper Chip'). This would mean that all manufacturers would use the same technique to encrypt, or scramble, electronic messages so that if intercepted by a third party they would be unreadable. However, the government (or a 'Trusted Third Party') would hold the key which would enable the security services to unscramble and read the messages, assuming they were legally entitled to do so. The objective was to prevent encryption from being used for criminal activity. This proposal too has floundered, mainly because of the vigorous opposition of the information technology industry which believes that the availability of secure encryption systems is vital to encourage confidence in the new services, particularly for commercial communications and transactions. This is particularly true of the Internet.

The European Commission, again perhaps benefiting from hindsight, is not currently proposing such legislation. However, it is considering proposals for the creation of Europe-wide Trust Services (ETS), the aim of which would be to guarantee the integrity and confidentiality of data sent over the new services. In contrast to the US, it is trying to improve the security of electronic information, as a way of increasing confidence in the information society. However, it is also looking at the idea of establishing a Trusted Third Party system at European level, where an independent third party would hold the keys to the different manufacturers' encryption algorithms, and could make them available to the security services in defined, limited circumstances (which is very similar to the current US proposal). The situation is obviously a complicated one, because a Commission Communication on these proposals which was originally scheduled for publication in the summer of 1996 was eventually published in October 1997.[25] The Commission has also recently produced proposals for a Directive on the legal protection of encrypted services in broadcasting and for a Directive on secure transactions including digital signatures in electronic commerce.[26]

A further difference between the US and EU approaches to privacy can be seen in the area of protection of personal data, which is again important for, though not confined to, the Internet. In the US, an anti-regulation mood prevails, with faith being placed in the market to resolve any problems. In Europe, however, there is a consensus that a legal framework is needed, and a landmark Directive on the protection of individuals with regard to the processing of personal data and on the free movement of such data[27] was adopted in October 1995. The Commission has described this as 'the first Community measure to deal primarily with a question of human rights'.[28] A key motivation for EU action was again the prevention of divergent national legislation from hampering the free flow of information services by harmonising the level of protection Europe-wide, the Commission stating that there is 'a clear economic justification for action. A failure on the part of those providing new on-line services to address privacy problems will inevitably act as a disincentive to potential consumers.'[29]

The Directive calls on Member States to protect the fundamental rights and freedoms of citizens, in particular their right to privacy with respect to the processing of personal data. It requires personal data to be processed fairly and lawfully, collected for specific and legitimate purposes, relevant for those purposes, accurate and up-to-date, and held for no longer than is necessary. It also defines criteria for legitimate data processing in circumstances where the subject has not given their explicit consent, and requires the data subject to be informed of the nature of data being held about them and to have access to the data. Data can be transferred between Member States, but only to third countries outside the Community if an adequate level of protection applies. This Directive must be transposed into Member States' law by October 1998. A Directive concerning the protection of personal data and privacy in the context of public digital telecommunications networks,[30] which mostly deals with data regarding telephone calls, was adopted by the Council in December 1997.

It seems clear that the outcome of EU policy on regulating the Internet is unlikely to lead to specific legislation censoring content on the Internet, or indeed any binding legislation targeted specifically at it. Rather, greater cooperation between Member States at police and judicial level and industry self-regulation will be encouraged, combined with exploitation of the technical possibilities offered by filtering systems. In its approach the Commission has been influenced by its overriding objective of promoting the growth of the Internet and ensuring the free circulation of services within the Community. It is also limited in that it cannot propose European-wide criminal law. In addition it has been able to see that direct censorship of the Internet is likely to be unworkable for both technical and political reasons. Of course the Commission's proposals represent only the start of the debate and a great deal of lobbying is likely to take place before they are made concrete. As such lobbying is traditionally dominated by industry it is unlikely that the result will be a more constraining policy.

This emphasis on self-regulation fits in with the general approach taken by the EU in the whole area of the information society. The growth of the Internet coincided with the espousal by the EU of deregulation as a central plank of policy in this field, particularly in the telecommunications sector. It was therefore unlikely that a heavily regulated approach would have been taken with respect to the Internet. This faith in deregulation stemmed in part from the prevailing fashion for neo-liberalism and the success of deregulation in the telecommunications equipment and value added services sectors. The Commission effectively used its competition powers to impose full telecommunications liberalisation in the face of hostility from some Member States, rather undermining its reputation as a harbinger of back-door socialism.

The Internet grew in Europe largely without political intervention or regulation and the phenomenal speed of its growth clearly took legislators at both EU and national level by surprise, making extensive retrospective regulation difficult to implement. The pace of technological and market developments makes predicting the nature of future services very difficult, and so it is hard to judge what type of regulation might be relevant. This combines with the fear of introducing legislation that might hamper the development of the new services. However, there are many different strands to the European Commission's approach and several proposals for legislation that will indirectly impact on the Internet. It is also possible that a further major scandal involving the use of the Internet for criminal purposes might create a momentum for censorship.

The transnational character of the Internet means that the problems faced in dealing with illegal and harmful activity within the EU will also exist between the EU and third countries and requires coordinated action at international level. On 6 February 1998, the European Commission proposed the adoption of an International Charter to Strengthen Worldwide Co-ordination. This initiative is the brainchild of Commissioner Martin Bangemann, who first called for an international charter for global communication in a speech in September 1997 in Geneva. The Commission wants to launch an international debate which could lead to the adoption of a charter in 1999, although reconciling the different political and cultural approaches to the Internet world-wide would not seem to be an easy task.

NOTES

1. European Commission, Press Release on Racism, Xenophobia and Anti-Semitism, IP/95/1387, 13 December 1995.
2. European Commission, 'Communication on The Implications of the Information Society for European Union Policies – Preparing the Next Steps', COM(96) 395, 24 July 1996.
3. Telecommunications Act 1996, Title V 'Obscenity and Violence', also known as the Communications Decency Act (CDA), which was put forward by US Senator Exon. The CDA has subsequently been challenged in the courts. On 12 June 1996 a Philadelphia court granted the Citizens Internet Empowerment Coalition a preliminary injunction against the implementation of the CDA on the grounds that it would unconstitutionally restrict the right of free speech. On 29 July 1996 a New York court, in *Shea* v. *Reno*, ruled the CDA unconstitutional. On 26 June 1997, the Supreme Court ruled in *Reno* v. *ACLU* that the federal CDA is unconstitutional, affirming a lower court decision.
4. Council Resolution of 22 July 1993 on the review of the situation in the telecommunications sector and the need for further development in that market, OJ C 213/1 of 6 August 1993 and the Council Resolution of 22 December 1994 on the principles and timetable for the liberalisation of telecommunications infrastructures, OJ C 379/4 of 31 December 1994.
5. European Parliament and Council Directive of 30 June 1997 amending Council Directive 89/552/EEC on the coordination of certain provisions laid

down by law, regulation or administrative action in Member States, concerning the pursuit of television broadcasting activities, 97/36/EC, OJ L 202/60, 30 July 1997.

6. European Commission, Information Society Trends Special Issue, 'An Overview of 1996's Main Trends and Key Events', December 1996.
7. 'Europe and the Global Information Society: Recommendations to the European Council', 26 May 1994.
8. European Commission, 'Communication on Europe's Way to the Information Society, an Action Plan', COM(94) 47, 19 July 1994.
9. European Commission, 'Communication on the Information Society: from Corfu to Dublin – The New Emerging Priorities', COM(96) 395, 24 July 1996.
10. European Commission, 'Communication on the Implications of the Information Society for European Union Policies – Preparing the Next Steps'.
11. Council Resolution of 21 November 1996 on new policy-priorities regarding the information society, OJ C 376/1 of 12 December 1996.
12. European Commission, 'Communication on Europe at the Forefront of the Global Information Society: Rolling Action Plan', COM(96) 607, 27 November 1996.
13. European Commission, Green Paper on the convergence of the telecommunications, media and information technology sectors, and the implications for regulation, COM (97) 623, 3 December 1997.
14. European Commission, 'Communication on Illegal and Harmful Content on the Internet', COM(96) 487, 16 October 1996.
15. European Commission, 'Communication Concerning a Regulatory Transparency Mechanism and Proposal for a Directive', COM(96) 392, 24 July 1996.
16. European Commission, 'Communication on Illegal and Harmful Content on the Internet'.
17. Ibid.
18. European Commission, 'Green Paper on the Protection of Minors and Human Dignity in Audio-visual and Information Services', COM(96) 483, 16 October 1996.
19. European Commission, Consultation on the Green Paper, SEC(97) 1207, 13 June 1997.
20. European Commission, 'Report of the Working Party on Illegal and Harmful Content on the Internet', http://www2.echo.lu/legal/en/internet/content/wpen.html, 2 November 1997.
21. European Commission, 'Communication on the Follow-up to the Green Paper of 18 November 1997', COM(97) 570 final.
22. Council Recommendation of 28 May 1998 on the development of the competitiveness of the European audio-visual and information services industry by promoting national frameworks aimed at achieving a comparable and effective level of protection of minors and human dignity, not yet published, http://europa.eu.int./en/comm/dg10/avpolicy/new_srv/recom-intro_en.html
23. European Parliament, 'Resolution on the Commission Communication on Illegal and Harmful Content on the Internet' of 24 April 1997, A4-0098/97.

24. European Commission, 'Action Plan on Promoting Safe Use of the Internet' of 26 November 1997, COM(97) 582, OJ C48/8 of 13 February 1998.
25. European Commission, 'Communication Towards a European Framework for Digital Signatures and Encryption', COM(97) 503 final.
26. European Commission, 'Proposal for a Directive on the legal protection of services based on, or consisting of, conditional access', provisional version of 9 July 1997, http://www2.echo.lu/legal/en/converge/condaccess.html
    European Commission 'Proposal for a Directive on a common framework for electronic signatures', COM(98) 297 final, 13 May 1998.
27. European Parliament and Council, 'Directive of 24 October 1995 on the protection of individuals with regard to the processing of personal data and on the free movement of such data', 95/46/EC, OJ L 281/31 of 23 November 1995.
28. Mario Monti, member of the European Commission, in a speech to the conference on 'The Information Society: New Risks and Opportunities for Privacy', Brussels, 18 October 1996.
29. Idem.
30. European Parliament and Council, Directive of 15 December 1997 concerning the processing of personal data and of the protection of privacy in the telecommunications sector, 97/66/EC, OJ L 42/1, 30 January 1998.

PART II

8 Political Participation and the Internet

Cathy Bryan and James Tatam

In this chapter we have constructed a narrow definition of political participation: our focus is on the individual's role in the political process rather than the political implications of the Internet for institutions.

Our definition encompasses five types of activity: voting; communicating with an MP, political party or government body; applying political pressure or influence, for example through lobbying or petition; accessing, retrieving and disseminating political information; and local political activity.

In this chapter we will assess current claims being made for the potential of a relatively new communications and information structure, the Internet, to impact upon the activities outlined above. History would suggest that some degree of scepticism is required if we are to avoid falling into the trap of technological determinism, and the naive belief that because something is technically possible it is either desirable or likely. In the 1960s the introduction of franchises for cable television in the US was perceived as an opportunity for viewer interactivity as well as for greater diversity of voices reaching the television screen. Whilst the concept of interactive television was not a political initiative, it was the basis of the utopian vision of the wired city, which sought to network citizens and representatives. The Internet is the 1990s embodiment of this vision. American Vice-President Al Gore was the first of the current generation of politicians to embrace the hyperbole of the new technology by coining that now ubiquitous term 'the information superhighway', since embraced by British Prime Minister Tony Blair and politicians world-wide.

In order to evaluate the impact of the Internet on political participation, we have undertaken a three-stage process. Firstly, we define the characteristics of the Internet. Secondly, we evaluate the possibilities for political participation in the UK using the five categories outlined above. Finally, we map the characteristics of the Internet onto the problems and opportunities outlined above.

CHARACTERISTICS OF THE INTERNET

The Internet is the first significant incarnation of the 'information superhighway' referred to and eulogised. Indeed, to many it is the superhighway. This is not true, and it remains to be seen to what extent the inherent characteristics of the Internet will feature in the digital communications networks of the future. We have identified seven key attributes of the Internet which have a bearing on its utility as an enabling tool for political participation. First, and most important, the Internet remains an open network, meaning that access (with all the provisos relating to socioeconomic conditions) is available to all. This is important because in theory it is a forum for political self-expression from which exclusion is not possible. This, as covered elsewhere in this book, creates its own problems, but essentially allows a diversity of viewpoints to sit side by side. Second, the Internet is a 24-hour medium; information retrieval and exchange is not confined to office hours or to broadcast schedules. Third, unlike the traditional mass media, the Internet is based on the telecommunications network, whose primary function is to allow two-way communications; the Internet therefore permits a dialogue. Fourth, it is instantaneous, allowing communication to take place between a number of individuals at the same time, in real time. This has implications for organisation of political activity. Fifth, the Internet is not location-dependent: for example, you can buy an English newspaper abroad only at inflated cost and, often, not until some time after it has been published in the UK. Information published on the Internet by comparison is available not only instantaneously, as we point out above, but also globally. The absence of geographical obstacles to accessing the Internet (again with the caveat that regulatory and infrastructural hurdles in some parts of the world make this problematic) has a number of implications for the locus of political activity. Our final two characteristics are related to each other: the first, quality of information, and the second, disintermediation, both relate to the fact that as an open network, information on the Internet comes directly from a variety of sources without passing through the filtering and editing processes of other, traditional media. The advantages of this removal of distorting effects need to be counterbalanced with the subsequent/related lack of criteria by which to judge the reliability, validity, authority and authenticity of information and its sources.

THE PROBLEMS OF POLITICAL PARTICIPATION

Looking at the characteristics we have outlined above, it is little wonder that the Internet has generated such excitement. To some extent the linking of the Internet to political participation has been brought about by the hype it has generated. But do these characteristics, and the way they have been employed so far, address the problems of political participation?

The failings in the way our political system accommodates participation on the part of citizens are widely recognised. Voting behaviour suffers from apathy, an ill-informed electorate and an unrepresentative electoral system. On top of this, there are certain groups of people whose ability to vote is hampered by physical disability. The propensity of individuals to communicate with those in authority – MPs and government representatives – is impeded by their expectations of a full, open and fruitful response. The existing channels for communication of this kind are seen as inefficient, bureaucratic and often impersonal. These factors make it difficult to identify the person most likely to provide a helpful response. For the expression of political opinion to be effective – anyone can stand on a soapbox in Hyde Park – requires considerable organisation, financial commitment and, most critically, knowledge of where best to apply political pressure. For any of the above activities to be meaningful, the participants need to be adequately informed. For instance, voting decisions require knowledge of the agenda and policies of both the political parties and their individual parliamentary candidates. For this to be the case, information needs to be inexpensive to retrieve and articulated in an accessible manner. Of course, these concerns apply to the local political environment where participation in elections is lower than at a national level.

POLITICAL RESOURCES ON THE WEB

The Internet is used extensively by political organisations and politically minded individuals. We approached this exercise as individuals who are fairly comfortable with the Internet landscape, our ability to find information is relatively sophisticated, and yet the results of our research should by no means be considered a definitive or exhaustive survey of political resources on the Web. This is because the Internet is organic, and changes constantly, and even the most sophisticated of the UK-based search and directory tools – for example Yahoo! UK, UK Plus and Yell – cannot give a complete picture of the political activity on the Internet.

All of the UK's main political parties – and some more marginal ones such as the Monster Raving Loony Party – have a presence on the World Wide Web. The Labour Party's site (http://www.labour.org.uk) gives details of Labour's policies and information on how to contact Labour MPs, including the e-mail addresses of the handful of those that are online. The ability to e-mail an MP is, on the surface, a possible solution to some of the problems associated with contacting those in authority because it appears to offer a direct route to an MP's desk. In reality, an MP's e-mail is more often than not mediated – by a secretary or assistant – in the same way as his or her regular mail, and the interval between sending a message and receiving a response is on a par with that of posted enquiries. A recent article in the *Guardian* newspaper reported that of a survey of 51 MPs only 19 responded to the journalist's e-mail enquiry within two weeks. Similarly, although both Paddy Ashdown and Tony Blair have participated in online question and answer sessions, there is little qualitative difference between such an event and a radio or TV phone-in. It is naive to think that professional politicians will perform any differently on the supposedly free and open Internet than they do elsewhere.

All of the Party Websites are useful in that they bring together basic information about who they are and what they think, but, if anything, the information posted online is even more superficial than printed material because people tend not to read a PC screen in the way that they would read a newspaper article. A preliminary conclusion from looking at these sites is that there is a trade-off between accessibility and depth of information. Whilst a Website has certain advantages over other media – for example it is available 24 hours a day – it is also constrained by the way in which people approach and interact with information on screen.

The government has its own, non-partisan presence on the Web at http://www.open.gov.uk, where it has made available government documents, press releases and a personnel directory for the Central Computer and Telecommunications Agency (CCTA) which operates the site. It also has links to quangos, regulators, government departments and some local authorities. The CCTA is also co-chair of the Government Online Project, one of eleven Information Society Pilot Projects launched by ministers from the G7 countries in February 1995. The open.gov site was launched in 1994 and registered two million hits a week in March 1997, a sixfold increase from a year ago.

One of the most extensive non-governmental Websites concerning UK politics is the UK Citizens Online Democracy site (http://www.democracy.org.uk), which is funded by the Joseph Rowntree Trust. One of the functions of this site is to provide a forum for citizens to voice opinions on a range of political issues. This ostensibly has the involvement of political figures as well as the public at large, but the site is tiered in such a way that barriers between different types of participants are created within the site and there are separate discussion forums for the public, organisations and politicians.

Finally, various Websites have been used to target groups in the community whose involvement in the political system is low – mainly young people and ethnic minorities. The 'apolitical charity' Rock The Vote (RTV) operates an extensive Website aimed at young voters in the US. In the UK, RTV used a

Website as part of its campaign to encourage young voters to enrol on the electoral register at both the 1992 and 1997 elections. The Websites provided links to other political resources on the Web, a form for registering to vote and streamed audio as background music for visitors to the site. Yet despite the efforts of RTV and the Labour Party's own bid for the youth vote, the percentage of 18- to 24-year-olds voting continues to decline – at the 1992 General Election only 57 per cent voted, compared to 69 per cent in 1987 and 73 per cent in 1970. The point exemplified in this instance is that even a clever and innovative use of the Internet to target a demographic that is broadly familiar with the technology, is hampered by the real world structures. If the same politicians are taking part in the same political processes, no Website in the world will be able to dispel citizens' cynicism toward them.

Before we go on to draw broader conclusions, it is worth highlighting some of the technology-based problems of using the Internet for the purposes of encouraging or facilitating political participation. The primary problem is one of reliability or authenticity of information. There are two reasons for this. Firstly, the Internet, as we have noted, is a publishing medium with fewer barriers to entry than newspaper publishing or television broadcasting, thereby allowing an enormous number of individuals and groups to post information on home pages and in chat forums. The difficulty lies in assessing the relative value of these sources in terms of their reliability, thoroughness and consistency. Secondly, there is the problem of authenticity; a recent stunt by a hacker who accessed the Labour Party's home page and altered the information on it, highlights the potential contamination of Internet-based resources posted by well-respected names and organisations. It is for this reason that using the Internet for that most central plank of political participation, voting, remains at this stage in our history an undesirable development, despite the obvious advantages to home-bound individuals and others for whom a trip to the ballot box is difficult enough to deter them from taking up their voting rights. Where this is the case the answer lies not in removing the trip to the ballot box but in ensuring that resources are allocated to assisting those for whom it is problematic. This emphasis on extending our efforts to make existing procedures work, rather than replacing them with a new set of processes with their own limitations, is central to our conclusions.

CONCLUSIONS

We have made no attempt to quantify or scale the problems of political participation outlined above, nor have we taken pains to match Web-based political resources with these problems. This is because we believe that such an exercise would be of dubious merit. We reject the technological determinism implicit in allocating a reformist role to the Internet as both naive and dangerous because it distracts attention from deeper analyses of impediments to political participation. Put simply, the Internet is a technological solution to what is in essence a societal problem.

What politicians need to address are the deep-seated feelings of distrust and ineffectiveness that are at the heart of political apathy. Widening the scope of the politically active should be a priority. Opportunities to participate fully in the political process exist without need for the Internet, but these opportunities are utilised by only a small number of people. Take-up of political rights is patchy and it remains the case that certain groups – notably the poor, ethnic minorities and the young – remain disenfranchised because they are less well equipped to make use of the opportunities available. Whilst we have acknowledged that the Internet could address some of the shortcomings of the present system – primarily in terms of time and cost efficiencies – we do not believe that in so doing it broadens the demographic catchment area for political activity.

Our scepticism is supported by statistics relating to PC ownership in the UK. A survey from research company Inteco shows that only 19 per cent of UK households own a PC. When these figures are broken down on an income basis, they show that PC ownership is skewed toward high-income households (38 per cent) while middle-income (7 per cent) and low-income (2 per cent) households are vastly under-represented. Moreover,

PC usage is still dominated by male users, and the most common place of usage is the workplace, which puts those without work at a disadvantage for obvious reasons. This will undoubtedly change over time and devices like the WebTV box, an Internet access device which can be attached to a television set and is currently on sale in the US for a quarter of the price of a PC, will increase overall penetration of Internet access and widen the user demographic. Although in theory, taking its characteristics neutrally, the Internet could change political participation for the better, the point is that the Internet has not been developed in a void and is subject to external pressures which will continue to shape its development, utilisation and ultimately its form. Already the commercial demands of large multinational corporations are leading to the fragmentation of the Internet in terms of technical standards, pricing and performance guarantees. For the Internet to be a tool for reinvigorating political participation, it must be ubiquitous, available on a non-discriminatory basis, inexpensive – if not free – to citizens, secure, private and not subject to commercial or political domination. While this may have seemed possible five years ago, before the Internet caught the eye of the media and the politicians, events since have and will continue to dilute the usefulness of the Internet as an empowering tool for citizens.

9 The Net Out of Control – A New Moral Panic: Censorship and Sexuality

Angus Hamilton

In August 1996 *The Times* reported on the 'problem' of paedophile and hard porn material appearing in newsgroups accessible through the Internet. The following month its sister paper, the *Sunday Times*, reported on an alleged 'invasion' of Internet Relay Chat (IRC) services by paedophiles and suggested that up to one-third of users were interested in such material. The tone of both pieces and of similar reports appearing elsewhere in the media neatly illustrate the popular conception of the law and other regulatory systems relating to the Internet. Such conceptions are based on a number of popular myths about both the law and the nature of the Net.

MYTH ONE:
THE NET IS STREWN WITH OFFENSIVE MATERIAL

The incidence of 'unsuitable' material on the Net has always been considerably exaggerated. A press story is deemed to be more attractive if it suggests major, almost unstoppable problems. The nature of the Internet is such that it is very difficult if not impossible to determine its size at any given moment. It is indisputable, however, that the Net has experienced extraordinary growth in recent years. In 1981 fewer than 300 computers were linked to the Net. By 1989 this figure had increased to 90,000; by 1993 1 million; by the beginning of 1996 9,400,000. This figure does not even include the personal computers used to access the Internet on an individual basis – that figure is expected to reach 200 million by 1999.

The growth of what is available on the Internet has been correspondingly exponential. There are now newsgroups on more than 18,000 different subjects, handling some 100,000 messages a day.

Within all this traffic pornography and other 'offensive' material is undoubtedly available – although you have to look reasonably hard to find it. Contrary to some popular conceptions a pornographic image does not pop up on to the screen the moment you log on. Communications over the Internet do not invade an individual's home or appear on one's computer screen unbidden. Users seldom encounter content by accident: a title or description of a document usually appears before the user takes the steps necessary to view it. Most newsgroups are reasonably explicitly titled: 'alt.binaries.nude celebrities' for example contains just what it suggests – shots of nude 'celebrities', predominantly women, although favoured males like Brad Pitt or David Duchovny occasionally make an appearance. The vast majority of the material can hardly be described as 'hardcore'. Most of the pictures are scanned in from mainstream magazines like *Playgirl* or 'grabbed' off commercial videos – items that are readily available 'over the counter' in this country. The material is posted in the spirit of anarchism which still predominates on the Net – why should a user with an interest in such images have to pay for or go through the embarrassment of buying *Playgirl* or *Playboy* when the material is on the Net for free?

Rough calculations suggest that about 0.002 per cent of newsgroups contain sexual images, with most of these being found in the alt.binaries area. Not wishing to avoid the issue, however, it is a fact that sexual images of children can also be found on the Net. But their incidence there probably reflects their incidence in society as a whole – arguably it is minuscule. Unfortunately, commentators and indeed the police in the UK do not seem to be too keen to acknowledge this point or to distinguish between material featuring consensual adult sexual activity and the material involving children. As a result, and in the maelstrom of a new moral panic, the former is often subjected to the same attempted or threatened censorship as the latter.

MYTH TWO: THE LAW – NOT BEING DESIGNED WITH THE NET IN MIND – IS HELPLESS TO ACT

The Net, in its present form, may be a beast of only a few years' standing, but the legal system is not far behind. The law is a remarkably flexible and adaptable creature – more akin to a rapidly developing organism than to some monolithic conservative structure. In the UK laws are developed – effectively 'created' – not only by the rather cumbersome process of government legislative proposals (White and Green Papers) followed by the passage of a Bill through Parliament, but also by the judges and courts interpreting and applying those laws – often to situations and technologies that simply did not exist at the time the original law passed on to the statute book. Where clarifying (as opposed to wholly new) legislation has been required it has been passed quickly – the Criminal Justice and Public Order Act 1994 contained several provisions designed to ensure that existing restrictions on pornography applied effectively to the Net.

That is not to say that the regulation of the Net by the implementation of existing legislation is wholly unproblematic. Such difficulties stem particularly from the international nature of the system and also its anarchic and transient characteristics. The authorities here are going to have severe practical difficulties in regulating the behaviour of someone in the US who is posting offensive material to a newsgroup which is accessible within the UK – their behaviour may be viewed as falling outside the jurisdiction of this country and not capable of prosecution within this country. Reporting the matter to the US authorities may not help as there is little uniformity in the regulation of offensive material between countries and the poster may not even be committing an offence in the US.

Nevertheless laws certainly exist which are adequate to regulate 'unsuitable' material on the Internet. Indeed as the case studies in this chapter illustrate, the law and, possibly more importantly, the threat of the law can act as very effective censorship tools.

Obscenity and Indecency

The principal piece of legislation regulating obscenity in the UK is the Obscene Publications Act 1959 (OPA). The Act makes it an offence to publish an obscene article or to have an obscene article for publication for gain. The latter prohibition may have limited relevance to Internet users as the vast majority of information on the Internet is, effectively, distributed free rather than as a commercial exercise. The producers of Websites that require some form of payment to enable access may, however, fall foul of this provision.

An article is deemed to be 'obscene' if its overall effect is to tend to deprave and corrupt a significant proportion of persons who are likely to see or hear the matter contained in the article. There have been attempts to define the terms 'deprave and corrupt', but such definitions have been largely tautological. In the prosecution brought against *Lady Chatterley*, 'deprave' was defined as 'to make morally bad, to pervert, to debase or corrupt morally'. 'Corrupt' was defined as 'to render morally unsound or rotten, to destroy the moral purity or chastity of, to pervert or ruin a good quality, to debase, to defile'.

Today what seems to be most commonly considered by juries in obscenity cases is whether the sexual activity depicted is lawful to practice. Even this principle does not adequately encapsulate the prevailing mood – in a quite startling decision in 1996, a jury accepted defence submissions that a scene of bestiality was not 'so much corrupting as preposterous'.

The most important distinction between printed or video pornography and that on the Internet is that material on the Net is obtainable in relatively uncontrolled circumstances, whereas shops selling printed porn or pornographic videos have to deny sales to those under 18. The standard of what is likely to deprave and corrupt those likely to have access to the Internet may accordingly be low. It is not yet clear whether ostensible targeting may be of any assistance on the Net – for example, making it clear who a particular site is intended for or giving 'offensive material' warnings. Arguably, such warnings unsupported by any real restriction on access are more likely to be viewed as an enticement than a deterrent.

The OPA has been amended by the Criminal Justice and Public Order Act 1994 (the '94 Act) so that publication is now clarified to include the transmission of electronically stored data which, on resolution into user viewable form, is obscene. The effect of the amendment is to render liable not only the sender of obscene material but also the organisation providing facilities which allow access to the Internet.

These bodies may be able to avail themselves of the defence under section 2 of the OPA if they can show that they did not examine the obscene material, and had no reasonable cause to suspect that its publication would lead to liability. The two elements of the defence effectively mean that it is not open to such bodies to 'turn a blind eye' if they suspect that their systems are being used to disseminate obscene material.

The OPA has been followed by two pieces of legislation which deal specifically with the current Net *bête noire* – material relating to children (legally defined as persons under 16). The Protection of Children Act 1978 makes it an offence to take or distribute indecent photographs or pseudo-photographs of children. The Criminal Justice Act 1988 renders mere possession (including on your hard disk) of indecent photographs or pseudo-photographs of a child an offence.

A 'pseudo-photo' is something that 'appears' to be a photo and 'appears' to show a child – even if it is not based on a child or indeed a real person. This means that electronically manipulated or created images will be caught.

Internet service providers (ISPs) will be at risk of prosecution for distributing child pornography if they 'channel' such images to individual users. There are, however, two potential defences open to companies charged under the legislation – the first being that they did not see the image and had no knowledge or suspicion that the image was indecent, and the second that there was a legitimate (for example medical) reason for possessing or distributing the image. The former defence is the pertinent one for ISPs, although again they are not going to be able to turn a blind eye – particularly with respect to the more explicitly named newsgroups or where the authorities have warned them about a particular site (see Case Study 1).

There have already been many instances where these pieces of legislation have been used against individual Net users who have either been in possession of or who have distributed 'child pornography' via the Net. No prosecutions have yet been brought against an ISP in this country – although the possibility has been suggested if ISPs fail to put their house in order (Case Study 1).

One of the practical difficulties that has arisen for the police in pursuing individual Net users has been gaining access to password protected files. There is no obligation to disclose passwords to the police in such a situation and although 'adverse inferences' can be drawn from a suspect's failure to answer police questions, the assumption that someone who refuses to allow access to their files is concealing child pornography is too large an inference to be drawn easily.

Exactly this problem arose with the prosecution of an alleged paedophile ring in London in March 1996. The police strongly suspected that computers seized contained indecent images of children but could not access the files to find out. Ultimately they were only able to seek the forfeiture of the computer hardware through the courts.

Case Study 1: Policing the Net

The investigation of criminal offences relating to pornographic and other offensive material on the Net fell by default to the Clubs and Vice Unit at Charing Cross Police Station in London. The Unit was 'hived off' from the former Obscene Publications Squad at New Scotland Yard and principally has the responsibility for regulating clubs, brothels and the distribution of pornography. In 1995 and 1996 the Unit developed something of a notoriety within London's gay community for the degree of interest they showed in the capital's gay clubs.

In August 1996 Chief Inspector French from the Unit sent out a standard letter to some 140 companies providing access to the Internet detailing 133 newsgroups that the police wanted ISPs to block. The list was cleverly arranged so that the first half page consisted of explicitly and unpleasantly titled paedophile newsgroups. The consequent reaction was typically distaste followed by support for the police action. It was only the persistent reader who would realise that the police also wanted to restrict access to newsgroups which clearly dealt with adult consensual sexual activities – many of them lesbian and gay interest groups.

The police action also failed to acknowledge the transient nature of many sites on the Net – even by the time the list was issued some were defunct (and doubtless others similar in nature had sprung up). The censorship demand also failed to take into account the technical difficulties of such action. Sally Weatherall, legal adviser to the 60-strong Internet Service Providers Association (ISPA), responded to the police letter by assuring cooperation with the police but also by pointing out the total impracticality of monitoring 18,000 newsgroups.

Nevertheless the police action has been reinforced with a clear threat that if ISPs do not cooperate over the proposed censorship then legal action against ISPs for publishing obscene and indecent material will be considered. Effectively, ISPs are being press-ganged into policing the Net on behalf of the police. No legal action has been taken yet and late 1996 saw a period of consultation taking place between the police and groups like ISPA and the British Computer Society (BCS). The feedback from these meetings, however, was less than positive, with one of those attending a BCS meeting describing Superintendent Hoskins from the Clubs and Vice Squad as 'wishing to assume the role of law maker as well as law enforcer'.

The pressure from the police also had a negative effect on the adoption of a coherent and united response by ISPs – in September 1996 Peter Dawe, formerly ISPA's political officer, resigned from the group to form the Safety-Net Foundation, the concept of which was akin to the Tory government's Benefit Fraud hotline, with Net users being invited to 'tell' on the posters and providers of porn.

Hate E-Mail

The Telecommunications Act 1984 makes it an offence to use a public telecommunications system to send grossly offensive, threatening or obscene material and this would seem to cover data sent via the Net. The 'public telecommunications service' requirement is likely to mean that offensive messages sent by one work colleague to another over an internal network would not be caught by this provision.

The Public Order Act 1986 also renders it an offence to use or to display threatening, insulting or abusive words or behaviour in the presence of a person likely to be caused harassment, alarm or distress thereby. This would not catch harmless teasing, however, because the legislation provides that a person is guilty of an offence only if they intend their behaviour to be threatening, insulting or abusive or are aware that it may be so.

To the best of the writer's knowledge no prosecutions relating to the use (or abuse) of the Net have been brought under these provisions. This may reflect the fact that between or within companies abusive e-mails are more likely to be dealt with as a matter of employment discipline.

Libel

The creation of a new medium by which one person could abuse another initially had libel lawyers rubbing their hands in gleeful anticipation. However, the reality, as far as the writer is aware, is that no Internet-based libel action has so far reached the UK courts.

In April 1995 Police Constable David Eggleton achieved an out-of-court settlement with supermarket chain Asda over a description of him that was circulated between its stores after he had complained about some meat he had purchased. Asda staff had apparently sought to suggest over their internal e-mail system that the officer's complaint was fraudulent.

In 1994 Dr Lawrence Godfrey, a former physicist at the German Electron Synchrotron Laboratory who was allegedly defamed in a notice on the Usenet system, was similarly compensated. Ironically, the alleged defamation originated from an employee of CERN (the European Particle Physics Laboratory), the organisation principally responsible for the introduction of the Net to Europe.

The lack of UK court cases may be a result of our legal aid system not extending to defamation actions – preserving libel actions as the exclusive territory of the very wealthy – or it may be a reflection of the somewhat *laissez-faire* attitude that prevails on the Net, or it may be a consequence of companies making e-mail libel, like other e-mail abuse, a disciplinary offence. Additionally, the very fact that the Internet, unlike print and broadcast media, permits the victim of defamation to respond immediately may remove the desire to sue. The notoriously litigious US is the only real source of Internet libel court cases and consequently of how the law of defamation may be interpreted in respect of such matters.

In *Cubby v. Compuserve*, a 1991 case, the complaint was that Compuserve provided an independently monitored bulletin board service dealing with journalism on which an unchecked and allegedly defamatory posting appeared. Compuserve maintained that it was an innocent distributor of the material and not a publisher and consequently could not be held responsible for matters appearing on the bulletin board that it did not actually know about or suspect.

The court considering the matter acknowledged the instantaneous nature of posting to the Net, accepted that it was simply not feasible for Compuserve to examine every posting and exonerated the company from liability.

The Compuserve case was, however, followed in 1995 by a case brought against online service provider Prodigy. Prodigy *was* held liable for defamatory allegations of fraud made against a company called Stratton Oakmont on a Prodigy-maintained bulletin board. The difference with the Compuserve case, the court held, was that Prodigy had specifically maintained that it regulated the contents of its bulletin boards so that it could market itself as a family-oriented system. Consequently, Prodigy was held to be a publisher and not a mere innocent distributor of the defamatory material.

One of the ironic consequences of this analysis is that many US-based service providers have been legally advised *not* to attempt to monitor postings to their bulletin boards, which is something of a blow to the self-regulation advocates.

The UK's Defamation Act of 1996 has attempted to clarify the issue of liability for Internet libels by proposing that system operators or ISPs should be viewed as only secondarily responsible for an Internet libel if they are only the transmitter and not the actual author or editor of the libel. A person with only secondary responsibility can then avoid liability for a Net defamation if they can show that, having taken all reasonable care, they did not know and did not suspect that the system was being abused.

As a result the 'hands-off' approach being advocated in the US may not have the same merit over here. Simply leaving everything unregulated may be viewed as not taking 'all reasonable care'. Conversely, checking everything may render a system operator or ISP liable as a de facto editor. In the UK the best approach for ISPs is probably to reserve the *right* to edit material – thereby demonstrating reasonable care – whilst emphasising the impracticality of checking everything and consequently not assuming the *obligation* to do so.

The new legislation has also been heavily criticised by David Shaw MP as being ineffectual against libels based, for example, on a US server that defames a UK citizen.

Case Study 2: A Very Special Type of Libel

At the start of 1996 officers from the Clubs and Vice Squad commenced an investigation into the Lesbian and Gay Christian Movement (LGCM) for allegedly assisting in the publication of a 'blasphemous libel'. The law on blasphemous libel criminalises slurs on the Christian religion but does not extend to any other faiths. In the case of LGCM the allegation was that they had provided a link from their Web page to another World Wide Web (WWW) site containing the James Kirkup poem 'The Love that Dares to Speak its Name'. That poem, which describes a Roman Centurion's lust for the figure of Christ on the cross, was held to constitute a blasphemous libel by the House of Lords in 1977 as the result of a prosecution brought against the now defunct *Gay News*. Lawyers representing the LGCM have expressed concern that the provision of a mere link to a controversial site could be viewed as a criminal offence. 'It's a bit like making it a crime to give directions to a Soho video shop', commented one representative.

It is believed that the investigation was instigated after pressure from a senior level within the Church of England. The investigation has yet to be resolved.

Copyright

Copyright issues are also a source of concern on the Net. Trademark infringement has become a particular problem with the development of the WWW. A trademark or business name may be established and registered in one country but unknown and unprotected in another. There may be accidental or deliberate clashes. Consider Apple Computers and Apple Records – which is entitled to the domain name apple.com? A practice has also developed of domain name 'warehousing' or 'cybersquatting' – where a far-sighted entrepreneur registers a domain name in anticipation that a popular company will itself require that or a similar name in due course and will buy the squatter out.

In 1996 the most infamous court case over Web-based trademark infringement was the action taken by Playboy Enterprises Inc. against the Italian-based Tatillo company for establishing the PLAYMEN Website which offered world-wide subscriptions to hard and soft porn online. The US courts had no hesitation in extending the protection already granted against PLAYMEN magazine to the new Website on the basis that the international nature of the Net meant the site was effectively being published in the US. What is not clear, however, from reading the court reports is how Playboy are going to enforce the court's ruling against the Italian company since the relevant server is based in Italy and the Italian courts are refusing to acknowledge Playboy as a registered trademark in Italy.

Case Study 3: Lovers of Lycra

In mid-1996 a member of staff at Birmingham University was dismissed after it was alleged that he had used the University's computer equipment to maintain a Website which contained references to Lycra. Dismissal followed after solicitors acting on behalf of DuPont, the manufacturers of Lycra, complained both to the technician and to the University about an infringement of their client's trademark and sought an undertaking that the use of the word Lycra would cease immediately. The complaint suggested that an infringement might have arisen by the technician describing pictures of men in cycling shorts as 'Lycra' wearers when they may in fact have been wearing other elastene fabrics. In reality it would appear that what was being objected to was the association of 'Lycra' with sexuality and in particular with a gay-oriented cycling shorts fetish. The site was entitled 'Gay Lovers of Lycra'. The dismissal of the technician also led to the loss of one of the most popular lesbian and gay resources on the Net – the WWW Lesbian Gay and Bisexual Guide to Britain. In the fever of paedophilia paranoia and the invariable association of 'gay man' and 'paedophile' the man's home was also raided by the police and he was arrested although later released without charge.

MYTH THREE: NOTHING ON THE NET IS SAFE OR SECURE

Atypically this particular myth is at least based on past truth and is only likely to become true myth within the next twelve months.

Expert testimony presented during the constitutional challenge to the US's Communications Decency Act (see below) indicated that at the beginning of 1996 neither Visa nor Mastercard considered the Internet to be sufficiently secure to process credit card transactions. Net technology develops very rapidly, however, and by July Microsoft and Netscape were announcing the release of 'secure' 128-bit versions of their Internet browsers. Meanwhile a Net user who finds his credit card details appropriated and misused still has a twofold protection. First, a UK-based credit card hacker is subject to the same criminal sanctions as if he or she had stolen the physical card and abused it. Most countries with a sizeable Net presence are likely to have similar criminal provisions. Second, most credit card companies limit the liability of their customers to a figure of about £50 for innocent losses and this policy will undoubtedly be extended to Net transactions as online shopping develops.

The other great fear of passing personal information through the Internet is that that data is being discreetly compiled by large-scale data holders intent on producing consumer profiles of Net users and thereafter submitting them to a barrage of junk 'real' or e-mail. This Orwellian scenario is not without foundation. Rosemary Jay, the senior lawyer with the Office of the Data Protection Registrar, reports two examples – one of a major organisation in the UK financial sector who wished to gather the e-mail addresses of all persons visiting their Website for marketing purposes and the other of a cereal manufacturer whose interactive Net game was specifically designed to encourage children to part with information which would allow the manufacturer to profile the child's family.

The Data Protection Act (DPA) came into force in 1986 and it regulated for the first time the storage and use of information about living individuals ('personal data') which is kept on computer. The Act gives rights to individuals to see information about them and to recover compensation if they suffer damage as a result of inaccurate information. The Act also sets standards for good personal data handling which must be adhered to by data users.

Most important is the requirement that personal data shall be obtained and processed fairly and lawfully. Several years ago the Data Protection Registrar formed the view that the indiscriminate sale of personal data by one mail order company to another was not a 'fair obtaining' of data and consequently all mail order reply coupons now carry an opt-out allowing you to indicate that you do not wish to be inundated with junk mail.

It was also due to an intervention from the Data Protection Registrar that police forces around the country were obliged to remove HIV+ 'markers' from the Police National Computer on the basis that the recording of this particular information was irrelevant to policing procedures since the police should have in place firm procedures to avoid the risk of HIV infection.

The DPA applies equally to an online environment as to traditional media, although this point does not appear to have been taken fully on board by many companies with a Net presence: Internet 'opt-outs' are still far and few between. Browsing programmes are also available which collect the addresses of those who take part in news and discussion groups. Where such programmes are being used individuals are not being informed that their data is being collected and will be used by others.

As well as seeking to explain to Net data gatherers their obligations under the DPA the Registrar is also encouraging the development of software which will provide a form of anonymity to Net users by placing an agent between them and the data gatherer, thereby avoiding the collectable 'electronic footprint'. Rosemary Jay also advocates the adoption of an internationally recognised 'suppression marker' in an e-mail address which would indicate unwillingness to have your data collected and sold on for junk e-mail purposes.

Data protection rules and regulation will also soon begin to take on a uniform international aspect with the implementation of a new EU Directive on Data Protection which must be incorporated into UK law in 1998.

Case Study 4: An Anti-Gay Spam

'Spamming' is the act of posting the same e-mail message, usually for commercial or marketing reasons, to a mass audience. It is a tactic that is generally disapproved of and often results in the sender receiving unsolicited mail, flames and bad publicity.

It is usually a harmless irritation. However, on 20 October 1996 thousands of gay men with e-mail addresses received a piece of 'junk' e-mail which suggested that they were on a list of known consumers of paedophile material and offering such material for sale. The 'spam' caused great consternation amongst the recipients, not least because it implicitly suggested that many of the gay men were on some unidentified list of paedophile material consumers and might therefore attract the unwarranted attention of the authorities.

The mailings appeared to originate from America Online (AOL), a US-based ISP, and many recipients complained to the FBI as a result. Subsequent investigation showed the spam to be a poorly conceived hoax, although the issue as to how so many individual gay men's e-mail details were gathered by the spoofers has not been satisfactorily clarified.

MYTH FOUR: OTHER COUNTRIES HAVE BEEN SPEEDY TO ACT TO REGULATE THE NET WHILST THE UK DAWDLES

Certainly other countries have attempted to deal with Net regulation by passing new specifically targeted legislation or adopting new strategies. On 8 February 1996 President Clinton signed into law the Communications Decency Act (CDA), which made it a crime to transmit 'patently offensive material' or to allow it to be transmitted over public computer networks where children might see it. It authorised the US government to restrict online speech and conduct with fines of $250,000 and gaol sentences of up to two years for anyone who made such material available to children online.

The American Civil Liberties Union (ACLU) responded by bringing an action against the US Attorney General seeking to have the Act thrown out as unconstitutional. In particular it claimed that the legislation offended against constitutional amendments prohibiting vagueness in laws and restrictions on free speech. Part of the ACLU's case was that existing US federal legislation already provided perfectly adequate sanctions in respect of obscene material and child pornography. The term 'patently offensive material' was condemned as unhelpfully vague. One example given (and accepted by the court) was that the phrase would interfere with the dissemination of information concerning HIV/AIDS which was specifically targeted at the young (13–20-year-olds account for 25 per cent of new HIV cases in the US). Another example related to the Pulitzer and Tony award-winning play *Angels in America*, which deals graphically with homosexuality and AIDS and which would undoubtedly, in the court's view, be caught by the CDA's net.

The US government responded by suggesting that it would be open to the American courts to interpret the legislation restrictively so that it was applied only to 'real' pornography. The government also emphasised the statute's defences which would exonerate ISPs who introduced systems of credit card verification or adult verification by password. These defences were subject to particularly stinging criticism from the court, which dismissed them as unworkable, costly, inefficient and, most importantly, unsupported by any currently commercially available software.

The three judges hearing the matter in Philadelphia delivered their unanimous judgment in June 1996 and granted a temporary injunction preventing the implementation of the Act. 'The Internet', commented District Judge Stewart Dalzell, 'may fairly be characterised as a never-ending worldwide conversation. The Government may not through the CDA, interrupt that conversation.' The decision will be the matter of further appeal to and review by the US Supreme Court, but the history of American case law relating to restrictions on broadcast and telecommunications media suggests that it is unlikely that the CDA will survive.

In July 1996 a similar fate befell France's proposed legislation to regulate the Internet. Telecommunication Minister Francois Fillon's plan for bringing order to the Net by forcing service providers to monitor and censor content was overturned by the French Constitutional Council. Yet again the legislation was criticised on constitutional grounds for being imprecise. Not all of the government's proposals were struck out, however – those requiring ISPs to offer clients software to block undesirable material remain, but otherwise it is anticipated that the French government will opt for voluntary compliance with an as yet unwritten international code of conduct for service providers.

By November 1996 the German authorities seemed to have taken on board the likely impracticality of seeking to regulate the content of the Net by imposing liability upon ISPs. The federal law proposals put forward in November 1996 render ISPs liable for materials which they themselves create but not for any other content unless they have actual knowledge of the presence of unlawful information and it is technically possible for them to block users' access to the offending material. Providers of hyperlinks to unlawful material are specifically exempted from liability – being seen as mere conduits.

Self-regulation appears to be the favoured strategy in the UK. City solicitors Denton Hall advised the Department of Trade and Industry on Net regulation in April 1996, having carried out a study into the incidence and control of different types of 'unsuitable' material on the Net, including pornography, seditious material, gambling and racist abuse. The firm came down in favour of a self-regulatory approach. The approach clearly has precedents in other parts of the media – the BBFC with film, the ITC with television and so on. In late 1996 Denton Hall were commissioned to carry out a further study on the possibility of EU-wide regulation for the European Parliament.

The industry has already been spooked by the spectre of legislation to come forward with self-regulatory proposals. PICS (the Platform for Internet Content Selection) has been formed by the WWW Consortium and includes many of the leading global players in the online industry – Microsoft, IBM, Netscape etc. Its aim is to develop a system for rating content on the Internet in a variety of ways. When fully implemented, PICS-compatible WWW browsers, Usenet News Group Readers and other Internet applications will provide parents with the ability to choose from a variety of rating and access restriction services. Non-rated sites will not be accessible. As the Net software market comes to be dominated by fewer and fewer manufacturers, the truly effective implementation of such controls looms ever nearer.

Case Study 5: Does Self-Regulation Still Mean Censorship?

In October 1996 US-based ISP Compuserve contacted the author of a Website which reproduced safer sex information for gay men which had originally been published by the Terrence Higgins Trust. The information, like much safer sex material, employed the use of clear but colloquial language. Compuserve's complaint was that much of the language was offensive and there was a risk of the ISP falling foul of indecency laws – not necessarily in the UK but in other jurisdictions. The British authorities have on the whole shown a reasonably tolerant attitude towards explicit text and imagery utilised for safe sex promotion, and it is unlikely that the material would have attracted their attention. Other jurisdictions, Compuserve felt, might not be so tolerant, and if they were to take action it would be against the ISP and not the UK-based Website author. Under threat of having the site closed altogether, the author withdrew the material.

10 AVIVA: The Women's World Wide Web

Kate Burke

I had the idea of an International Women's Listing Magazine whilst on my first visit to India in April 1996. My partner and I were there in the run-up to the General Election, and every day the papers were full of news about the political manoeuvring of the various parties. What made the news so interesting to me was the comprehensive coverage of women participants and women's issues. Phoolan Devi (the 'Bandit Queen') was one of the candidates and her rousing speeches about poverty and the struggles for equality by women were reported daily. The many women candidates were discussing issues around women's education, work, political and social inequalities, of which we never seem to have news through our UK media. It struck me that women everywhere would probably be interested to hear and compare the concerns of Indian women with their own preoccupations.

Unfortunately we never get the chance. News reports from India and other 'developing' countries seem to be confined to 'disaster news': poverty, famine, earthquakes, religious fanaticism, train/plane crashes etc. What we do not get to hear about are the energetic and vibrant contributions to political and social life made by the many women activists in India and elsewhere. 'Women's issues', at least in the UK, are generally restricted to fashion and 'domestic' themes in the mainstream media. Politics, the economy, the law, war, are everywhere formulated and directed by men with no account of the views *of* women, or the outcome *for* women of those policies.

Falling asleep one night under the tropical Indian sky, I was struck by the thought that it would be great if women everywhere – individuals and groups – could contact each other directly for an exchange of news and support about social problems in their own communities. In fact, as I realised in India, women in 'developing' countries have as much to offer in terms of experience and advice to women of the 'developed' world as vice versa. The ideal vehicle for such communication would be an international magazine for women where listings of women's groups would be free. Such a magazine could also be a vehicle for information about women's local events: exhibitions, music, theatre etc.; visitors and tourists, as well as locals, could find out about activities in the community.

When I discussed my idea of a magazine with my partner (a man), he immediately said 'Internet'. The major expense of running a magazine, he pointed out, are print and circulation costs. On the Internet those costs are minimal: one simply rents some space on a server – which is very cheap – then assembles the information and publishes it. Instantly one has the possibility of reaching millions of readers around the world. My immediate objection was that access to the Internet is limited to those who own PCs and modems, which are themselves expensive items. Therefore one would only be able to access an 'elite' which would defeat the object of the exercise, which is to access women everywhere, and publish news of resources and events.

It might be possible, I conceded, to recruit local agents, such as academics – who are the group most likely to have access to PCs – to print out and circulate copies of a magazine around local communities. As it happened, it would not be many months before news came of the development of technology in the US – TV Web – which will make the Internet accessible on TV screens for a few hundred dollars. Potentially, this will make it possible for TV viewers everywhere to access information published on the Internet. As I had already seen for myself, around the world in even quite remote regions, local bars and cafes where people gather often have the ubiquitous TV screen playing in the background.

Language would be another problem – to address an international readership it would be very helpful to be able to publish in local languages. But that would prove to be a lesser problem for an Internet publisher of the future in view of advancing technology – including instantaneous translation – than for print publishers. Anyway, I reasoned, even if a group or individual did not have access to a magazine, it would not preclude their advertising their offers or needs, since listings could be conveyed by post, fax, phone or e-mail to London in order to be published, via a third party if necessary.

Although I was at that time a user of PCs, in the form of word-processing, spreadsheets, financial packages etc., I had not yet progressed to using the Internet. 'Surfing the Net' held no attractions for me, as I would come to realise it does not for many women. My own experience seems to suggest that women, on the whole, use technology as the means to an end. For many men, my partner for one, technology is an end in itself – an adult, high-tech toy. However, now that I had an end in mind I applied myself to researching my new project on my return to London.

I support the work of several women's groups, and have many more connections through my organisation of Liberty's (National Council for Civil Liberties) women's seminars at the Rights Convention in June 1995 (I was also involved in gender studies as a part-time MSc student at Birkbeck College). I talked over my project with my many activist friends. Everyone was enthusiastic and supportive, with several offering ideas and help in providing information for listings. I discussed with friends the technical requirements, and have been fortunate enough to enlist the aid of Mark Rafter, an artist and designer turned Internet designer, who offered to design my site. I am also privileged in that my partner was anxious to install Internet facilities in my flat for his own use (Net-surfing), which would give me unrestricted access.

The name AVIVA came out of a brainstorming session where I and a group of friends searched for a name which would convey the creative energy of the project. We decided against acronyms, which would make sense only in English, and finally settled on a word which conveyed a feminine vision of 'life' in several languages, whilst being short and simple. A basic format evolved: information in AVIVA should consist of linked pages; first the international 'front page', with links to international news and the continents Africa, Asia, Europe, Australasia, Middle East, North America and Latin America. We determined that the magazine should not be Eurocentric, although of course it would initially be much easier to collect information about the UK through existing connections. One of the advantages of publishing on the Internet, however, must be the ease of communication, and therefore the accumulation of news and other information from around the world.

Listings of women's groups were the next priority, with a few words to explain their objectives. Resources offered/wanted listings would enable anyone to advertise their needs and have direct responses from interested parties. We were also anxious to advertise the activities of creative individuals and groups in terms of Arts events: exhibitions, music, theatre, dance etc. I have a long history of involvement with women's groups such as Julia Pascal's theatre company, and many other creative artists, so those free listings were the next category to be included. As a student of Women's Studies, I appreciate the importance of understanding the sources of women's inequalities in order to challenge them, so listings of Women's Studies courses were another essential. The last two categories, I hoped, might also prove sources of future advertising, which would supplement the free listings exposure of organisations to an international readership.

As a feminist, I discussed with other women the appropriate parameters for what I intended to be a 'feminist' publication. We agreed to exclude from free listings 'party' politics, religious parties and anti-abortion groups or events. I have no wish to display affiliation to any 'party' political agenda, and reserve the right to comment on political or social issues on the basis of their feminist content, i.e. their effect on women's struggle for equality and justice. Like many feminists world-wide, it is my opinion that *all* religions based on male omnipotence are oppressive to women, hence the exclusion of religious parties. Abortion is an issue of women's control over our own bodies, so the views of the anti-abortion lobby will not be supported in AVIVA. We decided unanimously that there should be no subscription charge for AVIVA, the news and information should be freely available to anyone with Internet access – who would then be free to print out and circulate sections of interest to others.

By this time it had become obvious that AVIVA should be formed into a company and have a written constitution, which would formalise the aims of the publication and outline the design. From the group of supporters evolved an all-women Board of Directors, which includes a journalist, an academic, a designer and an artist; the Board also has an international dimension which reflects the international constituency of the publication. The Directors have agreed to meet the editorial workers every few weeks to discuss the content of AVIVA, and consider future development.

Contacts around the world promised to send news of interest to others from their own regions, which would not be restricted to the conventional view of 'women's issues'. We are also interested in politics, economics and war – anything which affects our lives as citizens. While Mark set about designing a site (which would prove to be one of the most innovative and colourful on the Internet), I started collecting news and listings for the first issue of AVIVA – planned for a December 1996 publication at the end of November. This would prove to be more of a 'pilot' publication, since the collection of material world-wide was a daunting long-term mission.

I work part-time for International PEN, the international writers' organisation. I was fortunate enough to be going to their International Congress in Guadalajara, Mexico, in November 1996 to help with the financial organisation of the event. I saw this visit as the ideal opportunity to 'network', particularly at meetings of the Women's Committee, and recruit contributors to AVIVA from around the world. Since all PEN members are published writers, they would obviously be ideal for my purposes! PEN Congresses are also truly international assemblies, there being 130 centres around the world. In order to have representatives from every region, funds are made available by richer centres and international funders such as the United Nations Educational, Scientific and Cultural Organisation (UNESCO) and the Swedish International Development Agency (SIDA) to ensure the presence of delegates from every corner of the globe.

I had one thousand postcards printed with the bright AVIVA logo, and went to Guadalajara with a couple of hundred postcards to hand out. The Women's Committee gave me the opportunity to describe the AVIVA venture, and I handed out postcards to the many women activists who are among PEN's members. There was plenty of interest in the idea, and many promises of cooperation. After my return to London I had news direct from PEN members in Nepal, Peru, Palestine, Melbourne and South Africa. I was also able to publish interviews (on 'Women and Democracy') with speakers in Guadalajara such as Taslima Nasrin from Bangladesh and Molara Ogundipe-Leslie from Nigeria.

The Writers in Prison Committee of International PEN researches and reports on cases of imprisoned and persecuted writers around the world, including many women. AVIVA is the ideal vehicle for 'rapid action' initiatives. With information from Writers in Prison, Amnesty International and others our Action Alert section informs readers everywhere of human rights violations against women, and invites responses in the form of protest and petitions against the perpetrators of oppression. It seems appropriate that Internet publication should be the vehicle for the defence of women's rights to freedom.

Later in November 1996, we published the first issue of AVIVA. My partner had shopped around and found a service provider who would give me 10 megabytes of space for a Website, and e-mail facilities for £148 per year, plus VAT. I used the information I had collected so far, which of course was still rather limited. Since that time we have built up thousands of links with women and groups all over the globe. Information by e-mail, 'snail' mail, fax and phone now arrives daily. The Internet also has the facility for reciprocal 'links' with other sites, which means that, for instance, one can look at AVIVA and click on the Website address for 'Spinifex', an Australian feminist publisher, and vice versa.

During the Spring of 1997 we were joined in our work by Patience Agyare-Kwabi (a fellow student), who has experience as a journalist on African publications. Patience took on the listings of groups and courses – contacting institutions worldwide which run 'Women's Studies'. She has also taken charge of the 'Africa' news sections.

We have begun to get a few Classified and Display Advertisements, but have found sponsorship an uphill struggle – 'feminist' publications are never going to be appropriate marketing vehicles for the usual consumer goods: cosmetics, fashion items, plastic surgery, 'health' products etc., which subsidise the average women's magazine. Our attempts to form a charity in order to attract donations from charitable foundations were thwarted by the Charity Commission's objection to our 'Action Alert' section as being too 'political'. For those of us who are aware that even the 'personal is political' this decision actually made us laugh – particularly since 'religion' and 'education' are both classified as 'non-political' and suitable for charitable purposes. However, like others before us we shall be forming a charity purely to fund the educational aspects of work – which of course does constitute the major proportion of our publication.

One of the most interesting things one can observe by looking at women's issues on a global basis is the remarkable parallels between women's problems in different parts of the world. For instance, there have been revelations recently in both the US and the UK of the sexual harassment of women in the armed forces. The likelihood is that this phenomenon has always been a feature in military establishments, but it is only now that women have sufficient support to voice their protests; military establishments are being forced to listen through the increasing pressure of women's groups.

Religious fundamentalism is another universal feature of the news, particularly as it concerns the oppression of women. Western Christian leaders, who may take some comfort in favourable comparisons with the uncivilised behaviour of the Talibans in Afghanistan or the Mullahs in Iran or Saudi, should refrain from self-congratulation. The rise of Christian Fundamentalists in the US – who bomb abortion clinics – and in the UK, seeking to legislate on women's rights over their own bodies, is not a cause for complacency.

The issue of child abuse is also one which is international. In the 'developing' countries children are exploited and often treated as slave labour: UNICEF estimates that the number of child workers world-wide is 250 million, with many engaged in the sex trade. Save the Children estimates that the number of children serving in wars around the world is 250,000, some as young as five years old. But in the 'developed' world children are abused by their families and paedophile rings – very often in children's homes after they have been abandoned or neglected by their parents. Further, Western travellers to destinations in less affluent regions are responsible for the widespread abuse of children. 'Sex tourism' in the Philippines, for instance, is largely responsible for the numbers of child prostitutes which UNICEF estimates to be around 60,000 in that country alone.

In the UK, we have had reports about five children in Bedfordshire who are taking the UK government to Strasbourg for failing to protect them from their cruel parents. Reports from social workers, teachers, police and NSPCC had all been ignored; this echoes the plight of so many at the hands of the Wests of Gloucester. The fate of hundreds of former inmates of children's homes in North Wales is also coming to light, together with the refusal of government officials to defend the rights of children in spite of overwhelming evidence of their abuse at the time. Belgium and France have their own problems with child abuse, and again there is the likelihood of government officials being implicated in covering up the crimes.

On the Internet it is possible not only to access all this information, but to collate and publish it – cheaply. So far, women have been deterred from using the Internet in great numbers; it is claimed that 70 per cent of users are men (Graphics, Visualisation and Usability Centre at the Georgia Institute of Technology, US). The stories of unsolicited pornography deter many women, although I have to say that, not having yet found time to idly 'surf the Net', I have not stumbled across any offensive material.

The ease of access by millions of users makes it possible to spread subversive ideas (or at least, as in the case of AVIVA, news which is not readily available in the conventional press). For instance, we have been credited with a considerable part in preventing the deportation of Fateneh Fazelinasab from Canada. Ms Fazelinasab is an Iranian woman who had escaped imprisonment in her own country and made her way to Canada. Her return could have led to her death – and was prevented (in part) by the prompt action of AVIVA visitors, who petitioned the Canadian government.

We have discovered that amongst women's (and other) groups there exists a remarkable spirit of cooperation. Offers of reciprocal links with other sites are freely given. There are also 'List Servers' with whom one can sign up – without charge –

who e-mail to all members items of interest from other subscribers. For instance, the International Women's Tribune Centre (IWTC) in the US sends regular updates of initiatives which are the result of resolutions made at the Beijing Conference of 1995. Both HURINet (the Human Rights Network) and Amnesty International have given us permission to excerpt their reports for publication, with many more groups and individuals freely contributing news and information.

Our limited budget restricts us in our employment of staff, but the willingness of volunteers to join us has meant that we now have news editors for each section who originate from that region. Our listings have expanded to include thousands of women's groups and courses from around the world – which are often used printed out and used as a resource by educational institutions and others. Our 'Resources Offered and Wanted' sections have enabled a women's refuge in El Salvador to benefit from the help and advice of others in Central America; groups everywhere are making contact and corresponding across the world.

We have been able to add an 'Artful Women' section, which includes the AVIVA Global Gallery, and 'Artful Women' Register. Painter Mandy McCartin and designer Mark worked together on the opening exhibition. We were unfortunately turned down for National Lottery funding which would have enabled us to have regular exhibitions of women's arts and crafts: photographers, painters, sculptors, ceramics etc. The Internet is the perfect medium for the display of the visual arts, since reproduction of works is superior to that of the printed page. However, we are still seeking funding for an international gallery of women artists.

Patience is now moving back to Ghana to start her Centre for Women's Information, Resource and Support (CWIRS) in Accra, and will continue to edit the AVIVA 'Africa Section' – direct from the region. This is an arrangement which we are aiming for in every part of the world – and hope in the future to have funding for many more 'local correspondents'.

I was invited to the sixth Center for Global Leaders Institute at Rutgers University, New Jersey in June 1998. There I met a wonderful group of 23 other activists from around the world – some of whom had been the source of AVIVA news items –

such as journalist Rana Husseini from Jordan. Rana has been making groundbreaking reports on 'honour' killings in her country (whereby women are killed by male relatives for bringing 'dishonour' to the family, for example by talking to a man who is not her husband). Apparently these 'honour' killings are often a way of resolving a family property dispute by removing one of the claimants.

I have also been involved in the activities of an organisation called 'Women Connect' which is engaged in connecting up 20 UK women's groups, making available all the advantages of online communications that exist. It has been a fascinating experience to see women with no experience of technology, move very quickly from fear of the unknown to excitement and enthusiasm at the possibilities for contact and cooperation that await them. Many women's groups talked of their isolation in their work, and how the possibility of regular contact with other, similar groups, whether older, lesbian, disabled, refugee, Black, Asian, single parent or other, will prove beneficial to their activism.

Ironically, we have had plenty of interest from the mainstream media in AVIVA – having had pieces in both the *Independent* and the *Guardian*, as well as BBC Radio, the World Service and the UN radio. But we regard these contacts as the opportunity to promote our original agenda, which is the promotion of women's equality. Through AVIVA, we aim to bring together women academics, activists, artists and citizens from around the world. If we can publicise their work and experiences, and facilitate communication with each other, so much the better. Most important of all is the fact that we can all learn from each other. The Internet offers facilities to women users – whose numbers multiply daily – which makes contact more possible than any other media outlet has before.

At AVIVA, Patience, Mark and I are now joined by Joo from Malaysia, Laurie from the Middle East, Marja from the Netherlands and Ursula from Germany; we work through a schedule, updating all the sections for publication at the beginning of the next month. Thousands of visitors now visit our Website monthly, and many print out various sections for reference by others. We put together a press release each month – highlighting an 'Action Alert' case and featuring news items from around the world. Often it is difficult to find stories more optimistic than those of oppression of women in Algeria and Afghanistan, and drudgery for many others elsewhere.

But the news is not all bad. Where else do you read of the prodigious efforts of Israeli and Palestinian women who join together to challenge the destruction of the peace process? Or the women's rights activists in Peru who have successfully campaigned to eliminate from the law an article which allowed rapists to escape punishment if they *offered to marry* their victims? Unbelievably, the law had also allowed co-defendants in a gang rape to go free, if one of them had a marriage proposal accepted.

Finally, back to India. Phoolan Devi won her seat and is now an MP. The Prime Minister who made an election pledge that women would have one-third of seats in Parliament set aside for them – to win the support of women voters – later reneged. Nevertheless, the pledge is once again on the agenda. In the UK in spite of the dramatic rise in women MPs from less than 10 per cent to almost 20 per cent in the 1997 UK General Election which has brought in the 'New' Labour government, even the *promise* of parliamentary quotas is an achievement that eludes most Western women. We have a lot to learn from each other's experience – AVIVA exists to facilitate that process.

11 Women and the Internet

Clem Herman

The new information and communications technologies are rapidly transforming the way in which large numbers of people work and live as we move towards the information society and the Internet has begun to play a major role in this process. The most important challenge for us in this context is how we make the Internet fulfil its potential as a revolutionary and liberating form of communication, rather than watching it become simply another platform to reinforce current social inequalities.

On a global scale we are already witnessing a huge discrepancy between those who are part of the information revolution and those who are not – if half of the world's population have never made a phone call, just how accessible is the Internet in reality? For vast numbers of people, the infrastructure to use the Internet simply is not there. Even for those who do have telephone lines and access to a computer, the cost of a phone call to the nearest Internet provider makes regular online use impossible.

Whilst some of us are racing to keep up with the latest high spec computers to access the fastest and flashiest Java graphics online, huge numbers of people across the world are becoming increasingly marginalised from technological progress. Information technology, potentially a great equaliser, is in fact causing even greater polarisation between the haves and have-nots. In a world where information is power, we now have the growth of a new kind of poverty – the information disadvantaged, those for whom the online world is out of reach.[1]

One of the first initiatives in this country to try and bring the benefits of the online revolution to ordinary people began in Manchester in the early 1990s, with the creation of the Manchester Host and Electronic Village Halls, in response to increasing concern that the information disadvantaged were not just 'out there somewhere' but would soon be on our doorstep and in our communities. Many would not have the skills or confidence to know what to do with the technology and unemployed or low-waged people could never hope to afford their own computer, or the phenomenal phone costs that follow an online subscription. (Surely it has been no coincidence that the first and most frequent Internet users were university students who had free and unlimited online access and that most Net users these days are in a country where local phone calls are often free.)

The Manchester Host provided the technical services for e-mail and online information, and the Electronic Village Halls were to be points of access to the online world, providing resources – computers and modems – with support and training, and free or low-cost access. The rather quaint name Electronic Village Hall (EVH) comes from a clumsily translated Danish term describing a network of rural centres in isolated villages in Scandinavia, which were linked via faxes and modems to each other and the outside world. Manchester took the name and made it an urban phenomenon – but with virtual villages, communities of interest or neighbourhood within the urban context, catering for the needs of particularly disadvantaged groups. So, as well as the Women's EVH, there is a Disabled People's EVH, Bangladesh House EVH catering for Asian communities in Manchester, and other EVHs in community and adult education centres around the city, each providing public access to the online world. Common features are provision of basic information technology training and drop-in access to online services, but each retains its unique character and objective. There is also the Labour Telematics Centre which works nationally with the trade union movement to develop online resources. The Manchester Community Information Network has developed additional access points in libraries, hospitals and even local supermarkets.

The Women's EVH was set up because it was already clear that women were in danger of being excluded from participation in the new technologies – numbers of women studying computing and entering professions in computing were falling,[2] and most users of e-mail and the Internet were men. The Women's

EVH has provided the opportunities for women to learn skills, develop networks and use the technologies without having to compete for their own space.

There seems to be an apparent contradiction here – go into any office and you will find that most computer users in the commercial world are women. It is not that women are technophobic, but women are only trusted with the technology when it comes in word-processor shaped boxes. Apart from in low-paid and low-skilled jobs, women are consistently under-represented in all areas of work with computers, particularly in technical skills and at higher management levels where only 4 per cent are women.[3]

Meanwhile, the information superhighway is being built and unless women are included in its creation we will find ourselves left in the motorway service stations, or watching nervously from the slip roads.

Figures vary widely about how many women are actually out there in cyberspace, but what is clear is that it is still very much a male terrain. There are parts of the Internet, for example certain Usenet newsgroups (interactive conferences or chat lines), which are virtual no-go areas for women. Other areas, like the World Wide Web, which has became the fastest growing and most user-friendly service, are accessible and jargon-free, which prove to be less intimidating for women, but women are still much less visible.

A recent survey estimated that overall, 38.7 per cent of Internet users were women, a proportion which is steadily increasing.[4] Women are increasingly seeing the World Wide Web as an easily accessible and user-friendly place, but as one researcher put it, 'The average person on the Web is male, single, aged 25 to 30 and can't get a date', and therefore the content of vast areas of the Net reflects this profile and becomes self-perpetuating.[5]

Current estimates suggest that around 130 million people have Internet access.[6] Surveys of the most frequently visited sites show technical sites are the most popular – about 70 per cent of users regularly accessed these.[7] For many non-technical users, the huge amount of information available and the time it takes to find something relevant can be offputting after the first few attempts. This has been one of the key issues for women, certainly among women who have used our centre. Women have precious little free time, especially if they have children, and surfing the Net takes too long. Women need to see a use or a purpose for their interaction on the Internet, and are not interested in the millions of megabytes of information online simply for the sake of it.

One answer to women's apparent lack of interest in the Net may lie in the culture of computer games designed and marketed to boys, which in turn has spawned a generation creating the Internet in their own image, full of male interests which pass most women and girls by. Increasingly, studies have shown that women seem to see computers as just more 'toys for the boys'. Most home computers are bought for boys and it is the boys who develop the skills and the interest in technology. Fewer girls go on to study computer science at university level and many commentators believe there is a direct correlation between this and the gendered use of computers in teenage years.[8]

Yet the Internet has huge potential for women as a social and networking tool and also as a way to increase access to educational resources, to work flexibly from home, even for leisure and entertainment. At the Women's EVH we have seen the development of networking between women particularly in Eastern Europe, which would never have been possible without e-mail. For example, we worked with a group of women in the former Yugoslavia who organised a summer camp in Slovenia with participants from all across the world, organised by e-mail and including workshops and taster sessions for hundreds of women introducing them to telematics.

It seems clear that women have begun to make a space for themselves which can be found without too much trouble and this is an encouraging sign. A search on the word 'women' using a typical search engine brings up a variety of interesting sites, many of them created by American academics, covering a wide range of research areas and contacts, particularly in technical and scientific areas – a greatly needed resource for women working in otherwise male-dominated professions. There is also a significant number of women's networks, working in areas of community politics, and several international networks. Clearly women activists are out there and using the Net as a versatile, international networking tool.[9]

However, we cannot get away from another growing area of Internet use which has major implications for women but which is also being hijacked by those who advocate censorship. A search on the word 'girls' brings up a range of unsavoury sites that are not exactly Girl Guide groups – most links were to explicit pornographic pages and services. So, this is where we get into the tricky area of censorship and regulation – is the free speech and participation of girls and women on the Internet being impeded or hampered by the unregulated spirit of cyberspace? Does the knowledge that these images are around the corner affect women's participation, like in the local newsagents, when we feel the presence of men lurking and waiting till we go away so they can look at the top shelf?

For many women, the question of safety has not just been academic or theoretical – sexual harassment is just as much part of the virtual world as it is in reality. Just as women are aware of areas of their city where they would not walk alone at night, there are areas of the Internet that are not perceived as 'safe' for women. Online chat rooms can be the most dangerous places, especially if you dare to speak out, rather like speaking your mind in a crowded pub full of men. Women are being kept out of cyberspace by an electronic version of interruption and intimidation. Studies of interaction in certain Usenet newsgroups have shown that women were not able to get a word in, or were prevented from raising topics that were of interest to them. Women felt ignored, silenced, even abused in public online conversations. Flaming (vicious and angry e-mails) can be frightening and intimidating. But whenever these issues have been raised by women, the response is always 'if you can't stand the heat stay out of the kitchen'. Sexual harassment using computer networks has been well documented in college and university campuses, where more and more female students have online access but where the majority of those with technical skills are still male.[10]

Harassment online can range from so-called 'wanna fuck' e-mail – requests for a date or sex – to bitter hate mail and even threats of physical abuse or death: Stephanie Brail was harassed, threatened and abused when she dared challenge someone in a newsgroup. Determined to fight back, she taught herself how to track the perpetrator down and threatened police action which eventually made him stop, but she acknowledges that she has now censored herself and no longer participates in online discussion groups.[11] Like her, many women have learnt from bitter experience to develop strategies, online self-defence techniques – never to give their address or phone number online, learn how to programme their responses and trace messages. Some women even log on under gender neutral names to avoid being harassed. No wonder many women feel uneasy about entering this new territory. Any discussions about censorship must take into account issues of personal safety as well as rights to freedom of speech – for women who are being harassed there is no free speech.

As well as direct harassment via e-mail, the development of the World Wide Web has entered into the debate about women's safety and rights on the Net. Online pornography and the extent to which this is available is an area of much controversy. Recent estimates suggest that about 15 per cent of traffic on the Web is to these so-called 'adult sites', which is quite a substantial amount of online time.[12] The Internet has become the advertiser's dream – a huge untapped resource in which to market their products. And of course the easiest way to sell anything is to make it sexy, either literally or by implication – the Internet enables both. Pornographers can use the Internet to sell their wares, but equally the mere hint of sex and its availability on the Net attracts new customers and allows other products to be sold in its wake. Researchers are frantically working on sex via interactive virtual reality which has become the ultimate dream – sex sells the technology just as much as the technology sells the sex.

Feminists in the 1980s had complex debates about pornography and its role in the oppression of women, and have fought long and hard to have their own voices heard. Freedom of speech is a concept to which we all subscribe, but which in reality only those with privilege can enjoy. Pornography is just one of the many ways in which women's voices can be silenced. We have laws to protect the rights of minorities and vulnerable groups because as a society we have recognised our duty to do so, and the same rules should apply in cyberspace. What is clear is that Pornography is a huge multinational business, in which the bodies of vulnerable people simply become commodities. We could argue about the level to which an image is erotic or pornographic, how live video conferencing is safer than street walking or to what extent computer dating is a sad reflection of the demise of our social fabric, and it is clear that these issues should be debated. But we are witnessing an escalation of what is acceptable and easily accessible. The Internet has brought with it international racketeering in mail-order brides; interactive video conferencing; violent and abusive images available at the touch of a button. The increase in the market for these so-called 'products' is fuelled by their wider circulation via the Internet, creating a world wide web of exploitation and abuse.

Yet the rate of growth of the Internet and its capacity for such variety of uses means that the proportion of cyberspace being used in this way is diminishing. Although *Playboy* remains in the Top 50 sites visited, figures for visits to 'adult sites' have dropped since the beginning of 1996 from 25 to 15 per cent. After all, the Internet is just another vehicle which can be used in whichever way we choose and those of us working for social change and greater freedom for all must work to ensure that as many people as possible are able to benefit from its growth.

As Stephanie Brail says, 'Instead of withdrawing from the online world, with all its riches and opportunities, we can form our own networks, online support groups, and places to speak ... women cannot be left behind and we cannot afford to be intimidated.'[13]

We need to build more public access spaces for all people to get online – not just trendy cybercafes, but also terminals in launderettes and shopping centres, libraries and schools. We need to be creative about how to keep out unwanted information without bland censorship, and most importantly about how to empower people with skills to develop their own space and networks on the Internet.

NOTES

1. Recent estimates suggest that 2.4 per cent of the worlds population (130 million people) has access to the Internet (source: NUA Ltd). Percentages on a country by country basis range from 45 per cent (Iceland) or 30 per cent (USA) to 0.05 per cent (China) and 0.02 per cent India (sources: Gallup, Intelliquest, Yahoo/Reuters, *Wired*).
2. Research commissioned by Microsoft and carried out by NOP has revealed that the amount of women working in the IT industry has dropped from 30 per cent in 1989 to 15 per cent today (http://www.nua.surveys, 4 February 1998).
3. Frances Grundy, *Women and Computers* (Intellect, 1996).
4. 9th GVU WWW user survey. The same survey found, encouragingly, that 43 per cent of all users between the ages of 11 and 20 were female. In July 1998, Georgia Tech announced the results of their most recent survey which suggested that women now outnumber men in the new users category, with women comprising 52 per cent of all Internet users who had been online for less than a year.
5. Louise McElvogue, *Guardian OnLine*, 4 July 1996.
6. See note 1 above.
7. PCMC Marketing Services quoted in the *Guardian OnLine*, 11 July 1996.
8. Louise Eastin Moses, 'Gender, Video-Games and Software in the USA, an Overview', paper presented to the fifth IFIP International Conference on Women, Work and Computerization, 1994.
9. See Chapter 10 in which Kate Burke discusses the history and success of AVIVA, her pioneering International Women's Listing Magazine.
10. Stephanie Brail, 'The Price of Admission: Harassment and Free Speech in the Wild Wild West', in Lynn Cherny and Elizabeth Reba Weise (eds), *Wired Women: Gender and New Realities in Cyberspace* (Seal Press, 1996).
11. Ibid.
12. Louise McElvogue, *Guardian OnLine*, 4 July 1996.
13. Brail, 'The Price of Admission'.

15 Tinysex and Gender Trouble [1]

Sherry Turkle

From my earliest effort to construct an online persona, it occurred to me that being a virtual man might be more comfortable than being a virtual woman.

When I first logged on to a MUD, I named and described a character but forgot to give it a gender. I was struggling with the technical aspects of the MUD universe – the difference between various MUD commands such as 'saying' and 'emoting', 'paging' and 'whispering'.[2] Gender was the last thing on my mind. This rapidly changed when a male-presenting character named Jiffy asked me if I was 'really an it'. At his question, I experienced an unpleasurable sense of disorientation which immediately gave way to an unfamiliar sense of freedom.

When Jiffy's question appeared on my screen, I was standing in a room of LambdaMOO filled with characters engaged in sexual banter in the style of the movie *Animal House*. The innuendos, double entendres, and leering invitations were scrolling by at a fast clip; I felt awkward, as though at a party to which I had been invited by mistake. I was reminded of junior high school dances when I wanted to go home or hide behind the punch bowl. I was reminded of kissing games in which it was awful to be chosen and awful not to be chosen. Now, on the MUD, I had a new option. I wondered if playing a male might allow me to feel less out of place. I could stand on the sidelines and people would expect me to make the first move. And I could choose not to. I could choose simply to 'lurk', to stand by and observe the action. Boys, after all, were not called prudes if they were too cool to play kissing games.

They were not categorized as wallflowers if they held back and didn't ask girls to dance. They could simply be shy in a manly way – aloof, above it all.

Two days later I was back in the MUD. After I typed the command that joined me, in Boston, to the computer in California where the MUD resided, I discovered that I had lost the paper on which I had written my MUD password. This meant that I could not play my own character but had to log on as a guest. As such, I was assigned a colour: Magenta. As 'Magenta_guest' I was again without gender. While I was struggling with basic MUD commands, other players were typing messages for all to see such as 'Magenta guest gazes hot and enraptured at the approach of Fire_Eater.' Again I was tempted to hide from the frat party atmosphere by trying to pass as a man.[3] When much later I did try playing a male character, I finally experienced that permission to move freely I had always imagined to be the birthright of men. Not only was I approached less frequently, but I found it easier to respond to an unwanted overture with aplomb, saying something like, 'That's flattering, Ribald_Temptress, but I'm otherwise engaged.' My sense of freedom didn't just involve a different attitude about sexual advances, which now seemed less threatening. As a woman I have a hard time deflecting a request for conversation by asserting my own agenda. As a MUD male, doing so (nicely) seemed more natural; it never struck me as dismissive or rude. Of course, my reaction said as much about the construction of gender in my own mind as it did about the social construction of gender in the MUD.

Playing in MUDs, whether as a man, a woman, or a neuter character, I quickly fell into the habit of orienting myself to new cyberspace acquaintances by checking out their gender. This was a strange exercise, especially because a significant proportion of the female-presenting characters were RL men, and a good number of the male-presenting characters were RL women. I was not alone in this curiously irrational preoccupation. For many players, guessing the true gender of players behind MUD characters has become something of an art form. Pavel Curtis, the founder of LambdaMOO, has observed that when a female-presenting character is called something like FabulousHotbabe, one can be almost sure there is a man behind the mask.[4] Another experienced MUDder shares the folklore that 'if a female-presenting character's description of her beauty goes on for more than two paragraphs, "she" [the player behind the character] is sure to be an ugly woman'.

The preoccupation in MUDs with getting a 'fix' on people through 'fixing' their gender reminds us of the extent to which we use gender to shape our relationships. Corey, a 22-year-old dental technician, says that her name often causes people to assume that she is male – that is, until she meets them. Corey has long blonde hair, piled high, and admits to 'going for the Barbie look'.

> I'm not sure how it started, but I know that when I was a kid the more people said, 'Oh, you have such a cute boy's name', the more I laid on the hairbows [with my name] they always expected a boy – or at least a tomboy.

Corey says that, for her, part of the fun of being online is that she gets to see 'a lot of people having the [same] experience [with their online names that] I've had with my name'. She tells me that her girlfriend logged on as Joel instead of Joely, 'and she saw people's expectations change real fast'. Corey continues:

> I also think the neuter characters [in MUDs] are good. When I play one, I realise how hard it is not to be either a man or a woman. I always find myself trying to be one or the other even when I'm trying to be neither. And all the time I'm talking to a neuter character [she reverses roles here] ... I'm thinking 'So who's behind it?'

In MUDs, the existence of characters other than male or female is disturbing, evocative. Like transgressive gender practices in real life, by breaking the conventions, it dramatises our attachment to them.

Gender-swapping on MUDs is not a small part of the game action. By some estimates, Habitat, a Japanese MUD, has 1.5 million users. Habitat is a MUD operated for profit. Among the registered members of Habitat, there is a ratio of four real-life men to each real-life woman. But inside the MUD the ratio is only three male characters to one female character. In other words, a significant number of players, many tens of thousands of them, are virtually cross-dressing.[5]

GENDER TROUBLE [6]

What is virtual gender-swapping all about? Some of those who do it claim that it is not particularly significant. 'When I play a woman I don't really take it too seriously', said 20-year-old Andrei. 'I do it to improve the ratio of women to men. It's just a game.' On one level, virtual gender-swapping is easier than doing it in real life. For a man to present himself as female in a chat room, on an IRC channel, or in a MUD, only requires writing a description. For a man to play a woman on the streets of an American city, he would have to shave various parts of his body; wear makeup, perhaps a wig, a dress, and high heels; perhaps change his voice, walk, and mannerisms. He would have some anxiety about passing, and there might be even more anxiety about not passing, which would pose a risk of violence and possibly arrest. So more men are willing to give virtual cross-dressing a try. But once they are online as female, they soon find that maintaining this fiction is difficult. To pass as a woman for any length of time requires understanding how gender inflects speech, manner, the interpretation of experience. Women attempting to pass as men face the same kind of challenge. One woman said that she 'worked hard' to pass in a room on a commercial network service that was advertised as a meeting place for gay men.

I have always been so curious about what men do with each other. I could never even imagine how they talk to each other. I can't exactly go to a gay bar and eavesdrop inconspicuously. [When online] I don't actually have [virtual] sex with anyone. I get out of that by telling the men there that I'm shy and still unsure. But I like hanging out; it makes gays seem less strange to me. But it is not so easy. You have to think about it, to make up a life, a job, a set of reactions.

Virtual cross-dressing is not as simple as Andrei suggests. Not only can it be technically challenging, it can be psychologically complicated. Taking a virtual role may involve you in ongoing relationships. In this process, you may discover things about yourself that you never knew before. You may discover things about other people's response to you. You are not in danger of being arrested, but you are embarked on an enterprise that is not without some gravity and emotional risk.

In fact, one strong motivation to gender-swap in virtual space is to have TinySex as a creature of another gender, something that suggests more than an emotionally neutral activity. Gender-swapping is an opportunity to explore conflicts raised by one's biological gender. Also, as Corey noted, by enabling people to experience what it feels like to be the opposite gender or to have no gender at all, the practice encourages reflection on the way ideas about gender shape our expectations. MUDs and the virtual personae one adopts within them are objects-to-think-with for reflecting on the social construction of gender.

Case, a 34-year-old industrial designer who is happily married to a co-worker, is currently MUDding as a female character. In response to my question, 'Has MUDding ever caused you any emotional pain?' he says, 'Yes, but also the kind of learning that comes from hard times.'

> I'm having pain in my playing now. The woman I'm playing in MedievalMUSH [Mairead] is having an interesting relationship with a fellow. Mairead is a lawyer. It costs so much to go to law school that it has to be paid for by a corporation or a noble house. A man she met and fell in love with was a nobleman. He paid for her law school. He bought my [Case slips into referring to Mairead in the first person] contract. Now he wants to marry me although I'm a commoner. I finally said yes. I try to talk to him about the fact that I'm essentially his property. I'm a commoner, I'm basically property and to a certain extent that doesn't bother me. I've grown up with it, that's the way life is. He wants to deny the situation. He says, 'Oh no, no, no ... We'll pick you up, set you on your feet, the whole world is open to you.' But every time I behave like I'm now going to be a countess some day, you know, assert myself – as in, 'And I never liked this wallpaper anyway' – I get pushed down. The relationship is pull up, push down. It's an incredibly psychologically damaging thing to do to a person. And the very thing that he liked about her – that she was independent, strong, said what was on her mind – it is all being bled out of her.

Case looks at me with a wry smile and sighs, 'A woman's life'. He continues:

> I see her [Mairead] heading for a major psychological problem. What we have is a dysfunctional relationship. But even though it's very painful and stressful, it's very interesting to watch myself cope with this problem. How am I going to dig my persona's self out of this mess? Because I don't want to go on like this. I want to get out of it ... You can see that playing this woman lets me see what I have in my psychological repertoire, what is hard and what is easy for me. And I can also see how some of the things that work when you're a man just backfire when you're a woman.

Case has played Mairead for nearly a year, but even a brief experience playing a character of another gender can be evocative. William James said, 'Philosophy is the art of imagining alternatives.' MUDs are proving grounds for an action-based philosophical practice that can serve as a form of consciousness-raising about gender issues. For example, on many MUDs, offering technical assistance has become a common way in which male characters 'purchase' female attention, analogous to picking up the check at an RL dinner. In real life, our expectations about sex roles (who offers help, who buys dinner, who brews the coffee) can become so ingrained that we no longer notice them. On MUDs, however, expectations are expressed in visible textual actions, widely witnessed and openly discussed.

When men playing females are plied with unrequested offers of help on MUDs, they often remark that such chivalries communicate a belief in female incompetence. When women play males on MUDs and realise that they are no longer being offered help, some reflect that those offers of help may well have led them to believe they needed it. As a woman, 'First you ask for help because you think it will be expedient,' says a college sophomore, 'then you realise that you aren't developing the skills to figure things out for yourself'.

ALL THE WORLD'S A STAGE

Any account of the evocative nature of gender-swapping might well defer to Shakespeare, who used it as a plot device for reframing personal and political choices. *As You like It* is a classic example, a comedy that uses gender-swapping to reveal new aspects of identity and to permit greater complexity of relationships.[7] In the play, Rosalind, the Duke's daughter, is exiled from the court of her uncle Frederick, who has usurped her father's throne. Frederick's daughter, Rosalind's cousin Celia, escapes with her. Together they flee to the magical forest of Arden. When the two women first discuss their plan to flee, Rosalind remarks that they might be in danger because 'beauty provoketh thieves sooner than gold'. In response, Celia suggests that they would travel more easily if they rubbed dirt on their faces and wore drab clothing, thus pointing to a tactic that frequently provides women greater social ease in the world – becoming unattractive. Rosalind then comes up with a second idea – becoming a man: 'Were it not better / Because that I am more than common tall / That I did suit me all points like a man?' In the end, Rosalind and Celia both disguise themselves as boys, Ganymede and Aliena. In suggesting this ploy, Rosalind proposes a disguise that will be both physical ('A gallant curtle-axe on my thigh, / A boar-spear in my hand') and emotional ('and – in my heart, / Lie there what hidden woman's fear there will'). She goes on, 'We'll have a swashbuckling and martial outside, / as many other mannish cowards have / That do outface it with their semblances'.[8]

In these lines, Rosalind does not endorse an essential difference between men and women; rather, she suggests that men routinely adopt the same kind of pose she is now choosing. Biological men have to construct male gender just as biological women have to construct female gender. If Rosalind and Celia make themselves unattractive, they will end up less feminine. Their female gender will end up deconstructed. Both strategies – posing as men and deconstructing their femininity – are games that female MUDders play. One player, a woman currently in treatment for anorexia, described her virtual body this way:

> In real life, the control is the thing. I know that it is very scary for me to be a woman. I like making my body disappear. In real life that is. On MUDs, too. On the MUD, I'm sort of a woman, but I'm not someone you would want to see sexually. My MUD description is a

combination of smoke and angles. I like that phrase 'sort of a woman'. I guess that's what I want to be in real life too.

In addition to virtual cross-dressing and creating character descriptions that deconstruct gender, MUDders gender-swap as double agents. That is, in MUDs, men play women pretending to be men, and women play men pretending to be women. Shakespeare's characters play these games as well. In *As You Like It*, when Rosalind flees Frederick's court she is in love with Orlando. In the forest of Arden, disguised as the boy Ganymede, she encounters Orlando, himself lovesick for Rosalind. As Ganymede, Rosalind says she will try to cure Orlando of his love by playing Rosalind, pointing out the flaws of femininity in the process. In current stagings, Rosalind is usually played by a woman who at this point in the play pretends to be a man who pretends to be a woman. In Shakespeare's time, there was yet another turn because all women's parts were played by boys. So the character of Rosalind was played by a boy playing a girl playing a boy who plays a girl so she can have a flirtatious conversation with a boy. Another twist occurs when Rosalind playing Ganymede playing Rosalind meets Phoebe, a shepherdess who falls passionately in love with 'him'.

As You Like It, with its famous soliloquy that begins 'All the world's a stage', is a play that dramatises the power of the theatre as a metaphor for life. The visual pun of Rosalind's role underscores the fact that each of us is an actor playing one part or many parts. But the play has another message that speaks to the power of MUDs as new stages for working on the politics of gender. When Rosalind and Orlando meet 'man to man' as Ganymede and Orlando, they are able to speak freely. They are able to have conversations about love quite different from those that would be possible if they followed the courtly conventions that constrain communications between men and women. In this way, the play suggests that donning a mask, adopting a persona, is a step toward reaching a deeper truth about the real, a position many MUDders take regarding their experiences as virtual selves.

Garrett is a 28-year-old male computer programmer who played a female character on a MUD for nearly a year. The character was a frog named Ribbit, When Ribbit sensed that a new player was floundering, a small sign would materialise in her hand that said, 'If you are lost in the MUD, this frog can be a friend.'

When talking about why he chose to play Ribbit, Garrett says:

> I wanted to know more about women's experiences, and not just from reading about them ... I wanted to see what the difference felt like. I wanted to experiment with the other side .... I wanted to be collaborative and helpful, and I thought it would be easier as a female .... As a man I was brought up to be territorial and competitive. I wanted to try something new .... In some way I really felt that the canonically female way of communicating was more productive than the male – in that all this competition got in the way.

And indeed, Garrett says that as a female frog, he did feel freer to express the helpful side of his nature than he ever had as a man. 'My competitive side takes a back seat when I am Ribbit.' Garrett's motivations for his experiment in gender-swapping run deep. Growing up, competition was thrust upon him and he didn't much like it. Garrett, whose parents divorced when he was an infant, rarely saw his father. His mother offered little protection from his brother's bullying. An older cousin regularly beat him up until Garrett turned 14 and could inflict some damage of his own. Garrett got the clear idea that male aggression could only be controlled by male force.

In his father's absence, Garrett took on significant family responsibility. His mother ran an office, and Garrett checked in with her every day after school to see if she had any errands for him to run. If so, he would forego the playground. Garrett recalls these days with great warmth. He felt helpful and close to his mother. When, at ten, he won a scholarship to a prestigious private boarding school for boys, a school he describes as being 'straight out of Dickens', there were no more opportunities for this kind of collaboration. To Garrett, life now seemed to be one long competition. Of boarding school he says:

> It's competitive from the moment you get up in the morning and you've all got to take a shower together and everyone's checking each other out to see who's got pubic hair. It's competitive when you're in class. It's competitive when you're on the sports field. It's competitive when you're in other extra-curricular activities such as speeches. It's competitive all day long, every day.

At school, the older boys had administrative authority over the younger ones. Garrett was not only the youngest student, he was also from the poorest family and the only newcomer to a group that had attended school together for many years. 'I was pretty much at the bottom of the food chain', he says. In this hierarchical environment, Garrett learned to detest hierarchy, and the bullies at school reinforced his negative feelings about masculine aggression. Once out of high school, Garrett committed himself to finding ways to 'get back to being the kind of person I was with my mother'. But he found it difficult to develop collaborative relationships, particularly at work. When he encouraged a female co-worker to take credit for some work they had done together 'something', he says 'that women have always done for men' – she accepted his offer, but their friendship and ability to work together were damaged. Garrett sums up the experience by saying that women are free to help men and both can accept the woman's self-sacrifice, 'but when a man lets a woman take the credit, the relationship feels too close, too seductive [to the woman]'. From Garrett's point of view, most computer bulletin boards and discussion groups are not collaborative but hostile environments, characterised by 'flaming'. This is the practice of trading angry and often *ad hominem* remarks on any given topic.

> There was a premium on saying something new, which is typically something that disagrees to some extent with what somebody else has said. And that in itself provides an atmosphere that's ripe for conflict. Another aspect, I think, is the fact that it takes a certain degree of courage to risk really annoying someone. But that's not necessarily true on an electronic medium, because they can't get to you. It's sort of like hiding behind a wall and throwing stones. You can keep throwing them as long as you want and you're safe.

Garrett found MUDs different and a lot more comfortable. 'On MUDs', he says, 'people were making a world together. You got no prestige from being abusive.'

Garrett's gender-swapping on MUDs gave him an experience-to-think-with for thinking about gender. From his point of view, all he had to do was to replace male with female in a character's description to change how people saw him and what he felt comfortable expressing. Garrett's MUD experience, where as a female he could be collaborative without being stigmatised, left him committed to bringing the helpful frog persona into his life as a male, both on and off the MUD. When I met him, he had a new girlfriend who was lending him books about the differences in men's and women's communication styles. He found they reinforced the lessons he learned in the MUD.

By the time I met Garrett, he was coming to feel that his gender-swapping experiment had reached its logical endpoint. Indeed, between the time of our first and second meeting, Garrett decided to blow his cover on the MUD and tell people that in RL he was really male. He said that our discussions of his gender-swapping had made him realise that it had achieved its purpose.

For anthropologists, the experience of *depayesement* (literally, 'decountrifying' oneself) is one of the most powerful elements of fieldwork. One leaves one's own culture to face something unfamiliar, and upon returning home it has become strange – and can be seen with fresh eyes. Garrett described his decision to end his gender-swapping in the language of *depaysement*. He had been playing a woman for so long that it no longer seemed strange. 'I'd gotten used to it to the extent that I was sort of ignoring it. OK, so I log in and now I'm a woman. And it really didn't seem odd anymore.' But returning to the MUD as a male persona did feel strange. He struggled for an analogy and came up with this one:

> It would be like going to an interview for a job and acting like I do at a party or a volleyball game. Which is not the way you behave at an interview. And so it is sort of the same thing. [As a male on the MUD] I'm behaving in a way that doesn't feel right for the context, although it is still as much me as it ever was.

When Garrett stopped playing the female Ribbit and started playing a helpful male frog named Ron, many of Garrett's MUDding companions interpreted his actions as those of a woman who now wanted to try playing a man. Indeed, a year after his switch, Garrett says that at least one of his MUD friends, Dredlock, remains unconvinced that the same person has actually played both Ribbit and Ron. Dredlock insists that while Ribbit was erratic (he says, 'She would sometimes walk out in the middle of a conversation'), Ron is more dependable. Has Garrett's behaviour changed? Is Garrett's behaviour the same but viewed differently through the filter of gender? Garrett believes that both are probably true. 'People on the MUD have ... seen the change and it hasn't necessarily convinced them that I'm male, but they're also not sure that I'm female. And so, I've sort of gotten into this state where my gender is unknown and people are pretty much resigned to not knowing it.' Garrett says that when he helped others as a female frog, it was taken as welcome, natural, and kind. When he now helps as a male frog, people find it unexpected and suspect that it is a seduction ploy. The analogy with his real life is striking. There, too, he found that playing the helping role as a man led to trouble because it was easily misinterpreted as an attempt to create an expectation of intimacy.

Case, the industrial designer who played the female Mairead in MedievalMUSH, further illustrates the complexity of gender swapping as a vehicle for self-reflection. Case describes his RL persona as a nice guy, a 'Jimmy Stewart-type like my father'. He says that in general he likes his father and he likes himself, but he feels he pays a price for his low-key ways. In particular, he feels at a loss when it comes to confrontation, both at home and in business dealings. While Garrett finds that MUDding as a female makes it easier to be collaborative and helpful, Case likes MUDding as a female because it makes it easier for him to be aggressive and confrontational. Case plays several online 'Katharine Hepburn-types', strong, dynamic, 'out there' women who remind him of his mother, 'who says exactly what's on her mind and is a take-no-prisoners sort'. He says:

> For virtual reality to be interesting it has to emulate the real. But you have to be able to do something in the virtual that you couldn't

> in the real. For me, my female characters are interesting because I can say and do the sorts of things that I mentally want to do, but if I did them as a man, they would be obnoxious. I see a strong woman as admirable. I see a strong man as a problem. Potentially a bully.

In other words, for Case, if you are assertive as a man, it is coded as 'being a bastard'. If you are assertive as a woman, it is coded as 'modern and together'.

> My wife and I both design logos for small businesses. But do this thought experiment. If I say 'I will design this logo for $3,000, take it or leave it', I'm just a typical pushy businessman. If she says it, I think it sounds like she's a 'together' woman. There is too much male power-wielding in society, and so if you use power as a man, that turns you into a stereotypical man. Women can do it more easily.

Case's gender-swapping has given him permission to be more assertive within the MUD, and more assertive outside of it as well:

> There are aspects of my personality – the more assertive, administrative, bureaucratic ones – that I am able to work on in the MUDs. I've never been good at bureaucratic things, but I'm much better from practicing on MUDs and playing a woman in charge. I am able to do things – in the real, that is – that I couldn't have before because I have played Katharine Hepburn characters.

Case says his Katharine Hepburn personae are 'externalisations of part of myself'. In one interview with him, I use the expression 'aspects of the self', and he picks it up eagerly, for MUDding reminds him of how Hindu gods could have different aspects or subpersonalities, all the while having a whole self:

> You may, for example, have an aspect who is a ruthless business person who can negotiate contracts very, very well, and you may call upon that part of yourself while you are in tense negotiation, to do the negotiation, to actually go through and negotiate a really good contract. But you would have to trust this aspect to say something

like, 'Of course, I will need my lawyers to look over this', when in fact among your 'lawyers' is the integrated self who is going to do an ethics vet over the contract, because you don't want to violate your own ethical standards and this [ruthless] aspect of yourself might do something that you wouldn't feel comfortable with later.

Case's gender-swapping has enabled his inner world of hard-bitten negotiators to find self-expression, but without compromising the value he associates with his 'whole person'. Role playing has given the negotiators practice; Case says he has come to trust them more. In response to my question, 'Do you feel that you call upon your personae in real life?' Case responds:

> Yes, an aspect sort of clears its throat and says, 'I can do this. You are being so amazingly conflicted over this and I know exactly what to do. Why don't you just let me do it?' MUDs give me balance. In real life, I tend to be extremely diplomatic, non-confrontational. I don't like to ram my ideas down anyone's throat. On the MUD, I can be, 'Take it or leave it.' All of my Hepburn characters are that way. Thats probably why I play them. Because they are smart-mouthed, they will not sugarcoat their words.

In some ways, Case's description of his inner world of actors who address him and are capable of taking over negotiations is reminiscent of the language of people with multiple personality. In most cases of multiple personality, it is believed that repeated trauma provokes a massive defence: An 'alter' is split off who can handle the trauma and protect the core personality from emotional as well as physical pain. In contrast, Case's inner actors are not split off from his sense of himself. He calls upon their strengths with increasing ease and fluidity. Case experiences himself very much as a collective self, not feeling that he must goad or repress this or that aspect of himself into conformity. To use Marvin Minsky's language, Case feels at ease in his society of mind.

Garrett and Case play female MUD characters for very different reasons. There is a similar diversity in women's motivations for playing male characters. Some share my initial motivation, a desire for invisibility or permission to be more outspoken or aggressive. 'I was born in the South and I was taught that girls didn't speak up to disagree with men', says Zoe, a 34-year-old woman who plays male and female characters on four MUDs.

> We would sit at dinner and my father would talk and my mother would agree. I thought my father was a god. Once or twice I did disagree with him. I remember one time in particular when I was ten, and he looked at me and said, 'Well, well, well, if this little flower grows too many more thorns, she will never catch a man.'

Zoe credits MUDs with enabling her to reach a state of mind where she is better able to speak up for herself in her marriage ('to say what's on my mind before things get all blown out of proportion') and to handle her job as the financial officer for a small biotechnology firm.

> I played a MUD man for two years. First I did it because I wanted the feeling of an equal playing field in terms of authority, and the only way I could think of to get it was to play a man. But after a while, I got very absorbed by MUDding. I became a wizard on a pretty simple MUD – I called myself Ulysses – and got involved in the system and realised that as a man I could be firm and people would think I was a great wizard. As a woman, drawing the line and standing firm has always made me feel like a bitch and, actually, I feel that people saw me as one, too. As a man I was liberated from all that. I learned from my mistakes. I got better at being firm but not rigid. I practiced, safe from criticism.

Zoe's perceptions of her gender trouble are almost the opposite of Case's. Case sees aggressiveness as acceptable only for women; Zoe sees it as acceptable only for men. Comparison with Garrett is also instructive. Like Case, Garrett associated feminine strength with positive feelings about his mother; Zoe associated feminine strength with loss of her father's love. What these stories have in common is that in all three cases, a virtual gender swap gave people greater emotional range in the real. Zoe says:

> I got really good at playing a man, so good that whoever was on the system would accept me as a man and talk to me as a man. So, other guys talked to Ulysses 'guy to guy'. It was very validating. All those years I was paranoid about how men talked about women. Or I thought I was paranoid. And then, I got a chance to be a guy and I saw that I wasn't paranoid at all. [9]

Zoe talked to me about her experiences in a face-to-face interview, but there is a great deal of spontaneous discussion of these issues on Internet bulletin boards and discussion groups. In her paper 'Gender Swapping on the Internet', Amy Bruckman tracks an ongoing discussion of gender issues on the electronic discussion group rec.games.mud.[10] Individuals may post to it, that is, send a communication to all subscribers. Postings on specific topics frequently start identifiable discussion 'threads', which may continue for many months.

On one of these threads, several male participants described how playing female characters had given them newfound empathy with women. One contributor, David, described the trials and tribulations of playing a female character:

> Other players start showering you with money to help you get started, and I had never once gotten a handout when playing a male player. And then they feel they should be allowed to tag along forever, and feel hurt when you leave them to go off and explore by yourself. Then when you give them the knee after they grope you, they wonder what your problem is, reciting that famous saying, 'What's your problem? It's only a game.'

Carol, an experienced player with much technical expertise about MUDs, concurred. She complained about male players' misconception that 'women can't play MUDs, can't work out puzzles, can't even type "kill monster" without help'. Carol noted that men offered help as a way to be ingratiating, but in her case this seduction strategy was ineffectual: 'People offering me help to solve puzzles *I* wrote are not going to get very far.'

Ellen, another contributor to the rec.games.mud discussion, tried gender-bending on an adventure-style MUD, thinking she would find out:

> if it was true that people would be nasty and kill me on sight and other stuff I'd heard about on r.g.m. [an abbreviation of rec.games-.mud]. But, no, everyone was helpful (I was truly clueless and needed the assistance); someone gave me enough money to buy a weapon and armor and someone else showed me where the easy-to-kill newbie [a new player] monsters were. They definitely went out of their way to be nice to a male-presenting newbie .... (These were all male-presenting players, btw [by the way].) One theory is that my male character [named Argyle and described as 'a short squat fellow who is looking for his socks'] was pretty innocuous. Maybe people are only nasty if you are 'a broad-shouldered perfect specimen of a man' or something of that nature, which can be taken as vaguely attacking.

Ellen concluded that harassment relates most directly to self-presentation: 'People are nice if they don't view you as a threat.' Short, squat, a bit lost, in search of socks, and thus connoting limpness – Argyle was clearly not a threat to the dominant status of other 'men' on the MUD. In the MUD culture Ellen played in, men tended to be competitive and aggressive toward each other; Argyle's non-threatening self-presentation earned him kind treatment.

For some men and women, gender-bending can be an attempt to understand better or to experiment safely with sexual orientation.[11] But for everyone who tries it, there is the chance to discover, as Rosalind and Orlando did in the Forest of Arden, that for both sexes, gender is constructed.[12]

VIRTUAL SEX

Virtual sex, whether in MUDs or in a private room on a commercial online service, consists of two or more players typing descriptions of physical actions, verbal statements, and emotional reactions for their characters. In cyberspace, this activity is not only common but, for many people, it is the centerpiece of their online experience. On MUDs, some people have sex as characters of their own gender. Others have sex as characters of the other gender. Some men play female personae to have netsex with men. And in the 'fake-lesbian syndrome', men adopt online female personae in order to have netsex with women.[13] Although it does not seem to be as widespread, I have met several women who say they present as male characters in order to have netsex with men. Some people have sex as non-human characters, for example, as animals on Furry-MUDs. Some enjoy sex with one partner. Some use virtual reality as a place to experiment with group situations. In real life, such behaviour (where possible) can create enormous practical and emotional confusion. Virtual adventures may be easier to undertake, but they can also result in significant complications. Different people and different couples deal with them in very different ways.

Martin and Beth, both 41, have been married for 19 years and have four children. Early in their marriage, Martin regretted not having had more time for sexual experimentation and had an extramarital affair. The affair hurt Beth deeply, and Martin decided he never wanted to do it again. When Martin discovered MUDs he was thrilled. 'I really am monogamous. I'm really not interested in something outside my marriage. But being able to have, you know, a Tiny romance is kind of cool.' Martin decided to tell Beth about his MUD sex life and she decided to tell him that she does not mind. Beth has made a conscious decision to consider Martin's sexual relationships on MUDs as more like his reading an erotic novel than like his having a rendezvous in a motel room. For Martin, his online affairs are a way to fill the gaps of his youth, to broaden his sexual experience without endangering his marriage.

Other partners of virtual adulterers do not share Beth's accepting attitude. Janet, 24, a secretary at a New York law firm, is very upset by her husband Tim's sex life in cyberspace. After Tim's first online affair, he confessed his virtual infidelity. When Janet objected, Tim told her that he would stop 'seeing' his online mistress. Janet says that she is not sure that he actually did stop:

> Look, I've got to say the thing that bothers me most is that he wants to do it in the first place. In some ways, I'd have an easier time understanding why he would want to have an affair in real life. At

> least there, I could say to myself, 'Well, it is for someone with a better body, or just for the novelty.' It's like the first kiss is always the best kiss. But in MUDding, he is saying that he wants that feeling of intimacy with someone else, the 'just talk' part of an encounter with a woman, and to me that comes closer to what is most important about sex. First I told him he couldn't do it any more. Then, I panicked and figured that he might do it anyway, because unlike in real life I could never find out. All these thousands of people all over the world with their stupid fake names ... no way I would ever find out. So, I pulled back and said that talking about it was strictly off limits. But now I don't know if that was the right decision. I feel paranoid whenever he is on the computer. I can't get it off my mind, that he is cheating, and he probably is tabulating data for his thesis. It must be clear that this sex thing has really hurt our marriage.

This distressed wife struggles to decide whether her husband is unfaithful when his persona collaborates on writing real-time erotica with another persona in cyberspace. And beyond this, should it make a difference if unbeknownst to the husband his cyberspace mistress turns out to be a 19-year-old male college freshman? What if 'she' is an infirm 80-year-old man in a nursing home? And even more disturbing, what if she is a 12-year-old girl? Or a 12-year-old boy?

TinySex poses the question of what is at the heart of sex and fidelity. Is it the physical action? Is it the feeling of emotional intimacy with someone other than one's primary partner? Is infidelity in the head or in the body? Is it in the desire or in the action? What constitutes the violation of trust? And to what extent and in what ways should it matter who the virtual sexual partner is in the real world? The fact that the physical body has been factored out of the situation makes these issues both subtler and harder to resolve than before.

Janet feels her trust has been violated by Tim's 'talk intimacy' with another woman. Beth, the wife who gave her husband Martin permission to have TinySex, feels that he violated her trust when he chose to play a female character having a sexual encounter with a 'man'. When Beth read the log of one of these sessions, she became angry that Martin had drawn on his knowledge of her sexual responses to play his female character.

For Rudy, 36, what was most threatening about his girlfriend's TinySex was the very fact that she wanted to play a character of the opposite sex at all. He discovered that she habitually plays men and has sex with female characters in chat rooms on America Online (like MUDs in that people can choose their identities). This discovery led him to break off the relationship. Rudy struggles to express what bothers him about his ex-girlfriend's gender-bending in cyberspace. He is not sure of himself, he is unhappy, hesitant, and confused. He says, 'We are not ready for the psychological confusion this technology can bring.' He explains:

> It's not the infidelity. It's the gnawing feeling that my girlfriend – I mean, I was thinking of marrying her – is a dyke. I know that everyone is bisexual, I know, I know ... but that is one of those things that I knew but it never had anything to do with me ... It was just intellectual. What I hate about the rooms on America Online is that it makes it so easy for this sort of thing to become real. Well, in the sense that the rooms are real. I mean, the rooms, real or not, make it too easy for people to explore these things. If she explored it in real life, well, it would be hard on me, but it would have been hard for her. If she really wanted to do it, she would do it, but it would have meant her going out and doing it. It seems like more of a statement. And if she had really done it, 1 would know what to make of it. Now, I hate her for what she does online, but I don't know if I'm being crazy to break up with her about something that, after all, is only words.

Rudy complained that virtual reality made it too easy for his girlfriend to explore what it might be like to have a sexual relationship with another woman, too easy for her to experience herself as a man, too easy to avoid the social consequences of her actions. MUDs provide a situation in which we can play out scenarios that otherwise might have remained pure fantasy. Yet the status of these fantasies-in-action in cyberspace is unclear. Although they involve other people and are no longer pure fantasy, they are not 'in the world'. Their boundary status offers new possibilities. TinySex and virtual gender-bending are part of the larger story of people using virtual spaces to construct identity. Nowhere is this more dramatic than in the lives of children and adolescents as they come of age in online culture. Online sexual relationships are one thing for those of us who are introduced to them as adults, but quite another for 12-year-olds who use the Internet to do their homework and then meet some friends to party in a MUD.

CHILDREN AND NETSEX

From around 10 years of age, in those circles where computers are readily available, social life involves online flirting, necking, petting, and going all the way. I have already introduced a 17-year-old whose virtual affair was causing him to think more about the imaginative, emotional, and conversational aspects of sex. His experience is not unusual. A 13-year-old girl informs me that she prefers to do her sexual experimentation online. Her partners are usually the boys in her class at school. In person, she says, it 'is mostly grope-y'. Online, 'They need to talk more.' A shy 14-year-old, Rob, tells me that he finds online flirting easier than flirting at school or at parties. At parties, there is pressure to dance close, kiss, and touch, all of which he both craves and dreads. He could be rejected or he could get physically excited, and 'that's worse', he says. If he has an erection while online, he is the only one who will know about it.

In the grownup world of engineering, there is criticism of text-based virtual reality as 'low bandwidth', but Rob says he is able to get 'more information' online than he would in person.

> Face to face, a girl doesn't always feel comfortable either. Like about not saying 'Stop' until they really mean *'Stop there! Now!'* But it would be less embarrassing if you got more signals like about more or less when to stop. I think girls online are more communicative.

And online, he adds, 'I am able to talk with a girl all afternoon – and not even try anything [sexual] and it does not seem weird. It [online conversation] lends itself to telling stories, gossiping; much more so than when you are trying to talk at a party.'

A 13-year-old girl says that she finds it easier to establish relationships online and then pursue them offline. She has a boyfriend and feels closer to him when they send electronic mail or talk in a chat room than when they see each other in person. Their online caresses make real ones seem less strained. Such testimony supports Rob's descriptions of online adolescent sexual life as less pressured than that in RL. But here, as in other aspects of cyberlife, things can cut both ways. A 12-year-old girl files this mixed report on junior high school cyber-romance:

> Usually, the boys are gross. Because you can't see them, they think they can say whatever they want. But other times, we just talk, or it's just [virtual] kissing and asking if they can touch your breast or put their tongue in your mouth.

I ask her if she thinks that online sexual activity has changed things for her. She says that she has learned more from 'older kids' whom she wouldn't normally have been able to hang out with. I ask her if she has ever been approached by someone she believes to be an adult. She says no, but then adds: 'Well, now I sometimes go online and say that I am 18, so if I do that more it will probably happen.' I ask her if she is concerned about this. She makes it very clear that she feels safe because she can always just 'disconnect'.

There is no question that the Internet, like other environments where children congregate – playgrounds, scout troops, schools, shopping malls – is a place where they can be harassed or psychologically abused by each other and by adults. But parental panic about the dangers of cyberspace is often linked to their unfamiliarity with it. As one parent put it, 'I sign up for the [Internet] account, but I can barely use e-mail while my (14-year-old] daughter tells me that she is finding neat home pages [on the World Wide Web] in Australia.'

Many of the fears we have for our children – the unsafe neighbourhoods, the drugs on the street, the violence in the schools, our inability to spend as much time with them as we wish to – are displaced onto those unknowns we feel we can control. Fifteen years ago, when children ran to personal computers with arms outstretched while parents approached with hands behind their backs, there was much talk about computers as addicting and hypnotic. These days, the Internet is the new unknown.

Parents need to be able to talk to their children about where they are going and what they are doing. This same commonsense rule applies to their children's lives on the screen. Parents don't have to become technical experts, but they do need to learn enough about computer networks to discuss with their children what and who is out there and lay down some basic safety rules. The children who do best after a bad experience on the Internet (who are harassed, perhaps even propositioned) are those who can talk to their parents, just as children who best handle bad experiences in real life are those who can talk to a trusted elder without shame or fear of blame.

DECEPTION

Life on the screen makes it very easy to present oneself as other than one is in real life. And although some people think that representing oneself as other than one is is always a deception, many people turn to online life with the intention of playing it in precisely this way. They insist that a certain amount of shape-shifting is part of the online game. When people become intimate, they are particularly vulnerable; it is easy to get hurt in online relationships. But since the rules of conduct are unclear, it is also easy to believe that one does not have the right to feel wounded. For what can we hold ourselves and others accountable?

In cyberculture, a story that became known as the 'case of the electronic lover' has taken on near legendary status. Like many stories that become legends, it has several versions. There were real events, but some tellings of the legend conflate several similar incidents. In all the versions, a male psychiatrist usually called Alex becomes an active member of a CompuServe chat line using the name of a woman, usually Joan. In one version of the story, his deception began inadvertently when Alex, using the computer nickname Shrink, Inc., found that he was conversing with a woman who assumed he was a female psychiatrist. Alex was stunned by the power and intimacy of this conversation. He found that the woman was more open with him than were his female patients and friends in real life.[14] Alex wanted more and soon began regularly logging on as Joan, a severely handicapped and disfigured Manhattan resident. (Joan said it was her embarrassment about her disfigurement that made her prefer not to meet her cyberfriends face to face.) As Alex expected, Joan was able to have relationships of great intimacy with 'other' women on the computer service. Alex came to believe that it was as Joan that he could best help these women. He was encouraged in this belief by his online female friends. They were devoted to Joan and told her how central she had become to their lives.

In most versions of the story, Joan's handicap plays an important role. Not only did it provide her with an alibi for restricting her contacts to online communication, but it gave focus to her way of helping other people. Joan's fighting spirit and ability to surmount her handicaps served as an inspiration. She was married to a policeman and their relationship gave other disabled women hope that they, too, could be loved. Despite her handicaps, Joan was lusty, funny, a woman of appetites.

As time went on and relationships deepened, several of Joan's grateful online friends wanted to meet her in person, and Alex realised that his game was getting out of control. He decided that Joan had to die. Joan's 'husband' got online and informed the community that Joan was ill and in the hospital. Alex was overwhelmed by the outpouring of sympathy and love for Joan. Joan's friends told her husband how important Joan was to them. They offered moral support, financial assistance, names of specialists who might help. Alex was in a panic. He could not decide whether to kill Joan off. In one account of the story, 'For four long days Joan hovered between life and death.'[15] Finally, Alex had Joan recover. But the virtual had bled into the real. Joan's 'husband' had been pressed for the name of the hospital where Joan was staying so that cards and flowers could be sent.

Alex gave the name of the hospital where he worked as a psychiatrist. One member of the bulletin board called the hospital to confirm its address and discovered that Joan was not there as a patient. The ruse began to unravel.

All the versions of the story have one more thing in common: the discovery of Alex's deception led to shock and outrage. In some versions of the story, the anger erupts because of the initial deception – that a man had posed as a woman, that a man had won confidences as a woman. The case presents an electronic version of the movie *Tootsie*, in which a man posing as a woman wins the confidence of another woman and then, when he is found out, her fury. In other versions, the anger centres on the fact that Joan had introduced some of her online women friends to lesbian netsex, and the women involved felt violated by Joan's virtual actions. These women believed they were making love with a woman, but in fact they were sharing intimacies with a man. In other accounts, Joan introduced online friends to Alex, a Manhattan psychiatrist, who had real-life affairs with several of them.[16] In these versions, the story of the electronic lover becomes a tale of real-life transgression.

The con artist is a stock character who may be appreciated for his charm in fictional presentations, but in real life is more often reviled for his duplicity and exploitiveness. In this sense, Alex was operating as part of a long tradition. But when familiar phenomena appear in virtual form, they provoke new questions. Was the reclusive, inhibited Alex only pretending to have the personality of the sunny, outgoing, lusty Joan? What was his real personality? Did Joan help her many disabled online friends who became more active because of her inspiration? When and how did Alex cross the line from virtual friend and helper to con artist? Was it when he dated Joan's friends? Was it when he had sexual relations with them? Or was it from the moment that Alex decided to pose as a woman? At a certain point, traditional categories for sorting things out seem inadequate.

In the past 15 years, I have noticed a distinct shift in people's way of talking about the case of the electronic lover. In the early 1980s, close to the time when the events first took place, people were most disturbed by the idea that a man had posed as a woman. By 1990,1 began to hear more complaints about Joan's online lesbian sex. What most shocks today's audience is that Alex used Joan to pimp for him. The shock value of online gender-bending has faded. Today what disturbs us is when the shifting norms of the virtual world bleed into real life.

In 1993, the WELL computer network was torn apart by controversy over another electronic lover where the focus was on these shifting norms and the confusion of the real and the virtual. The WELL has a 'Women's Only' forum where several women compared notes on their love lives in cyberspace. They realised that they had been seduced and abandoned (some only virtually, some also in the flesh) by the same man, whom one called a 'cyber-cad'. As they discussed the matter with more and more women, they found out that Mr X's activities were far more extensive and had a certain consistency. He romanced women via electronic mail and telephone calls, swore them to secrecy about their relationship, and even flew across the country to visit one of them in Sausalito, California. But then he dropped them. One of the women created a topic (area for discussion) on the WELL entitled 'Do You Know this Cyber ScamArtist?' Within ten days, nearly one thousand messages had been posted about the outing of Mr X. Some supported the women, some observed that the whole topic seemed like a 'high-tech lynching'.[17]

At the time of the incident and its widespread reporting in the popular media, I was interviewing people about online romance. The story frequently came up. For those who saw a transgression it was that Mr X had confused cyberworld and RL. It was not just that he used the relationships formed in the cyberworld to misbehave in RL. It was that he treated the relationships in the cyberworld as though they were RL relationships. A complex typology of relationships began to emerge from these conversations: real-life relationships, virtual relationships with the 'real' person, and virtual relationships with a virtual other. A 35-year-old woman real estate broker tried hard to make clear how these things needed to be kept distinct:

> In a MUD, or chat room, or on IRC, it might be OK to have different flings with other people hiding behind other handles. But this man was coming on to these women as though he was interested in them

> really – I mean he said he was falling in love with them, with the real women. And he even did meet – and dump – some. Do you see the difference, from the beginning he didn't respect that online is its own place.

Mr X himself did not agree that he had done anything wrong. He told the computer network that although he had been involved in multiple, simultaneous consensual relationships, he believed that the rules of cyberspace permitted that. Perhaps they do. But even if they do, the boundaries between the virtual and real are staunchly protected. Having sex with several characters on MUDs is one thing, but in a virtual community such as the WELL, most people are creating an electronic persona that they experience as co-extensive with their physically embodied one. There, promiscuity can be another thing altogether.

Once we take virtuality seriously as a way of life, we need a new language for talking about the simplest things. Each individual must ask: What is the nature of my relationships? What are the limits of my responsibility? And even more basic: Who and what am I? What is the connection between my physical and virtual bodies? And is it different in different cyberspaces? These questions are framed to interrogate an individual, but with minor modifications, they are equally central for thinking about community. What is the nature of our social ties? What kind of accountability do we have for our actions in real life and in cyberspace? What kind of society or societies are we creating, both on and off the screen?

BEING DIGITAL

In this chapter we have seen people doing what they have always done: trying to understand themselves and improve their lives by using the materials they have at hand. Although this practice is familiar, the fact that these materials now include the ability to live through virtual personae means two fundamental changes have occurred in our situation. We can easily move through multiple identities, and we can embrace – or be trapped by – cyberspace as a way of life.

As more and more people have logged on to this new way of life and have experienced the effects of virtuality, a genre of cultural criticism is emerging to interpret these phenomena.

An article in the *New York Times* described new books on the subject by dividing them into three categories: utopian, utilitarian, and apocalyptic.[18] Utilitarian writers emphasise the practical side of the new way of life. Apocalyptic writers warn us of increasing social and personal fragmentation, more widespread surveillance, and loss of direct knowledge of the world. To date, however, the utopian approaches have dominated the field. They share the technological optimism that has dominated post-war culture, an optimism captured in the advertising slogans of my youth: 'Better living through chemistry', 'Progress is our most important product'. In our current situation, technological optimism tends to represent urban decay, social alienation and economic polarisation as out-of-date formulations of a problem that could be solved if appropriate technology were applied in sufficient doses, for example, technology that would link everyone to the 'information superhighway'.

We all want to believe in some quick and relatively inexpensive solution to our difficulties. We are tempted to believe with the utopians that the Internet is a field for the flowering of participatory democracy and a medium for the transformation of education. We are tempted to share in the utopians' excitement at the prospect of virtual pleasures: sex with a distant partner, travel minus the risks and inconvenience of actually having to go anywhere.

The new practice of entering virtual worlds raises fundamental questions about our communities and ourselves. For every step forward in the instrumental use of a technology (what the technology can do for us), there are subjective effects. The technology changes us as people, changes our relationships and sense of ourselves. The issues raised by the new way of life are difficult and painful, because they strike at the heart of our most complex and intransigent social problems: problems of community, identity, governance, equity and values. There is no simple good news or bad news.

Although it provides us with no easy answers, life online does provide new lenses through which to examine current complexities. Unless we take advantage of these new lenses and carefully analyse our situation, we shall cede the future to those who want to believe that simple fixes can solve complicated problems. Given the history of the last century, thoughts of such a future are hardly inspiring.

NOTES

1. This chapter was first published in Sherry Turkle, *Life on the Screen*, Simon and Schuster, New York, 1995, and subsequently in a paperback edition in Great Britain by Phoenix, a division of Orion books. Liberty would like to thank Professor Turkle and Orion books for permission to reprint it here.
2. For a general introduction to LambdaMOO and MUDding, see Pavel Curtis, 'Mudding: Social Phenomena in Text-Based Virtual Realities', available via anonymous ftp://parcftp.xerox.com/pub/MOO/papers/DIAC92; Amy Bruckman: Identity Workshop, Emergent Social and Psychological Phenomena in Text Based Virtual Reality, unpub ms, March 1992, available via anonynous ftp://media.mit.edu/pub/asb/papers/identity/workshop; and the chapter in MUDs in Howard Rheingold's *Virtual Community: Homesteading on the Electronic Frontier*, (New York: Addison Wesley, 1993). On virtual community in general, see Allucquere Roseanne Stone, 'Will the real body please stand up? Boundary Stories About Virtual Cultures', in Michael Benedikt (ed.) *Cyberspace: First Steps*, (Cambridge, Mass: MIT Press, 1992), pp. 81–118.
3. At the time, I noted that I felt panicky when female or female-presenting characters approached the gender-neutral me on the MUD and waved seductively. And I noted this with considerable irritation. Surely, I thought, my many years of psychoanalysis should see me through this experience with greater equanimity. They did not.
4. Pavel Curtis, op. cit.
5. Allucquere Rosanne Stone, presentation at 'Doing Gender on the Net' Conference, Massachussetts Insititute of Technology, Cambridge, Mass, 1995.
6. The term gender trouble is borrowed from Judith Butler, whose classic work on the problematics of gender informs this chapter. See Judith P. Butler, *Gender Trouble: Feminism and the Subversion of Identity* (New York: Routledge, 1990).
7. My thanks to Ilona Isaacson Bell for pointing me to this rich example.
8. William Shakespeare, *As You Like It*, Act I, Scene 3, lines 107–18.
9. Zoe does not MUD any more. She gave me two reasons. First, her MUDding succeeded in making her more assertive at work. Second, she doesn't want her MUDding to succeed in making her too much more assertive at home.

   I guess I got what I wanted out of MUDs. When I go to work I try to act like my MUD character, but that character is really a part of me now.

Well, more like a role model that I've had as a roommate. Not just as a teacher, but [someone] I actually lived with. For two years I did Ulysses for thirty hours a week, so it isn't so hard to do it for a few hours a week during meetings at work or on the phone with clients. But I didn't go all the way with Ulysses. It started to feel dangerous to me. My marriage is still pretty traditional. I am better at talking about my feelings and I think my husband respects me, but he is still Southern. He still likes the feeling of being superior. We need the money so my husband doesn't mind my working. But I do treat my husband more or less the way my father would have wanted me to. I want to have children. If I brought Ulysses home, it would upset my marriage. I don't want that to happen. I'm not ready for that now. Maybe someday, but not now.

10. With the increasing popularity of MUDding, this group has split up into many different groups, each looking at different aspects of MUDding: administrative, social, technical.
11. People feel different degrees of safety. Most MUDders know responsibility involves not logging sexual encounters and then posting them to public bulletin boards.

On an Internet bulletin board dedicated to MUDding, a posting of Frequently Asked Questions described Tinysex as speedwriting interactive erotica and warned players to participate with caution both because there might be some deception in play and because there might be the virtual equivalent of a photographer in the motel room.

> Realise that the other party is not obligated to be anything like he/she says, and in fact may be playing a joke on you (see log below).
>
> What is a log?
>
> Certain client programs allow logs to be kept off the screen. A time-worn and somewhat unfriendly trick is to entice someone into having TinySex with you, log the proceedings, and post them to rec.games.mud and have a good laugh at the other person's expense. Logs are useful for recording interesting or useful information or conversations, as well.
> [Jennifer Moira Smith, MUDFAQ, 1 December 1992.] This document posted regularly on rec.games.mud.tiny.

This last response refers to a client program. This is one of a class of programs that facilitate MUDding. A client program stands between a user's computer and the MUD, performing helpful housekeeping functions such as keeping MUD interchanges on different lines. Without a client program, a user's screen can look like a tangle of MUD instructions and player comments. With a client program a user's screen is relatively easy to read.

12. One of the things that has come out of people having virtual experiences as different genders is that many have acquired a new sense of gender as a continuum. In an online discussion the media theorist Brenda Laurel noted that media such as film, radio and television advertised the idea that sex and gender were identical and that the universe was bi-gendered. Brenda Laurel, The WELL, Conference On Virtual Reality (vr47.255), 15 January 1993.

13. Since many more men adopt a female persona than vice versa, some have suggested that gender-bending is yet another way in which men assert domination over female bodies. I thank my student Adrian Banard for his insights on this question. The point was also made by Alluquere Roseanne Stone, Presentation at 'Doing Gender on the Net' Conference, MIT, Cambridge, Mass, 7 April 1995.
14. Lindsay van Gelder. 'The Strange Case of the Electronic Lover', in Charles Dunlop and Rob Kling (eds) *Computerization and Controversy: Value Conflicts and Social Choices,* (Boston: Academic Press, 1991), pp. 366–7.
15. Allucquere Roseanne Stone, Presentation at 'Doing Gender on the Net' Conference, MIT, Cambridge, Mass, 7 April 1995.
16. Lindsay van Gelder, 'The Strange Case of the Electronic Lover', p. 372.
17. John Schwartz of the *Washington Post* reported that:

    In a telephone conversation, Mr X (who spoke on the condition of anonymity) again tried to put events in perspective. The cycle of fury and resentment and anger instantaneously transmitted, created this kind of independent entity ... These people went after me with virtual torches and strung me up. The emotional response is entirely out of proportion to what actually happened. It involved distortions and lies about what I did or did not do. I was wrong, he said. The cyber world is the same as the real world... I should have realised that the exact same standards should have applied. Mr X later announced that he would be leaving the WELL. He had already been shunned.
    [John Schwartz, 'On-line Lotharios Antics Prompt Debate on Cyber Age Ethics', *Washington Post*, 11 July 1993: A1.]

    I thank Tina Taylor of Brandeis University for pointing out to me in this case, as in others, the complex position of the virtual body. The virtual body is not always the same. It, too, is constructed by context. A virtual body in a MUD is not the same as a virtual body on IRC or on the WELL.
18. Steve Lohr, 'The Meaning of Digital Life', *New York Times*, 24 April 1995.

13 The Governance of Cyberspace: Racism on the Internet*

David Capitanchik and Michael Whine

The potential of the so-called 'Superhighway' to inform, educate, entertain and conduct business on a world-wide scale has caught the imagination of millions. At a relatively modest cost, and often at no cost at all, vast quantities of data can be transmitted around the globe – a multimedia form of communication combining all hitherto known means such as printing, the telephone, photography, radio and video. All that is required is a relatively cheap personal computer, a telephone line and a modem or connection to a cable operator.

Among other things, the Internet has provided a vast range of political parties and pressure groups with the unprecedented opportunity to disseminate their publications and messages to an international public, and even to interact with them on a one-to-one basis. The benefits of the Internet, it must be said, far outweigh its negative aspects. Nevertheless, these cannot be ignored.

In this chapter, we consider the current debates about free speech on the Internet and the issues raised by its exploitation by anti-Semitic and racist groups. Much attention has focused on the presence of pornography on the Net, especially in the so-called 'First Amendment' controversies in the US. However, in most European countries and around the world, incitement to racial hatred is also a criminal offence. To many, its appearance on the Internet is just as disturbing.

Although it has received less attention than pornography, 'hate' material, in the form of attractive Web pages and discussion groups or sent by e-mail, not only offends, but also seriously threatens racial harmony and provides neo-Nazis with the means to communicate, organise and distribute material which is illegal in jurisdictions other than that of the US.

The Internet has now emerged from the university laboratory into the public domain and the numbers of those with access to its various facilities are booming. Access to the Internet is provided for the domestic user by major international companies as well as in universities, colleges, and increasingly in schools.

This chapter concludes that because of its ubiquitous nature and, above all, its appeal to young people, it is essential now to formulate an Internet policy. It proposes a number of policy recommendations for organisations in the public, private and voluntary sectors which provide access to the Internet.

The Internet is probably the most powerful medium of communication to have been developed to date. Gutenberg's invention of the printing press gave to the many access to information and knowledge that was previously confined to a select few. The telephone made instantaneous communication possible regardless of the distance between the communicators. Now the Internet provides people with information unmediated by what publishers decide to print or the limitations of one-to-one communication by telephone.

This is a new dimension – an electronic, virtual world where time and space have almost no meaning. People in geographically distant lands communicate across time zones without ever seeing each other, and information is available 24 hours a day from thousands of places. The implications of this new global communication and information system are staggering.

In the early 1990s, the savings to be made from electronic mail (e-mail) alone were enough to encourage businesses, universities and many other organisations to invest heavily in the necessary equipment and network connections. By the spring of 1995, the number of people who could send an Internet e-mail message was widely acknowledged to be in excess of 32 million.

Electronic mail, however, is only one of the services the Internet provides. In fact it can deliver anything you can put into binary digits, which are simply bits of information flowing down wires. Already these include text, graphics, voices, music, radio broadcasts, digital photographs and moving video, and all can be readily accessed by means of a relatively low-cost personal computer and modem.[1]

THE INTERNET DEBATE

Inevitably, this powerful and ubiquitous medium has given rise to concern about its impact on thought and behaviour, and it should not be surprising that there is growing anxiety about the use of the Internet for undesirable anti-social purposes.

Pornography, according to a recent newspaper article, is fast becoming what the Internet is best known for.[2] Its dissemination has been the focus of much attention, if only because the Internet is accessed so easily by young people. Most of the material to be found on the Internet, however, originates in the US where the law and Constitution have been interpreted as upholding the right to virtually unlimited free speech. The Internet has become a First Amendment battleground. In particular, whether the Constitution protects repugnant or defamatory speech in this new medium has been the subject of controversy.

Elsewhere in the world such a defence does not exist. Most countries have strict laws against the publication and distribution, by any means, of pornographic and other anti-social material. Britain has seen its first successful prosecution and imprisonment of an individual for downloading pornography online.

In general, across the world there are signs of growing alarm among governments about pornography and other undesirable material on the Internet. According to a recent newspaper report, Germany is conducting an investigation of online services including America Online (AOL), the world's biggest, to see if such services 'can be held responsible for the material carried on their networks'. According to the German Research and Technology Minister Jurgen Ruttgers, Bonn respects free speech, but cannot tolerate a free-for-all on the Internet. Ruttgers wants to make it impossible to download child pornography 'and neo-Nazi diatribes such as Toronto-based Ernst Zündel's article "Did 6 Million Really Die?", which is illegal in Germany, but freely available on the

Internet'.[3]

Impressionable young people, whose manifest technology and communications skills mark them as potential leaders of the next generation, are obvious targets for political extremists using the Internet to avoid legal sanctions. Anxiety about this has been heightened by the increasing utilisation of the Internet by neo-Nazis intent on spreading race hate material.

Racist material on the Internet has not, until now, been subject to the same supervision as pornography and this has provided previously undreamed of opportunities for racists, terrorists and other extreme elements to promote their aims and ideals and to access each other's ideas and resources.

It is in the nature of the Internet that it is difficult to monitor. Its size and the ease by which the origins of messages can be disguised ensure that no agency has been willing or able to devote significant time or resources to investigate so-called 'hate' material. Neither the FBI nor the Metropolitan Police in the UK regularly monitor race hate bulletin boards (electronic notice boards), although the latter have recently confirmed that there has been internal discussion about the matter.[4] A first prosecution may be in the offing, however, following police raids on the homes of Nationalist Socialist Movement leaders David Myatt and Steven Sergant after complaints about their Website. Somewhat belatedly American government agencies have been investigating the publication of bomb-making manuals on the Net.[5] The German Office for the Protection of the Constitution (BfV) has noted the use being made of the Internet, and other electronic means of communication, to evade state surveillance.[6] It can be assumed, therefore, that they have been monitoring the Internet, at least for counter-terrorism purposes.

Concern appears to be growing about the provision of facilities for racist groups to access the Internet either deliberately, by non-racists acting on behalf of free speech, or inadvertently, by reputable companies unaware that their Internet publicity material might be just a 'click away' from the sites of hate organisations.

Some of America's leading universities, it seems, are being used by free speech activists to make Nazi propaganda available in Germany. A recent newspaper article states that through the activities of such activists the University of California, Carnegie-Mellon University and the Massachusetts Institute of Technology (MIT) have all become hosts to copies of a Nazi Website carrying Ernst Zündel's Holocaust-denial material which is illegal in Germany and to which the German telecommunications authorities have been trying to block access.

While many may accept the presence of neo-Nazis on the Internet as the price of free speech, it is doubtful whether reputable business organisations would welcome their logos appearing in such close proximity to hate groups as to create the appearance of sponsorship. This has been the subject of an article on Time-Warner's Pathfinder site on the Internet, which discusses a commercial Hollywood site called GeoCities. GeoCities offers 'Premier Communities' in the form of free pages for its users. Known as 'virtual homesteaders', some 25,000 groups have set up pages, the politically active ones residing in a 'Community' called 'Capitol Hill', which is devoted to political and national affairs.[7]

GeoCities' commercial sponsors are probably unaware that their banners are adorning sites which include, among others, Tom Metzger's White Racist Web Page, the New Aryan Movement, Zionwatch, the National Party, Independent White Racialists, Blood and Honour, and the Hate Page. The Resistance Records Home Page, which sells White Power records, will take credit card orders and the trademarks of both Visa and Mastercard are prominently displayed. They appear a few inches only below SS-style death skulls and record titles like 'Aryan New Storm Rising'.

THE FAR RIGHT AND THE INTERNET

The term 'far right' is generally used to describe groups with a neo-Nazi or radical nationalist and racist ideology or pedigree. Many of these groups regard themselves as successors to the Nazi regime of Hitler's Third Reich; others, especially in the US, are more influenced by the radical racist nationalism of national revolutionaries such as Julius Evola, and Georg and Gregor

Strasser. Still others follow the 'leaderless resistance' ideology of Louis Beam, formerly of the Ku Klux Klan, now of the Aryan Nations.

Skinheads have also been utilising the Internet for various purposes, although they have a less intellectual outlook. For them, Jews, anti-fascists and foreign workers are all 'scum' to be harassed, expelled or murdered; the vilification of 'others' serves to define their own identity in an ever-changing world. The membership and number of violent crimes attributed to skinhead groups have been rising fast. The Anti-Defamation League estimates that there are some 70,000 committed 'skins' around the world with branches active in 33 countries including New Zealand and Japan.[8] According to the anti-racist group Klanwatch, the likelihood of violence is enormous when skinheads get organised and the Internet is enabling them to get organised as they have never been before.[9]

For the far right the Internet is of considerable and far-reaching significance:

> The unique nature of the Internet makes this the information battle-ground of the future ... by contrast television and radio require the creation of broadcast quality programmes, and reaching listeners and viewers is tied to the amount of money one can afford to spend. Books, magazines and other printed materials are durable and inexpensive, but no way near so freely available, and can be confiscated by oppressive governments ... Internet users, though, enjoy free access to virtually all information on the system and new features are becoming available to allow researchers ... to find everything on the Internet in their areas of interest.[10]

Holocaust denial is the link which binds many far-right organisations. The denial of historical truth and the Nazis' crimes against humanity have been made a priority by today's neo-Nazis. Fifty years after the end of the Second World War they are seeking to re-establish their political legitimacy and they therefore portray the Nazi crimes as a myth or they belittle them in order to gain the support of a new generation.

During 1993, intense Holocaust-denial propaganda coupled with vehement anti-Semitism were published on the Swedish bulletin board FidoNet by two individuals using the aliases 'Fritz Goldman' and 'Oscar Andersson'. The former also uploaded a denial file to several bulletin boards which included an accurate Swedish translation of the Leuchter Report. This report is a major denial publication by Fred Leuchter, a self-proclaimed gas chamber expert, who claimed to have carried out a forensic examination of the gas chambers at Auschwitz from which he concluded that there were insufficient traces of cyanide for there ever to have been mass gassings of Jews. A subsequent court case in his home state of Massachusetts exposed Leuchter's lies. He has been expelled from the UK and a short time later he was fined and expelled from Germany. He was due to stand trial in Mannheim in September 1994 on other charges, but failed to return from America.

THE INTERNET AS A MEANS OF COMMUNICATION

So-called 'hotlines' and bulletin boards serve also as a means of communication between far-right groups. The Internet, and e-mail in particular, are now used extensively to provide local and international communications for the price of a local call.

According to a press article, two leading figures in the Scottish Anti-Nazi League were subjected to a campaign of telephone death threats from neo-Nazis after their names appeared online. This appears to be the first example of the use of the Internet for this purpose in the UK.[11]

On the whole, British neo-Nazis tend to be markedly less sophisticated and organised than their foreign counterparts, while German neo-Nazis are known to have been developing inter-computer communications since 1980. The so-called Thule Network was developed specifically to allow different German neo-Nazi groups to communicate with one another.[12]

The computer magazine *Chip* estimates that about 1,500 German far-right extremists are active on the Thule Network. This consists of at least 12 bulletin boards, and derives its name from the small elite 1920s movement considered to be the forerunner of the Nazi Party. Names of anti-fascist activists, code-named 'Zecken' (Ticks), as well as judges and journalists, can also be obtained. Code-names such as 'schöne Mädchen' (beautiful girls) have also been used to refer to the police.[13] It is believed that the Thule Network is located in Baden-Württemberg, Bavaria and North Rhine-Westphalia.

The precise planning of German neo-Nazis, and their strategy of remaining in small groups rather than amalgamating with one or two large umbrella organisations, has been facilitated by the use of the Internet.

> Police have recently been baffled by the precise, military-style planning of neo-Nazi actions. Provided with passwords such as Germania or Endsieg (final victory), from a post office box, personal computer schemes will display a calendar of forthcoming neo-Nazi events and list contact numbers of leading right wingers ... On Remembrance Sunday police saw in action, for the first time, computer-planned coordinated neo-Nazi action, involving the widespread use of secret codes and radio communication ... 'The advantage of electronic mail boxes is that they are free of censorship and bug-proof', said Karl-Heinz Sendbuhler of the National Democratic Party.[14]

PUBLICATION OF CONTACT LISTS AND HATE ARTICLES

The far right also uses the Internet for the publication of contact lists. Liberty Lobby, a major American racist organisation which funds other groups, sponsors the Logoplex bulletin board. Cyberspace Minuteman appears to be the most active American bulletin board and it is said to act as a contact point for much of the far right in the US, and possibly Europe. The neo-Nazi British National Party has a contact on it who uses the name 'D Man 1'.

The Internet is also being used to publish 'hate' articles. A not untypical example is entitled 'Rothschild – the Head of the Beast', which attacks the Rothschild family in terms similar to those used in classic pre-Second World War anti-Semitic texts:

> You must realize too that Rothschild agents are like cockroaches crawling around your home. These cockroaches crawl all over

> Europe, they are everywhere. They are all around the world: in the United States, in Europe, Asia, Africa, Japan and the Orient. They are constantly manoeuvring and working for the Rothschild purposes ...
>
> When this source speaks of the Rothschild purposes, it refers to those cohorts, the other twelve superworld families that associate or ride the coat tails of the Rothschilds.[15]

TERRORISM ON THE INTERNET

Bomb-making manuals have also been transmitted by computer links, although it is not certain whether via the Internet. What is certain is that much of this material emanates from the US, where the NSDAP-AO transmitted bomb-making plans in its magazine *Endsieg* by modem to Austria, Germany, France and Holland and one issue featured a bomb-making manual. It might have been from this manual that Austrian Nazis were able to construct the bombs used in the wave of terror attacks that took place throughout Austria in 1994 and in early 1995 after the imprisonment of the Austrian Nazi leader Gottfried Kussel.

REGULATING THE INTERNET

The Internet's global reach presents a seemingly insurmountable challenge to would-be regulators. As things stand, the Internet relies on the good sense of users to deal with those who 'abuse' its self-proclaimed ethos for their unacceptable ends. This anarchic situation allows neither the deletion of supposedly unacceptable messages, nor does it prevent further unacceptable messages from being posted. However, as the author of an article in *MacUser* magazine argued, cyberspace is not set apart from society, it is part of it.

> Virtual conferencing has real world results. Organised groups of fascists may be operating in a virtual environment but they intend actual physical harm to other people. That is why there should be no place for these groups in cyberspace.

She goes on to argue that users should use the freedom that is being defended to exercise some direct control: 'If there are Nazis in a conference you are joined to, drive them out.'[16]

The suggestion that the senders of hate messages be 'flamed out' by other users, that is, that their machines be bombarded with thousands of messages, even blank pages, thus tying up their phone lines, exhausting their fax machines and ultimately disabling their computers, is no long-term solution, although it has its appeal:

> The other day I encountered my first Nazi on the 'Net', a madman shouting hate. You know what happened? A bunch of Internet citizens ran him out of town. Chased him away, sent him packing. Gave him the big heave-ho.[17]

The practice of 'flaming' is

> a dangerous invitation to digital vigilantism and promiscuous computer violence. It turns cyberspace into a rude, lawless frontier town in which everyone carries a six-shooter and exacts his own revenge ... There is no discourse when everyone is free to interrupt and no one is appointed to keep order. No human activity can long remain unregulated ... Internet too is a form of human behaviour. Computers and modems do not remove them from the human orbit.[18]

Clearly the situation that has occurred recently where racists have broken into electronic mail accounts and fired off hate messages falls within the terms of the British Computer Misuse Act 1995. In 1994, at Middlesex University in the UK, the e-mail account of the University's Jewish Society was used to transmit racist messages. In an internal memorandum, Professor Michael Driscoll, Dean of the University, threatened disciplinary action, including exclusion, for the culprits.

In the UK there are legal provisions which can be used to prosecute those who transmit hate material; the authorities until recently failed to use these for fear of failing to secure convictions by juries. However, academic and practising lawyers and the police suggest that the provisions of Part III of the Public Order Act 1986 might be relevant where hate material, or Holocaust-denial material, is transmitted with the intention of inciting hatred against a group defined by reference to their colour, race or nationality, ethnic or national origins.

- Section 19 makes it an offence to publish or distribute written material where the intention is to stir up racial hatred.
- Section 21 makes it an offence to distribute visual images likely to incite racial hatred.
- Section 22 makes an attempt to broadcast threatening, abusive or insulting visual images or sounds on a cable programme service an offence.
- Section 23 makes it an offence to possess written material which is threatening, abusive or insulting or record visual images or sounds which are abusive or insulting, where it is intended that racial hatred be stirred up.

The Malicious Communications Act 1988 makes it an offence to send to another person:

- a letter or other article which conveys a message which is indecent or grossly offensive; a threat; or information which is false or known or believed to be false; or
- any other article which is, in whole or part, of an indecent or grossly offensive nature.

Section 43 (1) of the Telecommunications Act 1984 makes it an offence to send by means of a public telecommunications system a message that is grossly offensive or of an indecent, obscene or menacing character.

While there is no case law on the matter, the view of those consulted is that the medium by which the insulting message is transmitted is immaterial, and that a criminal prosecution of material on the Internet is possible provided that all evidential requirements are met.

Again, the view of those consulted is that the distribution of prosecutable information downloaded from a computer in Britain would be an offence, and therefore the owners of such host machines would have to consider their legal positions. The sending of such e-mail either internally or from this country abroad, while technically an offence, would be hard if not impossible to monitor, and therefore is unlikely to result in a prosecution.

Likewise, the receipt in this country of material sent from abroad would similarly be an offence, albeit hard, if not impossible, to prosecute. If, however, the material is subsequently transmitted or distributed by non-electronic methods, or if a UK-based recipient complains, a prosecution might be possible. The storage of such material in a physical computer might be considered akin to being in the public arena as are paper, video tapes and audio tapes, whereas the use of the Internet for communication is more ephemeral, as are telephone and face-to-face conversations.

Denial of the Holocaust, the glorification of the Nazi Third Reich, the falsification of history and the publication of Nazi and or racist literature are illegal in some European countries. An examination of each country's domestic legislation would be necessary to ascertain whether the definition of the mode of distribution includes or excludes e-mail and the Internet.

There is no case law in international law, but both the International Covenant on Civil and Political Rights and the Convention on the Elimination of all Forms of Racial Discrimination prohibit the incitement of race hatred, and these would also apply to the Internet.

CONCLUSION

For dedicated enthusiasts, the Internet exists within a virtual world of unregulated computer networks where the right to free speech is unlimited and no restrictive rules apply. In the real world, of course, societies have long-standing traditions and laws which they will inevitably seek to uphold. The rapid popularisation of the Internet – its emergence from the university research environment into the public domain – has provoked intense debate whenever legislators have sought to apply the same limitations on freedom of expression in cyberspace as exist in relation to the other electronic and printed media.

In all its various components, whether e-mail, the World Wide Web, bulletin boards or newsgroups, the Internet carries vast quantities of material, much of it of considerable value, and some – a much smaller amount – either useless or repugnant. The so-called 'superhighway' is utilised by a large and rapidly increasing number of business and commercial organisations worldwide; in Europe, North America and elsewhere virtually every academic institution provides some access to the Internet for its teaching and research staff, and students; and the sale of equipment and software to access the Internet at home is booming.

The anarchic nature of the Internet means that there is little or no control over the content of the many documents to be found there. Unlike publishing a book or newspaper article, where the author is subject to the control, taste and discipline of an editor, on the Internet authors are free to post their work directly into the public domain where there is a potential readership of tens of millions of people undifferentiated by age, sex, geographic, ethnic or religious affiliation. It is very difficult, if not impossible, to exclude from the Internet those who would seek to disseminate potentially offensive material via its various facilities. And, as we have seen in this chapter, the Internet has provided both an attractive format and a relatively regulation-free environment for both the publication of racist material and the organisation of the activities of neo-Nazi and other far-right organisations, terrorist and extremist groups.

It would not only be difficult to prevent such groups from using the Internet, but it might be undesirable to do so even if it were technically possible. Arguably, the freedom of speech provided by the Internet and its resistance to controls, especially by governments, should not be lightly abandoned. Throughout history, those in authority have sought to restrict, if not suppress altogether, the expression of independent, critical, and unfashionable ideas and beliefs. However, as has often been pointed out, the Internet epitomises the classic 'liberal dilemma'. In this case maintaining the principle of free speech means extending that right to those who would use it to 'promote violence, threaten women, denigrate minorities, promote homophobia and conspire against democracy'.[19]

However, the arguments in favour of unrestricted speech on the Internet have to be weighed against the evidence in this chapter of its abuse, albeit by a small minority. There are signs of continuing and increasing racism, xenophobia, intolerance and bigotry across the world. Across Europe anti-immigrant feelings are running high, with governments responding by introducing tighter controls on immigration and asylum-seekers.

The technical and libertarian arguments against attempting to control the posting of undesirable material on the Internet at source are compelling. It would be all too easy for groups who find their sites blocked or 'flamed' to change their Internet addresses (IPs), use encryption techniques to conceal the content of their messages from official prying eyes, and in general to go electronically 'underground'.

However, if it is either undesirable or technically impossible to restrict what goes on the Internet, there is a much stronger case for restrictions on what comes off it. Where countries have legislated against incitement to racial hatred or, indeed, against the publication and dissemination of pornography, those responsible for providing access to the Net would probably have a legal, as well as a moral, obligation to block such material from their machines.

Disturbed by what they have described as the unbridled promotion of 'racism, anti-Semitism, mayhem and violence' on the Internet, the Simon Wiesenthal Center in Los Angeles has called upon major access providers such as Compuserve, America Online and Prodigy, as well as universities, to ban those with an 'agenda of hate and violence'. Rabbi Abraham Cooper, Associate Dean of the Center, has proposed a 'code of ethics' to be applied largely against the Internet's World Wide Web, which is made up of publicly accessed pages of text and graphics, rather than against newsgroups, which consist of bulletin boards that encourage open debate.[20]

Already, some access providers and universities have banned certain material. One example is Compuserve's highly controversial ban on indecent photographs and other material under threat of prosecution in Bavaria. Rabbi Cooper argues that his ethical code is similar to that followed by bookshops when they refuse to carry certain books.

The Australian Broadcasting Authority (ABA) has been seeking public comment on the need for a code of practice for the development of the online services industry. The idea is that the code would represent a public statement of an industry's responsiveness to community needs and concerns and would provide for an appropriate complaints handling mechanism. In an issues paper, the ABA, which already has a classification scheme for broadcast material, lists a range of concerns expressed to the authority including material which racially vilifies.[21]

The Advertising Standards Authority (ASA) has applied the British Codes of Advertising and Sales Promotion to UK advertising on the Internet. The ASA has established a working group on self-regulation by advertisers on the Internet. In effect, the ASA has brought the Internet into line with press, poster and other non-broadcast media.[22]

A further classification scheme, this time to protect children from accessing unsuitable material on the Internet, has been considered by the powerful Microsoft Corporation, Netscape and Progressive Networks who have formed the Information Highway Parental Empowerment Group. They have been working on a new system which relies on Internet content providers conforming to a rating system that identifies the type of material they offer. It has been claimed that because Microsoft is so powerful, content providers can be persuaded or pressurised into the scheme which could then be about 95 per cent effective.[23]

Voluntary codes of behaviour may indeed work well in the majority of cases. However, they are unlikely to deter groups on the far right of the political spectrum who are determined to get their messages across. They have already condemned Rabbi Cooper's code of ethics as an attempt to quash free speech. Tom Metzger, director of the White Aryan Resistance, has said that 'We are not going to allow the Simon Wiesenthal Centre or the

Anti-Defamation League or any Jewish pressure group to limit our speech in any medium.'[24]

Those who are responsible for providing access to the Internet in the home and in public institutions such as schools, colleges, universities and public libraries cannot rely on voluntary codes of practice to prevent objectionable material being accessed on their machines. They will inevitably be held legally and morally responsible for the material they carry and such material, anyway, might well prejudice, among other things, their equal opportunities policies and their claim to be free of all racial prejudice or bias. Nor should they permit access to racist or pornographic material which they would not consider suitable to acquire for their library shelves.

Considerations such as these have led to a proliferation of new software initiatives designed to permit censorship at grass-roots level. While still incomplete, they already provide a good first line of defence. These so-called self-censoring programmes are designed to block out undesirable Internet sites and come with lists of such sites that are regularly updated. They should work particularly well with any new rating system introduced by, say, the Microsoft-led partnership referred to above. Already a number are on the market, some for domestic use and others intended for large networks. They range from the unfortunately named 'Net Nanny', a home product, to Cyber Sentry, WebTrack and Netscape Proxy Server, which are intended to be installed on servers in large organisations.[25]

Recently, Tim Berners-Lee, director of the World Wide Web Consortium at MIT, who is credited with having started the Web, has offered a free screening programme to people who want to keep objectionable material from entering their computers from the Internet.[26]

Censorship alone might not be the answer to the 'hate' sites on the Internet. Increasingly, the Internet itself is being used to assert historical truths and to put the record straight. In Canada, for example, the Nizkor project, established by Ken McVay, counters hate propaganda and Holocaust denial by education on the Internet.[27]

In general, it is desirable to keep censorship of the Internet to a minimum consistent with the values of liberal democratic societies. Moreover, the need for any kind of censorship whatsoever is strongly contested by civil liberties groups everywhere and especially in the US. The Internet, it is claimed, is unique in that it is technically impossible to impose any effective controls on it. It should therefore be protected as the last bastion of the absolute right to free speech, guaranteed in the US by the First Amendment to the Constitution. For others, this right is all too often abused by those seeking to disseminate racist and pornographic material. Thus it is important to reconcile the imperatives of free speech with the minimum controls necessary to limit the exploitation of the Internet by racists and pornographers.

AN INTERNET POLICY

What has clearly emerged both from this chapter and discussions with experts is that any policy designed to restrict, control or remove from the Internet material which is either illegal or repugnant must take account of some key principles:

- It is important to respect the right to freedom of speech. This right is not unconditional, even in democratic societies, and would not extend, for example, to the commission or promotion of criminal acts, or sexual, racial or other forms of discrimination deemed contrary to the public good.

- It is desirable to avoid state-imposed statutory controls or censorship of speech itself and the media through which it is expressed. Controls should be aimed at what can be accessed on the Internet, i.e. at the receiving end, since it is technically impossible to prevent material – which is illegal or specifically designed to offend – being put on the Internet at source.

- The Internet is used by far-right and other extremist groups to disseminate their ideas with a view to influencing opinion and recruiting new adherents. While there is little evidence at present to show that this is having much effect, this does not mean that we should be indifferent towards the presence on the Internet of material which is inherently offensive.

- The Internet should not be regarded differently from other means of publishing and disseminating speech and ideas. The same laws and controls which already apply to other means of publishing, whether electronic or printed, should be applied to the Internet.

Policy Proposals for Immediate Implementation

1 We urge the adoption now – by those in the public, private and voluntary sectors who own, control or manage institutions – of an interim Internet policy and accompanying code of good practice, pending the development of a more comprehensive policy (see recommendation 8). This policy would determine what materials can legitimately be accessed on their computers. We are not recommending that there should be a statutory requirement for such a policy. Instead, it would be similar to other initiatives such as policies which many institutions already have in place to provide for equal opportunities in employment or to regulate substance abuse. Indeed, institutions could adapt their policies relating to race and discrimination and extend these to cover the Internet.

2 Education authorities – as the initial base for public education – should take the lead in introducing an interim Internet policy. They have a particular responsibility for ensuring that they do not permit access to materials via the Internet that they would not consider suitable for their library shelves.

3 The policy should be reinforced by the use of so-called 'blocking software' which either only permits access to certain materials and denies access to everything else, or which permits access to everything except certain proscribed material.

4 Where open access is permitted, the criteria upon which any controls should be based should first be to exclude any material which is illegal (e.g. in England and Wales which falls under the Obscene Publications Acts 1959 and 1964, Computer Misuse Act 1990, incitement to racial hatred legislation included in the Public Order Act 1986, etc.). Second, it should exclude material which is designed to offend or contradicts other policies such as those relating to equal opportunities, substance abuse, etc.

5 The underlying principles upon which any exclusion policy should be based would be those which by regulation or custom govern the acquisition of materials for any libraries. In the case of some institutions, universities for example, special regulations already exist restricting access to certain materials.

6 In the Internet policy attention should be paid in the first instance to the graphical World Wide Web rather than the so-called newsgroups, bulletin boards, etc. Many organisations already exclude such groups from their servers altogether or allow access to a limited few. However, it is the increasingly professional and well-designed pages of the World Wide Web which give cause for concern. Their content cannot readily be refuted or debated as can the content of newsgroups, which anyway are essentially forums for discussion and debate.

7 Relevant groups should be widely consulted about the terms of any policy.

Longer-term Proposals

8 We recommend the establishment of a body to develop a comprehensive policy and accompanying model code of practice on Internet access for institutions in the public, private and voluntary sectors. Ideally, this body would be international in scope and might properly be under the

auspices of an organisation such as the Council of Europe or UNESCO. National bodies would also be required, and in the UK, an organisation analogous to the Press Complaints Commission or Broadcasting Standards Authority should be set up. Such bodies would monitor the dissemination of racist and pornographic material on the Internet and would investigate complaints. They should also consider a broader range of issues such as challenges to privacy versus freedom of expression, and copyright versus freedom of information.

9 For purposes of standardisation, on the national level, education authorities and bodies such as the Committee of Principals and Vice-Chancellors of the universities of the United Kingdom should be involved. In the private sector, business organisations such as the Confederation of British Industry and Chambers of Commerce should be involved in devising guidelines for employers. For them the issue is urgent because of the increasing commercial use of the Internet for advertising and the need for companies to observe prescribed advertising standards. However, given the global nature of the Internet and the multiplicity of different legal, moral and ethical systems involved, it is difficult to imagine that there could be any international agreement to control its contents. However, such agreement should be possible on a European level where the responsibility for setting guidelines could lie with agencies such as the Council of Europe.

10 As the Internet becomes more widely accessed internationally, police and similar authorities should be granted resources, currently not available to them, so that the surveillance they normally exercise over extremist groups can be extended to cyberspace.

11 We believe that Internet service providers have an obligation to prevent access, via the services they offer, to material which is either racist or pornographic. In view of this, we recommend that such service providers should be regarded as 'publishers' rather than 'common carriers' like the Post Office. Procedures should be established by the watchdog

body referred to in recommendation 8 above to ensure that service providers continue to prohibit access to such material once they have been put on notice.

NOTES

* This chapter is reproduced with the kind permission of the Institute for Jewish Policy Research.

1. Tracy Laquey (with Jeanne C. Ryer), *The Internet Companion: A Beginner's Guide* (Addison-Wesley, 1992), p. 2.
2. Paul Vallely, 'Sex on the Net: a Very Modern Morality Tale', *Independent*, 6 January 1996.
3. *Aberdeen Press and Journal*, 5 February 1996.
4. Conversations between M. Whine and the Metropolitan Police, 1994 and 1995.
5. Ibid.
6. Dr Eckart Werthebach, 'Verscharfen sich Extremismus/Terrorismus in einem Europa offner Grenzen?', BfV, 12 September 1994.
7. Steve Baldwin, 'Nazis in the Virtual Hood', *Digital Pulse*, 18 January 1996.
8. Michael McCormack and Crawford Killian, 'Fascism Begins at Home', *.net magazine*, October 1995.
9. Ibid.
10. *IHR Update*, California, February 1995.
11. 'Neo-Nazis Use Computer Linking in Campaign Against Left', *Scotsman*, 1 June 1994.
12. 'L'extrême droite se met sur ordinateur', *Le Figaro*, 21 May 1994.
13. *Anti-Semitism World Report 1995* (Institute of Jewish Affairs and American Jewish Committee, 1995), p. 136.
14. 'Neo-Nazis Go Hi-tech with Electronic Mailboxes', *Guardian*, 19 November 1993.
15. Newsgroup.alt.fan.rumpole, 24 October 1994.
16. Caroline Bassett, 'Censors in Space', *MacUser*, 8 July 1994.
17. Jim Carrol, 'I Know the Internet, and It's Not a Cauldron of Evils', *Globe and Mail*, Toronto, 21 March 1995.
18. Sol Littman, 'Some Thoughts on the Regulation of Cyberspace', unpublished paper, Simon Wiesenthal Center, Canada, 4 November 1995.
19. Keith Stone, 'Jewish Organization asks Internet Providers to Cut Access for Hate Groups', *Los Angeles Daily News*, 11 January 1996.
20. *Los Angeles Daily News*, 11 January 1996.
21. News Release, 20 December 1995.
22. Advertising Standards Authority Press Release, 15 July 1996.
23. *Internet Magazine*, November 1995.
24. *Los Angeles Daily News*, 11 January 1996.
25. *Internet Magazine*, November 1995.
26. CNN reporting an Associated Press Report, 11 February 1996.
27. *Anti-Semitism World Report 1996*, p. 19.

14 McSpotlight: Freedom of Speech and the Internet

Phil George

Information is power. Those that control information, control people. If people without money or 'power' choose to criticise those with it, would it surprise us if they could not get the information they required to prove their case? Time and time again vital information is withheld and injustices occur. The rich and the powerful have always controlled information, but the Internet changes this, which is what has excited so many activists. In the words of NBC: 'Taking on big business has always been a David versus Goliath battle. But in the age of the Internet, the rules of engagement have changed'.

What does the Internet do for you? Is it a tool enabling the information revolution, social change, freedom from censorship, protection against government intrusion, social interaction, free advice, corporate accountability, open debate, protection from repressive laws, alternatives from traditional media, freedom of association, electronic interactive experiences, anonymity, classless society, entertainment, sexual freedom, collective consciousness, information anarchy, freedom of information, irrelevance of gender, participatory democracy, borderless communities, privacy, adaptable systems, religious and political freedom, universal access, freedom of expression, mutual support, open education, freedom of speech, imaginative freedom, enhanced individuality, freedom of thought, cultural diversity, international communication, cooperative revolution?

McLIBEL

In 1990 McDonald's sued Helen Steel and Dave Morris for allegedly distributing a fact sheet entitled 'What's Wrong with McDonald's?', which criticised almost all aspects of the company's policies and practices. It examined:

- Multinationals and global trade: the connection between multinational companies like McDonald's, cash crops and starvation in the third world.
- Environment: the responsibility of corporations such as McDonald's for damage to the environment, including destruction of rain forests.
- Recycling and waste: the wasteful and harmful effects of the mountains of packaging used by McDonald's and other companies.
- Nutrition: McDonald's promotion and sale of food with a low fibre, high fat, saturated fat, sodium and sugar content, and the links between a diet of this type and the major degenerative diseases in Western society, including heart disease and cancer.
- Advertising and promotions: McDonald's exploitation of children by its use of advertisements and gimmicks to sell unhealthy products.
- Animal welfare: the way that animals are reared and slaughtered to supply products for McDonald's.
- Employment: the conditions that workers in the catering industry work under, the low wages paid by McDonald's and McDonald's' hostility towards trade unions.

McLibel is the longest trial of any kind, in English history. It has stimulated world-wide publicity and protests. As no legal aid is available in libel cases, Helen and Dave were forced to defend themselves, funded entirely by donations from the public.[2]

'Respected' industry analysts and legal representatives have commented that the whole McLibel case and the media coverage has been a complete disaster for McDonald's and a victory for the activist movement. McDonald's say that they were not trying to stifle debate through their court action; rather they were trying to protect their legitimate business interests by stopping the publication of false allegations made against them.[3] Whatever McDonald's were trying to achieve, they have not silenced their critics. It is against this backdrop that McSpotlight was created.

Type http://www.mcspotlight.org/ on the World Wide Web and you can judge for yourself.

McSPOTLIGHT

McSpotlight was launched on 16 February 1996, in London, Chicago, Helsinki and Auckland. The site was activated by the McLibel defendants outside a McDonald's store in Central London using a mobile phone and a laptop. The authors of the Internet's most contentious Website are spread round the world; most of them have never even met. They loosely refer to themselves as the McInformation Network.[4] The site is dedicated to providing uncensored information on the infamous 'McLibel' trial, on McDonald's itself and on other multinational corporations. There is even in-depth criticism of the McDonald's Web page. The makers of McSpotlight, with their line 'Judge for Yourself', have linked their site with that of McDonald's. McDonald's have not made a link from their site to McSpotlight, nor is there a return e-mail address or a debating room.

The site can be accessed from anywhere in the world by anyone with access to the Internet. The host server for the site is currently located in the Netherlands. Additionally, there are mirrors sites (complete, identical copies) available in:

- Finland: http://muu.lib.hel.fi/McSpotlight/
- USA: http://www.envirolink.org/mcspotlight/

- New Zealand: http://www.ch.planet.gen.nz/~mcspot/
- Australia: http://mcspotlight.va.com.au/

To save time downloading the pages, choose the nearest server to you. The site is constantly updated and is colossal already, containing about 21,000 files (about 120mb of data).

The information includes: the full court transcripts of the 313 days of the proceedings, closing submissions, daily reports of the closing speeches, approximately 90 McLibel witness statements, scores of other documents about the case, company publications, scientific reports, newspaper articles, cartoons, extracts from books, transcripts of TV and video appearances, plays and internal company memos.

In 'The Issues' section the information has been split up into relevant categories: Nutrition, Advertising, Employment, Environment, Animal Welfare, Free Speech, Multinationals and Global Trade, Capitalism and the Alternatives, and McDonald's International Expansion.

Other key features of McSpotlight include:

- the Debating Room, which is a moderated discussion group within the Website, providing a global forum for discussion and debate about McDonald's and all they stand for;

- the RealAudio Guided Tour – the McLibel defendants take you around the site, pointing out the key pages and features;

- exclusive interviews – with the McLibel defendants and others;

- video clips (quicktime movies);

- the Guided Tour of McDonald's own Website – McSpotlight takes you round McDonald's site (use Netscape 2.0, Internet Explorer v3, or any Frames-compatible browser) pointing out inaccuracies and untruths;

- the McQuiz – satirical quiz using quotes from McDonald's executives to emphasise the company's strategy and attitude;

- the site also features a powerful site-wide search engine, in order to help locate specific information.

All the evidence will continue to be available on McSpotlight and will enable anyone who cares to look, to judge the facts for themselves. Perhaps the one omission from the site is that of McDonald's' own expert witnesses. Those at McSpotlight asked for electronic copies of these voluminous texts but never received a reply from McDonald's or their lawyers.

Resources can be used to turn the 'McSpotlight' on other companies and industries. If you would like more information about the McLibel trial there is of course much more about the case on the McSpotlight site itself. You might also like to read the 'press backgrounder' produced by the McLibel Support Campaign.

You may wonder why McDonald's was picked on? At the Website it is explained that McDonald's was 'singled out' because, despite an annual global advertising budget of $2 billion dollars, they have made every effort to stifle public criticism – be it from campaigners, disgruntled workers and customers or from the media.

We take the view that over the years McDonald's has bullied its critics with threats of legal action and nobody has stood up to them. Those who have retracted statements include: Prince Philip, the BBC, Channel 4, the *Guardian*, the Vegetarian Society, labour research groups, trades unions, green groups and even a kids' theatre. The incident involving Prince Philip illustrates the disadvantages of being denied access to relevant information. The Prince is reported to have said to the President of McDonald's: 'So it is you that is tearing down the rain forest in Brazil.' Later he apologised after a pile of correspondence between the World Wide Fund for Nature and McDonald's in which the global corporation categorically denied that any store had ever used any beef reared on former rain forests. Indeed, during the trial, McDonald's maintained that any talk of Brazil was irrelevant and therefore inadmissible. In the absence of information to the contrary, the judge agreed. The defendants, however, received a lucky break. The plaintiffs (for McDonald's) accidentally passed a crucial document to them. The document showed that McDonald's UK had imported beef from Brazil in the 1980s. McDonald's had previously denied this. This led to the disclosure of further official company documents and information.

THE REACH OF THE INTERNET

It is difficult to calculate the number of visitors to any Web page. Most Websites simply publish the total number of 'hits', but these figures are misleading and need careful interpretation. In the 12 months following the launch of McSpotlight on 16 February 1996, the total number of hits (for all the McSpotlight sites) is conservatively estimated to have been at least 7 million, that is almost 600,000 hits per month. The total number of visitors in that period is calculated to have been in excess of 200,000. During that period, about 24,000 people have read the original fact sheet complained of by McDonald's. McDonald's themselves accessed the site 1,300 times in its first week alone.[5]

McSpotlight has received the most press coverage of any Website in the world. Some examples are: *USA Today* (front cover with photo), NBC TV, Channel 4 (Website of the week), ITV, BBC1 (prime time news), BBC2 (most informative Website), *Independent* (with photo), *Guardian*, *Observer* (Website of the week), *Daily Express*, *Chicago Tribune*, *San Jose Mercury News*, *Chicago Sun Times*, *Denver Post*, *Australian*, *Undercurrents*, *Times of India* (including cartoon), *Helsingin Sanomat* (Finland), *LA Weekly*, *Daily Telegraph*, BBC Radio 4. Many of these press articles are available in the press cuttings section of the Website.

Apart from what the architects have modestly described as 'the sheer unadulterated brilliance of the site's construction, design and layout there can be little doubt that the main "draw" is the content of its 21,000+ files. Time and time again people have observed that this is a site that goes into real depth about real issues that affect real people.' The site has won many awards.

The *Guardian* wrote: 'It is claimed to be "the most

comprehensive source of information on a multinational ever assembled" – and that doesn't sound like an exaggeration.' The fact that it is closely involved with one of the most well-known battles of modern times has certainly helped increase coverage. In our view the McLibel trial revolves around the question of the right of ordinary people to stand up to corporate censorship, and many press articles have picked up on McSpotlight taking this battle onto new territory – the seemingly unstoppable and uncensorable Internet.

PURPOSE

McSpotlight was created for several reasons: to support the heroic efforts of campaigners around the world attempting to expose the realities behind the glossy public images of multinational corporations; to show McDonald's and the world that legal action and bullying by big business in an attempt to censor and silence critics will not be accepted; and to show that such attempts can only fail now that the Internet provides an open and uncensored forum that need not rely on the scant attention that the traditional media gives to progressive campaigns.

McSpotlight was not created in the belief that it would drive McDonald's out of business, but to bring about a radical change in the way they do business. It is also hoped that this particular campaign will show people how to apply the principles of 'ethical consumerism' more widely when deciding what to buy and that companies will react by cleaning up their acts rather than by paying their public relations departments more to 'gloss-over' their practices. In these wider aims there are some signs of success. Indeed Enterprise Oil, the UK's largest independent explorer, published (March 1997) new internal guidelines stressing that all business should be conducted on an ethical basis. There are, it says, 'too many people, including shareholders and employees, monitoring our activity to do anything in a cavalier manner'.[6]

McSPOTLIGHT CENSORED?

McDonald's has shown itself to be very sensitive to criticism. Their success perhaps hinges upon a carefully manufactured image created by billions of advertising dollars. They react swiftly to destroy any threat to that image and would clearly love to destroy McSpotlight – but they know of no way to do it. A McDonald's spokesperson was reported to have said: 'People will find the real facts and figures from our Internet pages, we regret that there should be an inaccurate version but as the Internet cannot be controlled, it's difficult to do anything about it.'

The nature of the Internet makes successful censorship very difficult. The McInformation Network has, however, taken a number of steps to foil any attempt at shutting McSpotlight down: it operates from countries which have more liberal libel laws than in the UK; the mirror sites mean that if one is closed there are others; and the 'kit' allows the whole site to be downloaded. This virtually guarantees an effective barrier against any attempt from McDonald's to affect the site.

Any attempt to close McSpotlight would result in massive media attention and outrage from sympathisers and the Internet community. After all, it is obviously of vital importance that multinationals be subject to criticism and challenge.

THE VIRTUES OF THE INTERNET – JUDGE FOR YOURSELF

For years, access to information has been controlled by the few. The Internet changes this, and brings publishing to the many. A user has access to millions of other users, at a very low cost. All over the world people are using it to highlight injustices.

It is already clear that the Internet is a breakthrough in world communications. Like other technological advances, its use is not cash free and the power it gives can be abused. What uncensored access does allow is the power of individuals to judge for themselves from all the information that is available.

No longer must we be fed 'expert' advice from commercially sponsored politicians, scientists, doctors, priests or mechanics; we can make our own informed decisions.

So if you want to know about the McLibel court case and much more besides, McSpotlight is the place to go with its huge library of information and links to 'commercial' Web pages. You can truly judge for yourself.

NOTES

1. NBC News, 17 April 1996.
2. The defendants raised £35,000. McDonald's spent an estimated £10 million. Helen and Dave were denied a jury trial.
3. In June 1997, despite the legal odds stacked against the defence, the judge made some findings against McDonald's global core business practices. He ruled that they 'exploit children' with their advertising; pay 'low wages' in the UK; promote 'high fat, high salt' meals yet make deceptive nutritional claims and may be risking the health of their long-term customers, and are 'culpably responsible' for cruelty to animals. But he ruled that as other key points had not been proven, McDonald's had won the case. Subsequently, however, campaigners stepped up the protests: 400,000 leaflets were handed out in the UK alone on the weekend after the judgment. Within 28 days McDonald's abandoned all further legal action, including an attempt to halt the leafletting (their stated aim in bringing the case). The defendants have lodged an Appeal starting January 1999 against the unfairness of the UK libel laws, and are seeking to abolish the right of multinational corporations and other powerful bodies to sue for libel. Liberty has condemned the lack of availability of Legal Aid for defendants in libel cases and would be prepared to fight this point in the European human rights institutions.
4. The site was set up and run entirely by volunteers, and with no funding.
5. By the Autumn of 1998 the site had been accessed over 50 million times, including 2.2million times in the week of the judgment.
6. *Financial Times*, 18 March 1997.
7. The site is now available on CD ROM from London Greenpeace, 5 Caledonian Road, London N1 9DX. There is also a book by John Vidal: *McLibel, Burger Culture on Trial* (Pan Books, 1997), on which the author of this chapter worked as a researcher. A 53-minute video documentary *McLibel: Two Worlds Collide* is available from One Off Productions, BCM Oops, London WC1N 3XX.

15 Human Rights and the Internet

Conor Foley

This book examines some of the conflicting claims made about the impact which the Internet is likely to have on human rights. The Internet began as a creature of the Cold War. In 1957 the US responded to the Soviet Union's launch of Sputnik, the first artificial earth satellite, by establishing its Advanced Research Projects Agency (ARPA) within the Department of Defense to establish a lead for the US in military technology. In 1969 ARPANET was established as a network of computers capable of withstanding a nuclear attack. If one computer is blocked, the Internet attempts to find a way around the blockage. In 1972 an e-mail programme was developed to send messages across a distributed network of computers. In 1984 there were 1,000 hosts world-wide, by 1989 there were over 100,000. Since then, the Internet has been doubling in size every year. At the last count there were about 5 million 'host' computers connected to the Internet, of which about 70 per cent were in the US.

Despite its origins, the Internet has developed as a uniquely anarchic institution. The Internet has no single owner. It gives equal access to bulletin boards and databases for all people connected. It was built to treat all attempts at censorship as blockages to be circumvented. In some respects its design mirrors developments in radical politics in Britain during the 1990s.

In 1989 communism collapsed. The 'velvet revolution' was both directly and indirectly inspired by the flow of information and was also based on a rejection of authoritarianism and a positive assertion that the legitimacy of governments derives from the consent of those that they govern.

History was supposed to end the new world order, but instead new issues have thrown up new struggles, new concepts and new forms of protest. In the UK the last few years have seen tens of thousands of young people drawn into direct action protests around issues related to the environment, housing and land rights, animal welfare, exploitation of the third world, and most notably in the anti-roads campaign. In 1994 a remarkable coalition came together in defence of dissent and diversity, against the Criminal Justice and Public Order Bill. The strength of that movement lay in its spontaneity, its creativity and its complete rejection of the dominant value-system and culture of the last government.

Another striking feature about this counterculture was its willingness to appropriate the technologies associated with the Internet and to put them to work for the politics of protest. Theodore Roszack, who wrote the classic 1960s text *The Making of a Counter Culture: Reflections on the Technocratic Society and Its Youthful Opposition*, argued that youth in rebellion then were attempting to 'fight their way free of technocratic entrapment'.[1] A common theme of countercultures since the Second World War has been distrust of technology and rejection of consumerist materialism. We only need to think about the image which the mobile phone conjured up a few years ago – of shirt-sleeved Thatcherite yuppies – to see how so often the icons of technological progress are identified with the dominant groups in society and the political right.

That image was turned on its head during the last couple of years. The mobile phone, the hi-eight video camera and the Internet have become crucial tools of popular struggles, as simple, innovative and effective as flying pickets and sabotage in days gone by. Campaigning and media manipulation have become increasingly synonymous. Mobilising supporters quickly and secretly, recording their actions and stunts in high quality format, then disseminating this footage in time for the appropriate news bulletin are now the staple stock of the direct action campaigner. Groups like Road Alert, Earth First!, The Land is Ours and Reclaim the Streets have relied on the Internet, leaflets and word of mouth to publicise some of their most effective actions. In August 1996 a group of women were aquitted of causing criminal damage to British military aircraft destined for Indonesia on the basis of testimony they recorded on video during the action which they left behind after they had finished their protest.

Inevitably this culture is developing its own literature and the fad of 'cyberia' has gained popular currency in recent years. Because virtual reality involves accessing a fantasy world there is still a lot of fantasising about its potential. The hype and mystification can lead to elitism by the 'digiterati'. According to one writer:

> The mission of the cyberian counter-culture of the 1990s, armed with new technologies, familiar with cyberspace and daring enough to explore unmapped realms of consciousness, is to re-choose reality consciously and purposefully. Cyberians are not just actively exploring the next dimension; they are working to create it.[2]

This can and should be dismissed as hyperbole. However, a cursory reading of the *Financial Times* reveals a similar enthusiasm. Share values in cyberspace are rising like a real estate boom. In April 1996 it was reported that Yahoo, a fairly modest electronic catalogue of the World Wide Web, had been capitalised on Wall Street at over $1 billion.[3] In May 1996 another company, Cisco, which provides the 'plumbing' for the Internet, had a market capitalisation of $32 billion.[4] Financial interest in cyberspace has been described as the last great land rush of the twentieth century.

Of course booms tend to turn to busts and fads go out of fashion. Much of the problem with the current debate is that very few people fully understand the current state of cyberia. What can it do? What it its potential? Does it need to be subject to any form of legal control? And is it actually technically possible to do this?

The content of the Internet is entirely dependent on who its users are. Currently these are overwhelmingly male, white, middle class and young, and the messages and literature being posted reflect this. The system is becoming more user-friendly, and the numbers using it are growing, but it is still very much the preserve of a fashion cult with some similarities to CB radio.

While the Internet remains a minority pursuit there is little to be concerned about. People who wish to participate in specialist discussions can do so while others seem to make a hobby of monitoring the Internet for views which they disagree with in order to refute them. In principle there is no difference between these types of arguments and those which take place in any other semi-public arena and there seems to be no point in trying to regulate or control such discussions. The point at which this argument is no longer tenable is when cyberia goes mainstream.

Many cyberians – particularly American libertarians – conflate their own opposition to regulation of cyberia with the physical problems of achieving it. As John Perry Barlow, for example, argues, 'Your legal concepts of property, expression, identity, movement and context do not apply to us.'[5] On the other hand, 'moral panic merchants' argue for control of this type of media, or even to shut it down, precisely because they do not understand the phenomenon.

Fear of the harmful effect of new technology, particularly in the field of communications, has been a recurring historical theme since the invention of the radio. Down the years, it has been argued that each development will destroy our moral fibre, atomise society and corrupt the nation's youth. In that sense, cyberia just provides a displacement activity for Mary Whitehouse. However, there are three specific areas where the technologies associated with the Internet will clearly make a difference and where the development of international human rights jurisprudence provides some broad guidelines for action.

FREEDOM OF INFORMATION

This is discussed more fully in Andrew Ecclestone's chapter. The Internet provides an extremely cost-effective way of finding and disseminating information. It is possible to get information from around the world at a fraction of the time and cost. You can trawl library databases and networks to download information in an hour which it would take weeks to accumulate any other way.

For campaigners, in our present media-friendly world, speed and quality of information are everything. Non-governmental organisations, such as Greenpeace, have long understood the media's potential and invest considerable resources in ensuring that their stunts and actions get the correct news 'spin'. The technologies associated with the Internet make it possible for anyone who has access to a computer, modem and telephone to get real news, testimonies and pictures in an accessible format from across the world as fast as a government or a major news corporation can.

Amnesty International is making increasing use of the Internet for its Urgent Actions because the speed with which it can register protests can literally mean the difference between life and death. When we consider the efforts that are put into news management by governments during conflicts such as the Falklands in 1982 or the Gulf War in 1991 it is easy to see the potential impact this can have for campaigners and for freedom of information in general.

In July 1996 the British government published a parliamentary report, *Information Society: Agenda for Action*, on the Internet for the first time. The report followed a parliamentary inquiry of the House of Lords' science and technology committee into the digital revolution. It focused on the applications for the technologies associated with the Internet for government and concluded that everything the government does – from informing citizens to collecting taxes – can be transformed by screen-based technology.

With the publication of the minutes of meetings between the Chancellor of the Exchequer and the Governor of the Bank of England, a principle has been established that it is possible to bring sensitive high-level policy documents into the public domain within a reasonable time period. Other departments, such as the Central Statistical Office, the Central Office of Information and the Treasury, also all have their own Websites.[6] There is no cost argument against putting more official information online. It is collected and stored electronically anyway, so why should it not be free?

Protection of Crown Copyright may become a sensitive issue with privatisation of Her Majesty's Stationary Office (HMSO). However, the argument that we should have to pay for more than the production costs of public information which the government holds on our behalf is ludicrous and may soon acquire the force of King Canute's authority towards cyberia's rising tide.

FREEDOM OF EXPRESSION

The second issue which is a particular dilemma for civil libertarians revolves around freedom of expression: where, if at all, should the line be drawn? The contributions in this book provide a number of different perspectives on this question, but this still leaves the problem of enforcement. Cyberspace is virtually an uncensorable form of media. Short of impounding computers, it is technically impossible to prevent information being posted onto the Internet and then downloaded from it. The Internet is already beginning to subvert some archaic forms of censorship in British society – such as the use of injunctions and seizure of publications. At the same time the increasing ease of communicating highlights the weakness of our current statutory protection of individual privacy, equal opportunities and the right of groups in society not to be subject to harassment and intimidation.

In December 1995, for example, Friends of the Earth announced that they would ignore a ruling by the Advertising Standards Authority instructing them to remove an advert from the Internet which highlights the brutality of mahogany loggers in Brazil.[7] There have been questions in the House of Commons about bomb-making instructions appearing on the Internet[8] and Conservative MPs have complained that a Website established by Sinn Fein supporters in the US breaches the Prevention of Terrorism Act.[9]

Many groups are currently exploring the Internet's potential as a tool for subversion. This includes neo-Nazis and white supremacists who have a particular interest in targeting the social groups who use the Internet most frequently. The Internet also contains substantial pornography, including child pornography, and, as Clem Herman argues, lack of regulation may result in its current users excluding others from participating in it.

Exercising the right of freedom of expression carries with it special responsibilities, such as respect for the rights of others, as set out in Article 19 of the International Covenant on Civil and Political Rights, but the principles of 'publish and be damned' have been recognised as important to generations of radicals. If people break the law, then they should face the consequences after the event. There is no place for book burning in a democratic society.

As the implications of this become more apparent, it is likely that other forms of media will begin to demand parity of treatment, pointing the way towards possible law reform. The British government's attempts to injunct Peter Wright's memoir *Spycatcher*, and in particular the allegation that sections of MI5 plotted treason against the last Labour government, eventually collapsed because the book was so widely available in the rest of the world. Similarly, one can imagine a situation where the courts begin to reject imposing injuctions on the printed word because the information is already widely accessible online.

However, existing laws on pornography, race hate, libel, breach of confidence, contempt of court and so on still mean that people can be held accountable for information that they have posted so long as this has been done from within the UK. In May 1996, for example, two men were sentenced to terms of imprisonment for distributing child pornography in Britain after a court rejected the argument that the images did not constitute photographs.[10]

However, if cyberia should be subject to the same forms of regulation as other forms of speech, it is important to clarify what type of media it is. The law is different as it applies to the written, spoken and broadcast word, and it also applies with different degrees of rigour in different contexts. The broadcast media are already subject to considerable regulation and restriction. There are requirements covering quality standards, impartiality, diversity, balance, breadth and range of programmes. The funding of the British Broadcasting Corporation (BBC) through the licence fee, and the positive public service obligations on terrestrial broadcasters, have provided a range of safeguards against commercial competition being the main force determining programming.

The publishing industry is subject to fewer restrictions, which are principally to be found in the civil and criminal law in relation to obscenity, libel, blasphemy, state security, court proceedings and the incitement of racial hatred. However, these are subject to considerable variations. For example, people can be prosecuted in Britain for inciting racial hatred but prosecutions are rare and usually only take place if there is a likelihood that violence will be stirred up. Prosecutions can only be mounted with the permission of the Attorney-General and successful defences have been mounted on the grounds that racist comments were 'humorous', were not 'threatening, abusive and insulting', or would not affect their target audience.[11]

Prosecutions on grounds of obscenity are much more frequent and literature is often seized, by police or customs officers, on the grounds that it is obscene. Britain's laws on libel and restricting information on grounds of national security are amongst the toughest in the world and there is considerable evidence that overt censorship, prior restraint, and other restrictions have inhibited freedom of expression in British society in an unjustifiable way.[12]

PRIVACY

Finally, the Internet also reshapes the debate about privacy in British law. Until now this has focused on invasions of privacy by the newspaper media. However, the Internet makes everyone a potential publisher, and people still have the right to protect their reputations. Those who post messages on the Internet can currently be prosecuted in the same way as if they have published information in another media (so long as they can be identified). Given the amount of material on the Internet, there is a need for public figures to show less sensitivity about their reputations to prevent the courts being swamped with cases. In particular, the Internet highlights the urgent need for an overhaul of the libel laws and the limiting of libel awards.

But cyberia is an international phenomenon and this is increasingly forcing governments to consider the final area of differing global standards. Any attempt at regulation immediately poses questions about international human rights jurisprudence. The global nature of the Internet could lead to conflicts about the acceptability of differing forms of 'speech' in different jurisdictions. There may be some attempt to harmonise the different legal standards which apply in different parts of the world and there is likely to be increased intergovernmental cooperation to monitor communications on the Internet. Penny Campbell's chapter in this book describes how this is already happening within the European Union with the Bangemann report[13] and the Commission's Action Plan on the Information Society.[14]

The fact that the Internet is currently being used by global paedophile rings and the far right is hardly startling. As a cheap global means of communication it is likely that the Internet will be used for all sorts of purposes. Sarah Hogg, former advisor to the last Conservative Prime Minister and a member of the House of Lords' committee on science and technology, has commented:

> The Internet, for example, has thrived on creative anarchy ... Some question whether there is any role for national regulation in an era of satellite broadcasting and global telecommunications. But racial and subversive material finds its way on to information superhighways. New ways will have to be found of dealing with it. Parents will have to exercise more responsibility but service providers are already providing sophisticated filters, the protection of intellectual property and privacy; sanctions on libel and obscenity – such issues can only be dealt with by governments acting together.[15]

There is a need to ensure that such intergovernmental initiatives do not unnecessarily infringe on individual privacy and freedom of expression, and that the formulation of a global policy in this area is informed by civil liberties concerns.

In August 1996 anti-paedophile campaigners at the World Congress Against the Commercial Sexual Exploitation of Children agreed to establish an international monitoring group to 'police' cyberia.[16] The Congress agreed that the censorship of the Internet was 'unrealistic and undesirable' but decided to establish a 'tip off' line where people could report child abusers so that the information could be passed on to the police in their respective countries. The industry itself is working to ensure that software is available so that people do not get bombarded with unwanted literature from anonymous sources, and can use the Internet without encountering literature or images which they find offensive. The Platform for Internet Content Selection (PICS) is one solution based on clear signposting and restricted access to certain Websites. This is a solution which the industry itself has devised and it allows for regional and cultural variation to take into account the different standards of different societies.

This is not a perfect solution. Children will probably have hours of fun attempting to outwit Net Nanny and the other software their parents have installed to control their access to certain sites. But the bank has not been built that cannot be robbed. The Internet merely exaggerates existing problems by technical means.

However, clearly there is a need for the development of some form of legal principle to deal with the globalisation of standards. Perhaps a new International Covenant is needed – possibly through the United Nations – on international electronic freedom of expression? This could lay down the broad principles governing freedom of expression, which are currently expressed in Article 19 of the International Covenant of Civil and Political Rights (ICCPR), and lead to the establishment of a committee which could then develop jurisprudence in this area.

Some countries may be unwilling to sign up to such a Covenant. The US, for example, only ratified the ICCPR in 1994. The Covenant would also need to contain certain provisions for opt-outs and derogations, to take account of different countries' cultures and traditions. However, the advantage of this approach is that it would allow jurisprudence to develop over time, allowing standards to evolve at the same time as the technology develops. It would also facilitate the maximum public debate about the principles governing electronic freedom of expression.

The alternative is likely to be intergovernmental agreements – concluded behind closed doors – and establishment of unaccountable global policing bodies to eavesdrop and monitor transnational communications. An inevitable corollary of the globalisation of society is the globalisation of government, just as the internationalisation of crime has led to the internationalisation of policing. The democratic deficit here is enormous and, in this sense, human rights in cyberspace concerns us all.

NOTES

1. Theodore Roszack, *The Making of a Counter Culture: Reflections on the Technocratic Society and Its Youthful Oppositions* (London, 1970), p. 73.
2. Douglas Rushkoff, *Cyberia, Life in the Trenches of Hyperspace* (Harper, 1994), p. 7.
3. 'Land-rush in Cyberspace', *Financial Times*, 18 April 1996.
4. 'Providing the Plumbing for the Internet', *Financial Times*, 14 May 1996.
5. 'Surfing with the Blinkers On', *New Scientist*, 6 April 1996.
6. http://www.hmsinfo.gov.uk/hmso/document/inforsoc.htm
7. 'Banned Advert Still on Internet', *Independent*, 1 December 1995.
8. *Hansard*, Written Answer, 24 January 1996, cols 261–2.
9. 'Ulster Security Details Posted on the Internet', *The Times*, 25 March 1996.
10. 'Two Jailed for Child Porn on Internet', *Daily Telegraph*, 25 May 1996.
11. In one case two men who made speeches referring to 'coons', 'wogs', 'niggers' and 'black bastards' were acquitted after arguing that their language was so extreme that it was more likely to arouse sympathy than hostility. Others have argued that, for example, distributing anti-Semitic literature exclusively to Jews is not an offence because it is not inciting anyone else to hate them.
12. See, for example, Conor Foley, *Human Rights, Human Wrongs: The Alternative Report to the United Nations Human Rights Committee* (Liberty and Rivers Oram Press, 1995), pp. 238–316.
13. Martin Bangemann (Chair), *Europe and the Global Information Society, Recommendations to the European Council*, Brussels, 26 May 1994.
14. *Europe's Way to the Information Society: An Action Plan*, Communication from the Commission to the Council and European Parliament and to the Economic and Social Committee and the Committee of the Regions, Brussels, 19 July 1994.
15. 'Relaxed Hand on the Wheel', *Financial Times*, 31 July 1996.
16. 'Hackers Called in as Cybercops to Drive out Porn', *Observer*, 1 September 1996.

Glossary of Internet Terms

Anonymous remailer A forwarding service which allows e-mail to be sent anonymously (or received pseudonymously). Cryptographic keys protect the identity of sender or receiver even if the e-mail is intercepted.

Application Applications are also called 'apps' or simply 'programs'. Some common Internet applications include FTP, e-mail, and Telnet. Netscape Navigator and Microsoft's Internet Explorer are also common Web applications.

Bandwidth A measurement of the amount of data that can be transferred over a network connection. The pipe analogy is a good one – the bigger the pipe, the more water can flow through it. Bandwith is usually measured in bits-per-second (bps).

Bit (Binary digIT) A bit is the smallest unit of measure for computer data. Bits are represented by binary digits, and can be either on (1) or off (0). Bandwidth is usually measured in bits-per-second (bps).

Browser Internet software which enables a user to view hypertext documents and information on the Internet. Popular browsers are Netscape and Microsoft Explorer.

Bulletin boards A system that lets you post and read messages. You can read other messages, or wait until someone responds to your 'post'. Most software/hardware vendors maintain a bulletin board to provide technical support and allow registered users to download patches and updates.

CDA Computer Decency Act, USA.

Cipher Allows encryption of an arbitary message using a scheme and a key.

Client When you and your computer are searching for or accessing information on another computer, you are the client.

Clipper Chip US government proposal to put encryption chips into computers, telephones and fax machines, where the government would keep each copy of each decryption key.

Code The correspondence of a fixed repertoire of messages to a set of previously agreed symbols.

Cryptanalysis 'Code breaking', that is decrypting messages without knowing the key, through mathematical analysis, or exploitation of lapses in security.

Cryptography Science and study of secret writing, 'means that communications and data can be encoded so that only certain people can read the message.

Cyberspace A term coined by William Gibson in his 'cyberpunk' novel *Neuromancer*, to describe the abstract landscape of information created by networks of computers, and the culture of the inhabitants.
Data Encryption Standard (DES) Widely used commercial cipher with 56-bit keylength, now considered inadequate and insecure (cracked in three days with $250,000 hardware).
Decryption The reverse process to encryption, returning a scrambled message to its original state.
Digital signature A private cryptographic key is mathematically applied to a document, to produce a value which can be verified against the corrresponding public key, proving that the document was authored by the key owner (and has not been altered).
Discussion groups The Web's version of bulletin boards. Users post messages and respond to other users' posts about specific topics and interests.
Downloading Copying a program or document file from the Internet (or any remote computer) to the user's local machine.
E-mail or electronic mail A basic Internet service which allows users to exchange messages electronically. An e-mail address might be me@machine.kme.co.jp. In this case, me is the user's name; machine is the name of the computer; kme is the company that provides the user with internet access; co means that the 'site' is a corporation and jp (Japan) is the country.
Encryption The encoding or scrambling of data prior to transmission so that it cannot be read or recognised if intercepted during transmission.
Escrow The voluntary or compulsory surrender of private encryption keys to a private or government authority, who may release a key under warrant to law enforcement agencies.
File Transfer Protocol (FTP) The most common way to download and upload (get and put) files on the Internet.
Filtering software Software that can filter out documents based on key criteria given by the user (or access provider). Key criteria may include certain words, images or labels.
Flaming An e-mail or newsgroup posting of sarcastic, abusive or querulous nature. Usually an indication of intemperate disagreement, but may also be malicious (see Troll).
Frame A bordered panel within a Web page, which may be browsed while the outer region remains fixed (often used to show advertising).
Gateway A switching computer which connects a local area network to a larger network (such as the Internet).
Gopher A facility for searching and accessing data on remote computers. Largely supplanted by the Web, but still used for specialised textual databases.
Hacker Original meaning was merely a resourceful and ingenious programmer; now used to describe person who gains unauthorised access to systems through security flaws.
Hits The number of times a document is accessed by different users.

Home page Starting page of a Website, containing navigation links and search buttons.

Host Usually refers to a server machine that allows client machines to visit, access, and share files.

HTML (HyperText Markup Language) The language of the World Wide Web. Websites and pages are created using HTML, which sounds a lot more complex than it really is. Plain text is 'marked-up' using hypertext tags. Items in the document can be text, images, sounds, and links to other HTML documents on the Internet.

HTTP (HyperText Transport Protocol) HTTP is the protocol that the servers and the clients of the Internet use to transfer those great looking hypertext documents all over the Web.

Internet A global network of interconnected networks linking millions of computers in hundreds of countries. It provides services such as the World Wide Web, File Transfer Protocol, electronic mail, newsgroups and Internet Relay Chat.

Internet Protocol (IP) The Internet Protocol is what allows the many computers on the Internet to communicate across the various networks and different operating systems. It allows data to travel in packets routed across different networks, then reach its final destination to be reassembled.

Internet Relay Chat (IRC) IRC allows you to communicate in chat rooms with other users. Everything is in real time and only limited by your typing skills and the rules of the room. The room operator can boot you out if you step out of line.

Internet service provider (ISP) The general idea is that the ISP forks out the cash for all the equipment, and then the rest of us pay them a fee for the right to access the Internet through their network.

Java Programming language oriented to objects, for the realisation of applications for the Internet. It is necessary, of course, that the navigation software (browser) supports Java.

Links Hypertext links can occur in all hypertext documents and are a way of moving from one document to another by clicking on a highlighted word in the document.

Mainframe computer Generalised term for a large centralised computer system.

Megabytes/Bytes/Gigabytes A measure of storage volume. It is applied commonly to computer memory and disk storage space.

Mirror sites Mirror sites come into play when a particular Web or FTP site becomes extremely popular. When the site is so popular that it puts particular strain on the server, often the site providers will put the same information and content on another server, and create a 'mirror site' to accommodate more users.

Modem Short for 'MOdulator, DEModulator', modems convert digital data into analog wave forms that can be transmitted over our current phone lines. They let your computer communicate and share information with other computers on the Net.

Moderated discussion groups/bulletin boards Discussion lists, interest groups, mailing lists, or Usenet newsgroups that are managed or administered by someone.
Netiquette A whole set of rules and manners for interacting with people on the Internet.
Newsgroups Large collections of discussion groups (usually centring around a particular topic) which can involve millions of people. Postings are made by e-mail messages, and replies can be made to particular postings. There are two types: moderated and unmoderated discussions.
Packet A chunk of data easily sent over network. Imagine some brown paper packages but instead of snail mail addresses, they have the IP address of where they came from and the one they are going to digitally stamped with bits and bytes.
Platform for Internet Content Selection (PICS) Software that labels sites according to their language, violence, and sexual content.
Posting Tacking up a message on a bulletin board or discussion group, or submitting an article to a Usenet newsgroup.
Pretty Good Privacy (PGP) A popular 'public key' encryption program. It allows messages to be sent confidentially by scrambling them, however, unlike conventional ciphers, there is no need for sender and receiver to share a secret key.
Protocols A protocol is a common set of rules and 'language' agreed upon by networked computers to allow communication. With so many different types of computers and operating systems on the Internet, agreed protocols are a must.
RSA System used for most public key cryptography, named after the inventors Rivest, Shamir and Adleman.
Search engines A service provided on the World Wide Web in order to search through the many millions of Web pages and newsgroups. Key words are typed in, and a summary of relevant documents (with links) is created.
Servers A computer system attached to the Network which provides a service to other computers on the Network on demand. There are FTP servers, Web servers (which serve up Web pages) Usenet servers (which serve up discussion groups) etc.
Signature A file added to the end of an e-mail message that contains personal information about the sender such as their full name, company name, mailing address, phone number, etc. Not to be confused with digital signature.
Spam Unsolicited e-mail or scatter-gun newsgroup postings, usually containing get-rich-quick scams or advertisements for pornography. Named after the Monty Python sketch featuring singing Vikings in a café where all the items on the menu contain varying amounts of ... spam.
Troll A disingenuous opinion or bogus rumour, intended to provoke a 'flame' from the recipient.
Uniform Resource Locator (URL) Standard method to show the

logical address of a specific resource on the Internet, for example a Web page or an FTP server. 'Logical address' means that the resource is identified by name rather than by numerical address indicating its position on the Net.

Uploading The transfer of a document from one system to another higher in the control hierarchy. Thus a document is uploaded from a PC to a server.

Upstream control Preventing harmful material from being published.

Usenet A UNIX-based messaging system of thousands of distributed discussion groups – rather like bulletin boards that you can subscribe to.

Web TV A hybrid of Web and conventional broadcast services aimed at a mass market and offering limited interactivity, delivered to the home via satellite dish or cable.

White listing The practice of blocking users' access to all documents except those that have been approved.

World Wide Web A hypertext-based system consisting of pages of information. The user can access text, graphics, video and sound from the web. It lets users download files, listen to sounds, view video files, and jump to other documents or Internet sites by using hypertext.

Index

Index compiled by
Sue Carlton